OHIO IN THE UNITED STATES

STUART ZIMMER

MARK JARRETT, Ph.D.

JAMES KILLORAN

JARRETT PUBLISHING COMPANY

EAST COAST OFFICE
P.O. Box 1460
Ronkonkoma, NY 11779
631-981-4248

SOUTHERN OFFICE
50 Nettles Boulevard
Jensen Beach, FL 34957
800-859-7679

WEST COAST OFFICE
10 Folin Lane
Lafayette, CA 94549
925-906-9742

www.jarrettpub.com
1-800-859-7679   Fax: 631-588-4722

The authors wish to thank the following educator for her comments, suggestions, and recommendations which proved invaluable to this manuscript.

Karen Fiedler
K–8 Social Studies Curriculum Coordinator, Columbus City Schools
Columbus, Ohio

Layout, maps, graphics, and typesetting: Burmar Technical Corporation, Sea Cliff, N.Y.

This book is dedicated…

to Joan, Todd, and Ronald,
and my grandchildren Jared and Katie — *Stuart Zimmer*

to Malgorzata, Alexander, and Julia — *Mark Jarrett*

to Donna, Christian, Carrie, Jesse,
and my grandchildren Aiden, Christian, Olivia,
Rutland, Shannon, and James — *James Killoran*

ISBN 1-935022-20-2   [978-1-935022-20-6]
Printed in the United States of America
First Edition
10 9 8 7 6 5 4 3   17 16 15

ALSO BY ZIMMER, JARRETT, AND KILLORAN

Ohio: Its Land and Its People
Ohio: The Buckeye State
Mastering Ohio's Grade 5 Social Studies Achievement Test
Ohio: Its Neighbors Near and Far
Mastering World Regions and Civilizations
Mastering Ohio's Grade 8 Social Studies Achievement Test
Mastering Ohio's 9th Grade Citizenship Test
Mastering Ohio's 12th Grade Citizenship Test
Mastering Ohio's Graduation Test in Social Studies
Mastering the Grade 8 TEKS in Social Studies
Mastering the TEKS in World Geography
Mastering the TEKS in World History
Mastering the TEKS in United States History Since 1877
Mastering the Grade 8 TAKS Social Studies Assessment
Mastering the Grade 10 TAKS Social Studies Assessment
Mastering the Grade 11 TAKS Social Studies Assessment
Texas: Its Land and Its People
Learning About New York State
Mastering New York's Elementary Social Studies Standards: Grade 5 Edition
Mastering New York's Grade 7 Social Studies Standards
Mastering New York's Intermediate Social Studies Standards
The Key to Understanding Global History
Mastering Global History
A Quick Review of Global History
The Key to Understanding U.S. History and Government
Mastering U.S. History
A Quick Review of U.S. History and Government
North Carolina: The Tar Heel State
Michigan: Its Land and Its People
Mastering the Social Studies MEAP Test: Grade 5
Mastering the Social Studies MEAP Test: Grade 8
Mastering Michigan's High School Test in Social Studies
Mastering the Grade 5 MCAS History and Social Science Test
Mastering the Grade 5 CRCT in Social Studies
Mastering the GHSGT in Social Studies
Los Estados Unidos: Su Historia, Su Gobierno
Historia y gobierno de los Estados Unidos
Claves Para La Comprension de historia universal
Principios de Economia
Mastering the Internet

TABLE OF CONTENTS

HOW THIS BOOK WILL HELP YOU

Ohio in the United States will help you master Ohio's Fourth Grade Learning Standards in social studies. In the activities in this book, you will learn about the geography of Ohio, the main events that led to the settling of Ohio, and some of the challenges the people of Ohio have faced since achieving statehood. You will also learn about Ohio's diverse ethnic heritage and the importance of respecting the traditions and achievements of others.

You are about to set off on an exciting journey in which you will travel through 28 activities. Each activity has been designed to provide you with an opportunity to cooperate, discuss, brainstorm, debate, research, and learn what you need for passing the *Fourth Grade Ohio Achievement Test in Social Studies*.

THE ORGANIZATION OF EACH ACTIVITY

The book is broken down into four strands. Each strand covers the four main themes of social studies — **history**, **geography**, **government** and **economics**. Each activity has several unique features, designed to help you better learn the information in that activity.

FOCUS QUESTION

At the start of each activity, you will find a thought-provoking focus question. This focus question or "aim" question is the "engine of the lesson." It "drives" the activity by supplying the purpose and direction of the activity.

CONTENT STATEMENT

At the beginning of each activity, there is also a gray box. This box contains a *Content Statement* from the Ohio Learning Standards. This statement tells you the essential knowledge you are expected to learn in that activity.

KEY TERMS

Can you imagine playing a game without knowing its rules? That would surely be very confusing. Social studies has many unique and specialized terms and concepts. Mastering these terms and concepts is important to understanding the content of the activity. Therefore, at the start of each activity, you will find a list of **bolded** terms and concepts found in the activity. These terms and concepts highlight the most important information you should look for as you work your way through that activity.

CONTENT SECTIONS

Each activity includes text explaining the Content Statement. This text is divided into several smaller sections. Here you will find clear and insightful information that will help you to master the main ideas and facts that you should know. The text is accompanied by maps, diagrams, and illustrations to help you visualize about what you are reading.

CHECKING YOUR UNDERSTANDING

In each activity you will find one, two or more questions that ask you to apply what you have just read. These *Checking Your Understanding* exercises encourage you to review what you have just read.

THINKING IT OVER

Thinking It Over exercises ask questions that provoke you to think more about what you have read and to express your own opinion. They encourage you to interact with what you just read.

STUDY CARDS

Study Cards identify the major facts, terms, concepts, and people at the end of each activity. You can use these *Study Cards* alone to quiz yourself, or with a group of classmates. You will learn more about how to use these cards later in this introduction.

MAKING CONNECTIONS

At the conclusion of each activity is a *Making Connections* section. This section extends and reinforces a part of the subject matter in that activity. Here you are challenged to do something extra, such as visiting a museum or interviewing a business person or going to a library to research a topic.

LEARNING WITH GRAPHIC ORGANIZERS

Most activities have an exercise that asks you to complete a graphic organizer summarizing the most important information in the activity.

EXPRESS YOURSELF

Some of the activities conclude by asking you to write something about what you just learned. You are given an opportunity to express your views. These exercises often deal with the core of information that you will need to master the fourth grade test in social studies.

HOW TO USE YOUR STUDY CARDS

During this school year, you will learn about important past events and the many people who have influenced the development of Ohio. With such a large amount of information, it is sometimes difficult to identify and remember all the things that are important. Learning how to use *Study Cards* will help you to do that.

At the end of every activity you will find two or more *Study Cards*. These *Study Cards* highlight the most essential information you should know about a fact, term, or concept in the activity. You should make a habit of building a collection of these *Study Cards* by copying by hand or photocopying them.

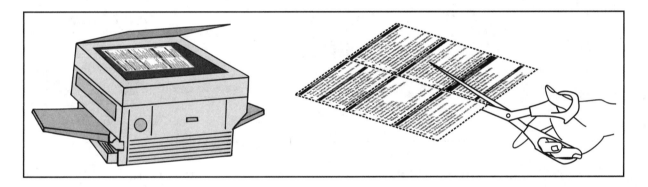

After you duplicate these *Study Cards*, you should use the back of each card to illustrate the main point of what appears on the front of the card.

Why should you draw your own illustration? Turning written information into a picture can help you to better understand the term or concept. Many students learn better when they can visualize something. By "seeing" the term or concept, you create an impression in your mind that helps you to remember it better. In drawing these illustrations, do not be concerned with your artistic ability. That is not important. What is important is that your illustration captures the main idea of the term or concept.

There are many ways to use *Study Cards* to recall information when it comes to a class quiz or test. One method is to sort your cards into two stacks, based on how well you recall the information on each card.

First, gather your *Study Cards* into one pile. Try to recall the information on the card at the top of the stack. If you can recall it, place the card in the "Know It" stack. If you have trouble recalling the information, place the card in the "Don't Know It" stack.

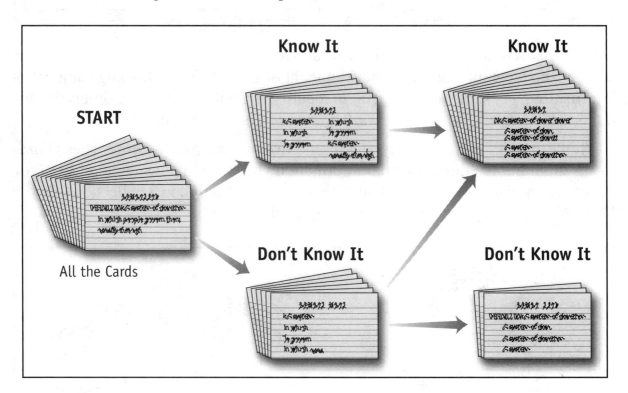

Review the cards in the "Don't Know It" stack every time you study. Review the *Study Cards* in the "Know It" stack every other time you study. As you move closer to the day of the quiz or test, you should see the number of cards in the "Don't Know It" stack start to grow less. This will give you even more time to study the ones you know the least.

Ohio in the United States will provide you with all the essential information you will need to know about *history*, *geography*, *government*, and *economics*. With this book as your guide, you should be well prepared to face the challenges presented by the *Fourth Grade Ohio Achievement Test in Social Studies*.

Name _Jafferi James Kinyuy_

UNIT 1

GEOGRAPHY

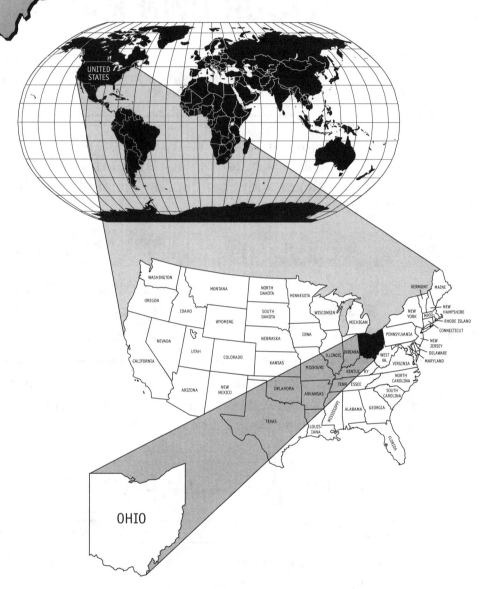

Where we live often determines how we live. The study of geography comes from the need to know "where." Geography tells us where different places are located and what they are like. This knowledge helps us because we come into contact with people and products from many different places.

ACTIVITY 1A

CAN YOU CREATE YOUR OWN MAP?

■ A map scale and cardinal and intermediate directions can be used to describe the relative location of physical and human characteristics of Ohio and the United States.

In this activity, you will learn how to create your own map of your community. After completing this activity, you will be able to measure distances on a map using the map's scale. You will also learn about cardinal and intermediate directions to describe the location of places in Ohio.

KEY TERMS

- ■ Map
- ■ Globe
- ■ Legend
- ■ Key
- ■ Symbol
- ■ Direction Indicator
- ■ Cardinal Directions
- ■ Intermediate Directions
- ■ Map Scale

Your teacher has asked you to make a map of an imaginary community as a school project. You tell yourself: "This seems like a fun and interesting project. But what do I have to do to create a map? How do I even start?"

WHAT ARE MAPS?

You ask your teacher for advice on how to begin. Your teacher explains that a **map** is simply a small diagram of a larger place. It shows where things are located. The easiest way to understand a map is by mapping things in a small area. For example, you might start by making a map of your desktop. You can begin by drawing a box to represent the top of your desk.

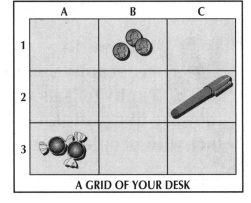

A GRID OF YOUR DESK

Suppose there are three objects on the top of your desk. Pretend you are a bird, flying over the desk. Could you describe exactly where the objects are located?" At first, you might find this hard to do. The first mapmakers had the same difficulty.

To locate places on a map, mapmakers today make a **grid** like the one for the "desk map" above. A grid uses straight lines that cross each other. The crossing lines form boxes. The rows along the top and side are given letters or numbers.

CHECKING YOUR UNDERSTANDING

Write down the number and the letter of the grid box that contains:

- the candy _____
- the coins _____
- the pen _____

HOW TO USE A MAP

Maps come in different sizes and shapes. Some maps show where countries, states and cities are located. Other maps show geographic features such as mountains, oceans and rivers. Still others show airports, parks and schools. A **globe** is a special kind of map. It is a three-dimensional sphere that shows the entire Earth.

THE TITLE

To understand a map, you should first look at its title. The title tells you what area is shown on the map.

THE LEGEND

The secret to using any map is understanding its symbols. Instead of writing the word "highway" or "railroad" each time one of these appears

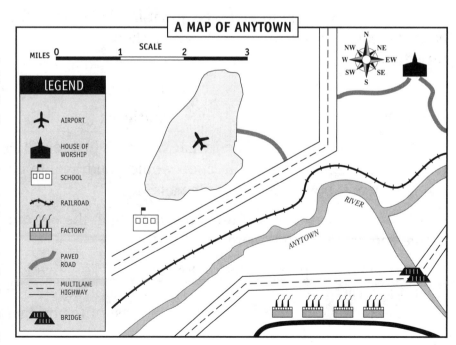

on a map, mapmakers use symbols to represent them.

A map **symbol** is a drawing that stands for an actual place or thing. For example, the symbol for an airport might be a small airplane. Symbols may appear as shapes, lines, dots, dashes or pictures. Each map will have its own set of symbols. Mapmakers provide a legend to explain what each symbol means. The **legend** or **key** explains what the symbols used on the map represent. The legend "unlocks" their meaning.

CHECKING YOUR UNDERSTANDING

1   What is the title of the map on the previous page?_____

2   There are 8 symbols on the map of Anytown. Draw the symbol used for:

   • a factory _____   • a school _____

   • a bridge _____   • an airport _____

FINDING DIRECTIONS

To make it easier to find directions on a map, mapmakers provide a **direction indicator**. This shows the four **cardinal directions**. These are the four main points of the compass.

• **north** (N)   • **south** (S)

• **east** (E)   • **west** (W)

Sometimes we need to find places that fall in between the four basic directions. A compass rose may also show four **intermediate directions**:

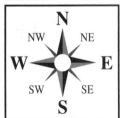

• **northeast** (NE)   • **northwest** (NW)

• **southwest** (SW)   • **southeast** (SE)

How well do you understand what you have just read? On the Anytown map on the previous page, in which direction would you travel to go from the bridge to the school? Here is how to figure out the answer:

• Most maps show north at the top and south at the bottom, but you should check the compass rose to be sure.

• Look at the compass on the Anytown map. If you traveled from the bridge, found in the eastern part of Anytown, to the school, located in the western part, you would be traveling west. The school is west of the bridge.

Name ___Jarves___

Activity 1A: Does Geography Affect How People Live?   **9**

CHECKING YOUR UNDERSTANDING

In what direction would you travel from the:

- house of worship to the bridge? _____

- airport to the bridge? _____

- factories to the school? _____

- school to the factories? _____

MEASURING DISTANCES ON A MAP

As you have seen, a map is a small diagram of a larger space. If a map were the same size as the area it shows, it would be too large to use. Imagine a map of your school that was the same size as your school! Instead, mapmakers shrink distances on their maps. For example, mapmakers may use one inch to represent one real mile. On a map of a large area, one inch may represent 100 miles or more.

Mapmakers provide a **map scale** to show what the dis-

tances on a map stand for in real life. A map scale shows the relationship between a unit of length on the map and the actual length on the map on the Earth's surface.

The map scale can be used to figure out the distance between any two places on a map. Scales tell us the real distance, usually in miles or kilometers. Map scales are often shown as a line marked: "Scale of Miles."

Let's see how we can find the distance from Cleveland to Youngstown. First, put a ruler under the map scale. You will notice that one inch on the Scale of Miles represents a distance of 50 miles.

Put a piece of paper on the map. Line up the edge until it touches both Cleveland and Youngstown. Mark both spots on the paper with a pencil or pen. Now place the same edge along the scale of the map. Mark off the first 50 miles. Then move the paper over to see how many more miles are needed to reach the spot marking the end of the distance. You can see it is just 15 more miles. Since the total distance between the two marks is about one and a quarter inches, we can conclude that the distance from Cleveland to Youngstown is about 65 miles.

CHECKING YOUR UNDERSTANDING

Using the map on the previous page, what would be the distance from:

- Toledo to Cleveland _100 miles_
- Columbus to Akron _120 miles_
- Dayton to Cincinnati _50 miles_
- Youngstown to Cincinnati _250 miles_

DRAWING A MAP OF YOUR IMAGINARY COMMUNITY

You now know enough to draw a map of your own imaginary community. You will map an imaginary town named after yourself. For example, if your name was Brian, you would call the town Brianville. Use the following steps to create your map:

- Decide how many different features you want to show on your map.
- Think of where you will place each feature.
- Create symbols for a legend or "key" to explain the features on your map.
- Add a direction indicator (*compass rose*) showing both **cardinal** and **intermediate directions**.
- Include a **scale of miles**.
- Finally, put a title at the top of your map: **MAP OF ___?___ VILLE**

Name _____

MAKING CONNECTIONS

DIRECTIONS TO A "MYSTERY CITY"

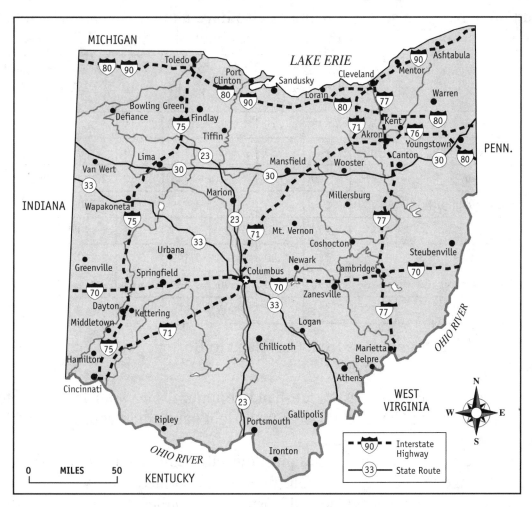

Above is a road map of Ohio. A **road map** shows the major cities, towns, chief roads, and places of interest in an area. It also indicates the distance from one place to another. In this *Making Connections*, your teacher will divide your class into small groups. In each group, one student will challenge the others in the group by identifying a starting city. From that city, the student will provide directions to the other students in the group to reach the "Mystery City."

If you provide accurate directions, the other students using your directions should end up at the correct destination. Each student in your group must locate the "Mystery City" by using only the map scale and the cardinal and intermediate directions provided to them.

For example, assume your starting city is Columbus. (**1**) Travel 75 miles east on Route 70. (**2**) Then travel 50 miles north on Route 77. (**3**) Travel 3 miles northwest.

Based only on these directions, what is the "Mystery City"? _Clinton_

INTERPRETING A MILEAGE CHART

In addition to having a scale, some maps also have a mileage chart. The following mileage chart shows the approximate distances between 8 major U.S. cities.

	Atlanta	Boston	Chicago	Cleve.	Dallas	Detroit	LA	NY
Atlanta, GA	•	1,075	715	730	830	745	1,980	865
Boston, MA	1075	•	980	645	1,870	710	3,130	215
Chicago, IL	715	980	•	345	345	280	2,190	820
Cleveland, OH	730	645	345	•	1,225	165	2,980	505
Dallas, TX	830	1,870	940	1,225	•	1,195	1,490	1,650
Detroit, MI	745	710	280	165	1,195	•	2,450	635
Los Angeles, CA	2,185	3,130	3,130	2,490	1,435	2,450	•	2,915
New York, NY	865	215	820	505	1,650	635	2,915	•

To find the number of miles from Cleveland to Boston, you can use the information in the mileage chart above.

- First, find Cleveland along the left-hand column. Using your left hand, hold a finger on the name Cleveland. Using your right hand, slide your finger along the top line until you reach Boston.
- Now move your right finger straight down the column of numbers and slide your left finger straight across. Your fingers should meet at "645." The distance between the cities of Cleveland and Boston is 645 miles.

CHECKING YOUR UNDERSTANDING

1   What is the distance from Boston to Atlanta? _____

2   What is the distance from Chicago to Los Angeles? _____

3   Which is a longer trip: from Dallas to Chicago or Boston to New York?

_____

STUDY CARDS

Maps

- What is a map? <u>It's a small diagram of a larger place.</u>

- Name the four main parts of a map.

1 <u>Compass Rose</u>   3 <u>Ledgend</u>
2 <u>Map scale</u>   4 <u>Title</u>

LEARNING WITH GRAPHIC ORGANIZERS

Directions: Complete the graphic organizer by identifying each part of a map.

Title: <u>Tells you what area is shown on the map</u>

Legend (Key): <u>Explains what the symbols on a Map represent</u>

Main Parts of a Map

Cardinal Directions:
1 <u>North</u>   3 <u>East</u>
2 <u>south</u>   4 <u>West</u>

Intermediate Directions: (NE)
1 <u>Northwest</u> (NW)   3 <u>Northeast</u> (NE)
2 <u>Southwest</u> (SW)   4 <u>Southeast</u> (SE)

Map Scale: <u>Show what the distance on a stand for in real life.</u>

ACTIVITY 1B

WHERE IS OHIO LOCATED?

■ A map scale and cardinal and intermediate directions can be used to describe the relative location of physical and human characteristics of Ohio and the United States.

In this activity, you will write a letter to an imaginary pen pal living in Mexico. After completing this activity, you will understand the meaning of relative location. In addition, you will be able to describe the relative location of Ohio in relation to other states and countries.

KEY TERMS

■ Relative Location
■ Country

■ Physical Regions
■ Region

■ State
■ County

DETERMINING RELATIVE LOCATION

Juan, your pen pal from Mexico, has sent you an email. In his email, Juan tells you of his school project — to pick an area in the world and describe its relative location.

RELATIVE LOCATION

Relative location is where a place is found in relation to other places. It is a way of describing a place using reference points. Cardinal and intermediate directions like north, south, northeast, and southwest help to describe relative location. For example, my house is one mile northeast of the mall. Or you can tell someone to meet you at Starbucks, next to the state park. Or, Ohio is located south of Canada, and north of Mexico.

Relative location uses such terms as *near*, *by*, or *at the corner of* to identify a location. The relative location of your school can tell us if it is near a highway, or how far it is from the nearest bus stop. We use relative location to see how two places are connected. For example, the cities of Columbus, Ohio and Anchorage, Alaska are about 4,000 miles apart. Anchorage is northwest of Ohio.

Knowing that you live in Ohio, Juan has decided to pick Ohio for his project. In Juan's email, he asks you to help him describe Ohio's relative location. You decide to use your computer's "Geography-Information" program to help you find where Ohio is located relative to other states and countries. Here is your first computer screen:

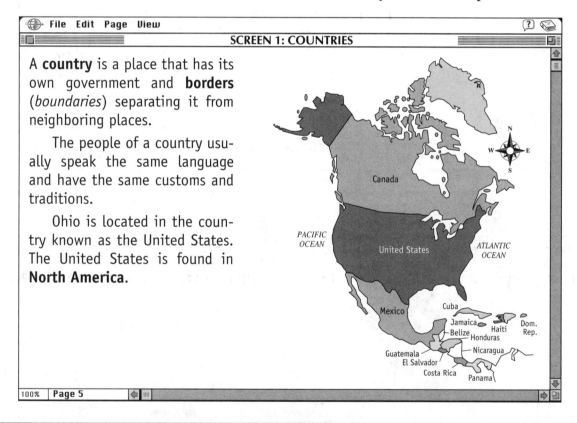

File   Edit   Page   View

SCREEN 1: COUNTRIES

A **country** is a place that has its own government and **borders** (*boundaries*) separating it from neighboring places.

The people of a country usually speak the same language and have the same customs and traditions.

Ohio is located in the country known as the United States. The United States is found in **North America**.

100%   Page 5

CHECKING YOUR UNDERSTANDING

Use the map and information in **Screen 1** to answer the following questions:

1 What country borders the United States to the north? _____

2 What country borders the United States to the south? _____

3 Describe the relative location of the United States to the Pacific Ocean:

_____

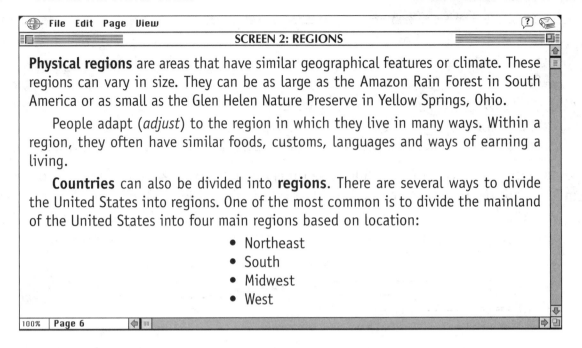

File   Edit   Page   View

SCREEN 2: REGIONS

Physical regions are areas that have similar geographical features or climate. These regions can vary in size. They can be as large as the Amazon Rain Forest in South America or as small as the Glen Helen Nature Preserve in Yellow Springs, Ohio.

People adapt (*adjust*) to the region in which they live in many ways. Within a region, they often have similar foods, customs, languages and ways of earning a living.

Countries can also be divided into **regions**. There are several ways to divide the United States into regions. One of the most common is to divide the mainland of the United States into four main regions based on location:

- Northeast
- South
- Midwest
- West

100%   Page 6

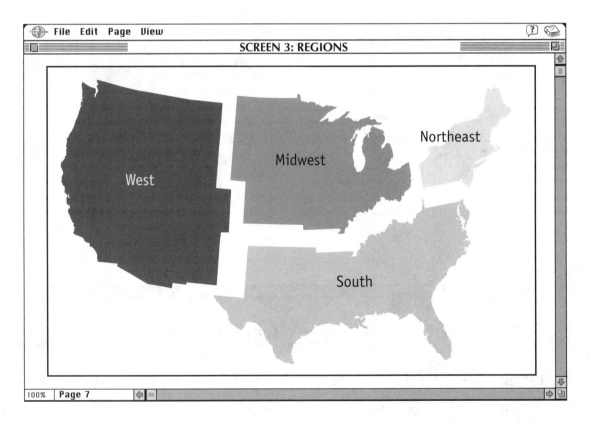

File   Edit   Page   View

SCREEN 3: REGIONS

West

Midwest

Northeast

South

100%   Page 7

CHECKING YOUR UNDERSTANDING

Use the map and information in **Screen 3** to answer the following questions:

1　What is a physical region? _____

_____

2　In which region of the United States is Ohio located? _____

3　Describe the relative location of that region to the West: _____

_____

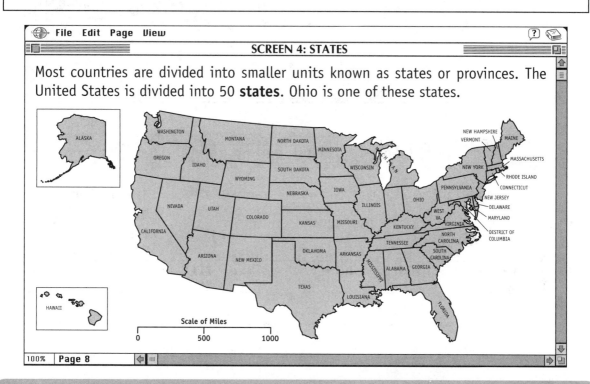

File　Edit　Page　View

SCREEN 4: STATES

Most countries are divided into smaller units known as states or provinces. The United States is divided into 50 **states**. Ohio is one of these states.

100%　Page 8

CHECKING YOUR UNDERSTANDING

Use the map and information in **Screen 4** to answer the following questions:

1　Describe relative location of Ohio to Alaska. _____

_____

2　Describe the location of Ohio relative to two of its neighboring states:

_____

_____

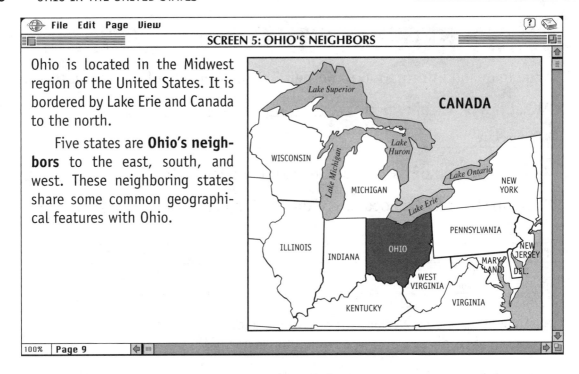

File   Edit   Page   View

SCREEN 5: OHIO'S NEIGHBORS

Ohio is located in the Midwest region of the United States. It is bordered by Lake Erie and Canada to the north.

Five states are **Ohio's neighbors** to the east, south, and west. These neighboring states share some common geographical features with Ohio.

100%   Page 9

CHECKING YOUR UNDERSTANDING

Use the map and information in **Screen 5** to answer the following questions:

1   Which five states border the state of Ohio?

    A _____

    B _____

    C _____

    D _____

    E _____

2   What body of water borders the state of Ohio? _____

3   Describe the location of Ohio relative to that body of water:

    _____

    _____

WRITING YOUR RETURN EMAIL

You now have enough information to describe Ohio's relative location. Write an email to Juan describing Ohio's location relative to other countries, states and bodies of water. In your letter, be sure to use both cardinal and intermediate directions to describe Ohio's location.

from: You
subject: Ohio's location relative to other countries, states, bodies of water
to: Juan
cc: Your Teacher

Dear Juan,

Your friend,

MAKING CONNECTIONS

USING RELATIVE LOCATION TO LOCATE YOUR COMMUNITY

Each of the 50 states of the United States is divided into smaller governing units called **counties**. Below is a map of the 88 counties that make up in Ohio. Examine the map closely. Then answer the questions that follow on the next page.

CHECKING YOUR UNDERSTANDING

1 Name the county where you live: _____

2 Describe its location relative to the other counties on this map. Be sure to identify all those counties bordering your county.

_____

_____

3 Which county is directly north of Wayne? _____

4 Which county is nearby Lawrence? _____

5 Which county would you come to first if you were to travel northeast of

Lake County? _____

6 Ask an adult family member, neighbor or family friend to describe any type of changes that have occurred in the community, such as new highways, new buildings, or new businesses, over the last several years.

_____

_____

STUDY CARDS

Relative Location

- Define relative location? _____

_____

- List two examples using relative location:

    1 _____

    _____

    2 _____

    _____

Ohio's Relative Location

• Name two tools used to locate a place.

1 _____   2 _____

• What country borders the state of Ohio? _____

• Which five states border Ohio?   3 _____

1 _____   4 _____

2 _____   5 _____

LEARNING WITH GRAPHIC ORGANIZERS

Directions: Complete the graphic organizer below by adding the missing information.

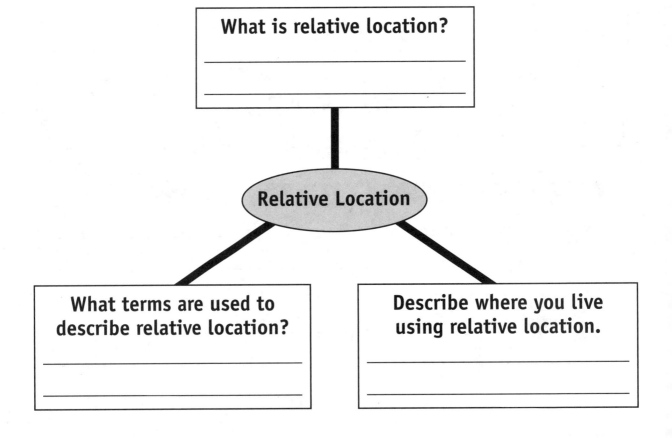

What is relative location?

_____

_____

Relative Location

What terms are used to describe relative location?

_____

_____

Describe where you live using relative location.

_____

_____

Name _____

ACTIVITY
1C

HOW HAS OHIO CONTRIBUTED TO THE ECONOMIC DEVELOP-MENT OF THE UNITED STATES?

■ The economic development of the United States continues to influence and be influenced by agriculture, industry, and natural resources of Ohio.

In this activity you will create a poster showing how Ohio has influenced the economic growth of the United States.

KEY TERMS

- ■ Natural Resources
- ■ Ohio River
- ■ Mineral Resources
- ■ Iron Ore
- ■ Forests
- ■ Farming
- ■ Fishing
- ■ Manufacturing
- ■ Transportation

Imagine there is a contest for fourth-grade students to create a poster showing how economic factors in their state have helped to develop the American economy. You are excited to enter the contest. To enter this contest, your teacher divides the class into small groups. Each group must create its own poster showing how Ohio's natural resources, agriculture, and industry contributed to the economic development of the United States.

Before your group begins, it needs to obtain information about Ohio's role in the development of the nation's economic growth. To help with this task, imagine that your teacher provides several handouts about Ohio's economy. This information will serve as the basis of your poster.

NATURAL RESOURCES

The economic development of the United States has been greatly influenced by Ohio's natural resources.

WATER RESOURCES

One of Ohio's leading natural resources is its plentiful water resources. These have played an important role in the economic development of the United States.

The **Ohio River** is the state's most important river. Most of Ohio's rivers and streams drain into the Ohio River. The Ohio River flows more than 450 miles along the state's southern border. It separates Ohio from Kentucky and West Virginia.

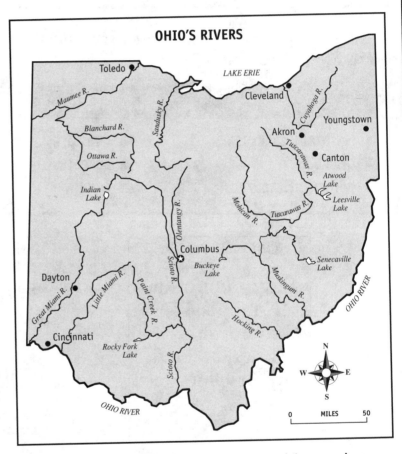

OHIO'S RIVERS

The Ohio River flows into the Mississippi River and provides an important shipping route from Ohio all the way south to the Gulf of Mexico. By the 1800s, the Ohio River became a major route for both farmers and manufacturers. Crops and manufactured goods were sent on flat boats and barges down the Mississippi River to New Orleans. Once in New Orleans, they were loaded onto ocean-going ships for delivery to other states.

PAGE 1

After the invention of the steamboat and the completion of the Erie Canal in 1825, goods could also be sent from Ohio into the Great Lakes, across the Erie Canal, and down the Hudson River to New York City.

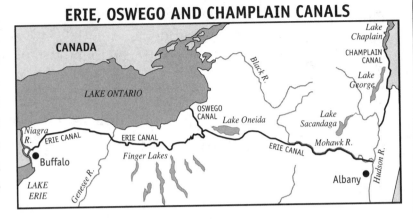

ERIE, OSWEGO AND CHAMPLAIN CANALS

The location of Lake Erie, the Ohio River and other rivers in the state greatly influenced settlement patterns. Early settlers first came to Ohio by traveling along the Ohio River. People tended to settle in Ohio along the shores of Lake Erie and on the banks of Ohio's major rivers. These locations served as important transportation routes and provided plenty of fresh water for drinking and farming. The population of Ohio surged after the Erie Canal was built.

MINERAL RESOURCES

The economic development of the United States has also been greatly influenced by the abundance of mineral resources found in Ohio. Large deposits of coal, salt, limestone, sandstone, sand, clay, and gypsum helped make Ohio an early leader in mining and manufacturing. These minerals were equally important to the production of goods in other areas of the United States.

Workers in an Ohio coal mine.

Coal and natural gas are two of Ohio's most valuable resources. Heat and electricity can be produced when they are burned. Coal from Ohio was once used to power many of the nation's factories, and to power the ships and trains that carried both raw materials and finished products.

PAGE 2

Ohio also has an abundance of **iron ore**. Iron ore is needed to make iron and steel products. America's growth as an economic superpower can be traced to the rise of its steel industry. Ohio's supply of iron ore and its other minerals helped it to become a center of heavy industry. In the years after the Civil War, the American steel industry grew with astonishing speed.

Iron ore

FORESTS

Ohio's once plentiful forest lands also had an important influence on the nation's economic development. Its trees were used to make houses and other buildings. Ships loaded with lumber from the forests of Ohio sailed to Europe where their cargoes were sold. For 150 years, the forests of Ohio were cut down to clear farmland. Wood from trees was a major source of energy, and was often used to build fences and houses. As settlers moved into the Ohio River Valley, forests were cleared for planting and to build homes. No attempt was made to stop the destruction of these forests until the mid-1800s.

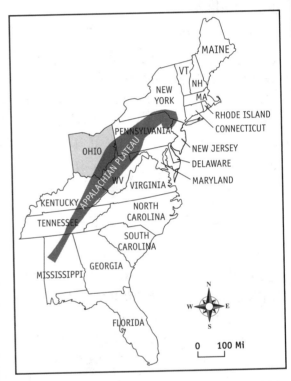

Eastern Ohio is part of the Appalachian Plateau. Today, much of its land is again covered with forests, making it a good source of lumber. About 93% of the forest land in Ohio is privately owned. Ohio's forests are the basis for its multi-billion dollar wood industry, employing thousands of workers.

PAGE 3

CHECKING YOUR UNDERSTANDING

How have Ohio's natural resources helped the nation's economy to develop?

_____

_____

FARMING AND FISHING

The economic development of the United States has been further influenced by Ohio's agriculture. The first farmers in Ohio were part of America's westward expansion. Farming back then was different from today. Early farmers lacked large machinery. Human and animal power were needed to raise a crop.

Most of the early settlers in Ohio grew wheat, corn, and other grain crops. They played an important role in feeding the nation's expanding population. By 1849, Ohio produced more corn than any other state, and it ranked second in wheat production. In 1885, the most commonly grown crop in Ohio was corn, followed by wheat, oats, potatoes, barley, rye, and buckwheat.

Fertile farm land remains one of Ohio's most valuable resources. The state's soils are well suited to agriculture. Farming continues to be an important occupation in Ohio. The state today has almost 80,000 farms. Half of Ohio's land area is still farmland. Ohio is a leader in the farming of soybeans, one of its largest crops, and corn.

Ohio farmers also continue to grow wheat, oats, barley, and hay. They raise livestock such as cattle, hogs, and poultry. Milk is a leading product. Many farmers also grow vegetables and fruit. Ohio's greenhouse and nursery (*a place where plants and trees are grown*) products earn about one dollar in every ten earned from farming.

FISHING

The fisheries of Ohio have had an important influence on the economic development of our nation. Because of its location along the Great Lakes, and its many rivers and streams, Ohio's fisheries played an important role in helping feed the nation's expanding population. The growing demand for fish helped encourage Ohio's economy. Ohio's largest source of fish is Lake Erie.

CHECKING YOUR UNDERSTANDING

How have the farms and fisheries of Ohio contributed to the economy of the United States?

_____

_____

_____

INDUSTRY

MANUFACTURING

Manufacturing is one of Ohio's most important economic activities. Ohio's rich water resources helped to power the machines in its factories. This allowed manufacturers to produce more goods for less money. As goods became cheaper, demand for them increased, leading to the creation of more jobs. Cities grew up around factories, as people moved to where they could find work.

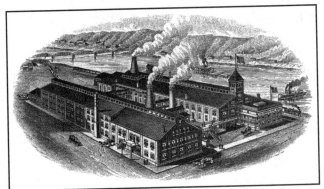

Factories such as this appeared throughout Ohio in the middle to late 1800s.

The nation's growing demand for manufactured goods led to the rise of many industries in Ohio. Today, manufacturing still accounts for about one out of every four jobs in Ohio. Factory workers make goods such as steel and rubber products. Others work in factories turning steel or iron into products such as cars and washing machines. Ohio's largest manufacturing industry is making transportation equipment, including automobiles, car parts, and aircraft parts.

Several factors help explain why Ohio became a leading manufacturing state. Ohio's central location, natural resources, and skilled and educated workforce made it a good location for manufacturing. Today, more than 800 companies do business in Ohio. These businesses include Honda, Bridgestone, Hitachi, Mitsubishi, Chrysler, Rolls-Royce, and Nestlé.

CHECKING YOUR UNDERSTANDING

How did Ohio's industries help the American economy to grow?

_____

_____

_____

TRANSPORTATION

Ohio's transportation system has had an important influence on the economic development of the United States. As the nation expanded, travel overland became a problem. Travel by road was expensive and time-consuming. In 1806, the federal government built a national road from Maryland across the Appalachians to Ohio. Completion of this and other roads encouraged economic growth by making it easier to ship goods.

Workers building the National Road.

The nation's growing economy led to the expansion of Ohio's transportation system. In the early 1800s, it was easier to ship goods by water than by land. Advances, such as the steamboat, greatly contributed to Ohio's economic growth. In 1825, New York completed a 360-mile canal connecting Lake Erie at Buffalo to the Hudson River. The **Erie Canal** made it possible to ship crops by water from the Great Lakes to population centers along the East Coast. While a 3 mph speed was slow, canal boats could carry 10 tons of goods, making them more efficient than wagons traveling over dirt roads.

As a result, Ohio's population grew. The example of the Erie Canal was copied by Ohio and other states. Along these canals, many new cities arose. People moved to these cities because jobs were readily available. Ohio soon became the third most populated state, owing much of its growth to its canals.

PAGE 6

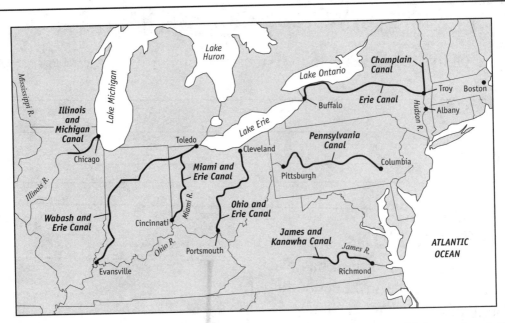

Today, the Great Lakes and St. Lawrence Seaway connect Ohio to the Atlantic Ocean and to the east. The Great Lakes and Ohio River link Ohio with other north-central states and Canada. The Ohio River carries coal, oil, chemicals, and building materials to the Mississippi River, which flows south into the Gulf of Mexico.

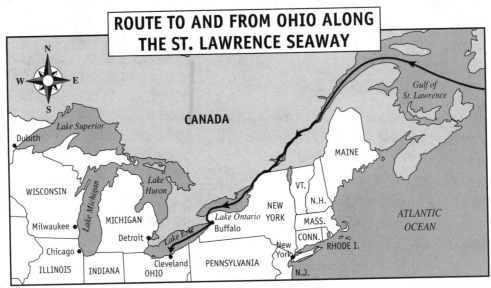

Ohio is recognized as a having an ideal business location that delivers easy access to customers and markets. Centrally located between the eastern and western United States, Ohio is within 600 miles of more than half of all American and Canadian manufacturing. Ohio's modern, multi-lane highway system crisscrosses the state. The state's airports link Ohio to all parts of the world.

CHECKING YOUR UNDERSTANDING

How did Ohio's transportation system help promote the nation's economic development?

_____

_____

_____

DESIGNING YOUR POSTER

Now that you have reviewed the information needed for your poster, it's time for you and the other members of your group to get to work. Your group should think about which information would best illustrate how Ohio helped the economy of the United States to grow. In creating your poster, keep in mind:

■ Artistic talent is not as important in designing your poster as creating an interesting and thought-provoking poster.

■ Remember that a poster is not just a paper stuck on a board. Your poster has to show, not simply tell. It should express your points in an illustrated (*to show something in pictures or diagrams*) manner.

■ Your poster should display the basic message in the title, headings and graphics. Each main heading should use large type-face. The details should be in visually smaller type-face. The headings must explain the main points, rather then having the viewer hunt for your message.

■ You can search magazines, newspapers and the Internet for pictures to use in creating your poster. Members of your group may want to ask their parents for help. Parents help should be limited to suggesting ideas or providing photographs for use in the group's poster.

■ After all the groups have finished, each group should present its poster to the class. Then the class should vote on what they believe is the best.

Your group may want to create a **PowerPoint presentation** instead of a poster presentation. You'll first need a PowerPoint application. After the program starts up, if a blank presentation does not appear in front of you, select "new" from the file menu. You can find more information on making a PowerPoint presentation at: http://www.worldofteaching.com

MAKING CONNECTIONS

CHALLENGES FACING OHIO AND THE NATION

Have you ever heard of the expression: "Two heads are better than one"? This means that some tasks may be accomplished more easily if two or more people are working together than one working alone.

In this part of the activity, you are going to **brainstorm** with others, listing as many ideas or solutions as you can think of. When brainstorming, people suggest as many ways of solving a problem as they can think of.

Today, Ohio and the United States face many problems. Two of these problems involve global competition and the greater use of biofuels. Your teacher will divide the class into groups. Each student in the group will read the background below about these problems. Then, all the members of the group will brainstorm — trying to come up with as many ideas as they can think of. Finally, the class will hold a discussion of each group's solutions and come up with the best ones.

FIRST CHALLENGE: GLOBAL COMPETITION

Rapid changes have made the world's nations more interdependent than ever before. As the world has grown "smaller," events taking place in one area of the world have a greater impact on other parts of the world. In the past, Ohio and the United States were leaders in the production of automobiles, rubber, steel and heavy equipment. However, competition from Europe and Asia now threaten the leadership of Ohio and the United States in these industries.

What can Ohio and the United States do to regain their leadership in the production of automobiles, rubber, steel and heavy equipment?
_____
_____

_____

_____

_____

_____

_____

SECOND CHALLENGE: THE MOVE TO BIOFUELS

People in Ohio and the United States are becoming more sensitive to threats to the atmosphere posed by "fossil fuels" like coal and oil. A significant part of Ohio's corn was once used to feed the growing population of the United States. Today, an increasing amount of corn and soybeans are now used to produce **biofuels** — fuels made from living organisms such as plants. Although these fuels are burned, the plants that make these fuels absorb carbon dioxide and create oxygen when they are grow-

ing. The effect is more balanced than burning fossil fuels. In recent years, American farmers have converted millions of acres of grassland into corn and soybean fields.

What are the costs and benefits of producing corn and soybeans for fuel?

STUDY CARDS

Impact of Natural Resources on Ohio and the United States

What impact have Ohio's natural resources had on Ohio and the United States?

_____

_____

_____

_____

Agriculture

What impact has agriculture had on Ohio and the United States?

_____

_____

_____

_____

Manufacturing and Transportation

What impact have the following had on Ohio and the United States?

Manufacturing: _____

_____

_____

Transportation: _____

_____

_____

Name _____

Activity 1C: Ohio's Contribution to the Nation's Economic Growth   **35**

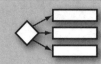 # LEARNING WITH GRAPHIC ORGANIZERS

Directions: Complete the graphic organizer below by explaining the influence of Ohio on the development of the economy of the United States.

Natural Resources:

_____
_____
_____
_____
_____
_____

Agricultural Industries:

_____
_____
_____
_____
_____
_____

Ohio's Influence on the Economic Development of the United States

Transportation Systems:

_____
_____
_____
_____
_____
_____

Manufacturing Industries:

_____
_____
_____
_____
_____
_____

EXPRESS YOURSELF

The economic development of the United States was greatly influenced by different economic factors in the State of Ohio. Some of the factors include Ohio's natural resources, agricultural products, industries, and transportation systems.

Choose **two** of these economic factors. For each factor selected, show how that factor promoted the economic development of the United States.

Name _____

ACTIVITY 1D

DOES GEOGRAPHY AFFECT HOW PEOPLE LIVE?

■ The regions which became known as the North, South and West of the United States developed in the early 1800's largely based on their physical environments and economies.

In this activity, you will learn how to make inferences. After completing this activity, you will also be able to describe how the North, South, and West of the United States developed differently in the 1800s. In addition, you will examine how the geography of each area affected how people in each region lived.

KEY TERMS

- ■ "Data Literacy"
- ■ Infer
- ■ Physical Map
- ■ Political Map

- ■ The North
- ■ The South
- ■ "King Cotton"
- ■ Slavery

- ■ The West
- ■ "Bread Basket"
- ■ Product Map
- ■ Legend

Information today comes in many different forms. Charts, graphs and pictures as well as text can provide us with information. Today, people need to have "**data literacy**" — the ability to find, manage, and interpret various types of data.

THE SKILL OF MAKING INFERENCES

A key part of "data literacy" is the ability to "make inferences" from data. To **infer** is to make a logical guess about something based on knowledge and experience, even though it is not directly stated. Writers often provide hints that help readers to understand what they are trying to communicate. To be "data literate," you have to act like a detective and carefully examine the clues to infer what is happening.

Let's take a look at a sample story to see this process. Suppose one night relatives you have not seen for a long time are visiting your family. Everyone in your family has stayed up late to catch up on past family events with these relatives.

The next morning, you are awakened by the noise of your mother banging on your sister's bedroom door. As you look out of your bedroom window, you see the school bus leaving without your sister in it.

CHECKING YOUR UNDERSTANDING

What can you *infer* from these facts about the reason why your mother is banging on your sister's bedroom door?

_____

_____

_____

You probably inferred that your sister was still asleep and failed to get up on time for school. She has missed her school bus. As you can see, an inference is a kind of an "educated guess." It is something you can suppose happened based on the facts you know. When you examine a new piece of data, you should therefore ask yourself:

What can I infer from this information?

Let's practice the skill of making inferences by looking at several pieces of data about different regions of the United States in the 1820s. Then see what you can infer about the geography of the areas and its impact on the people living in each region.

THE NORTH

SOURCE 1: PHYSICAL REGIONS OF THE UNITED STATES

In 1820, there were 23 states in the United States. The total population of the United States stood at just under 10 million people. Most of the land west of the Appalachian Mountains consisted of territories, not yet states.

Below is a political and physical map of the nation in the early 1800s. A **physical map** shows the physical features of an area, such as elevation, rivers and mountains. A **political map** shows borders between states.

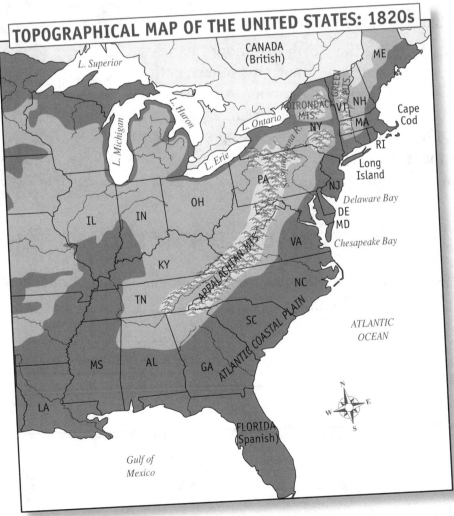

TOPOGRAPHICAL MAP OF THE UNITED STATES: 1820s

CHECKING YOUR UNDERSTANDING

What can you *infer* from Source 1 about the location of most Northern states (*today, referred to as the Northeast*) in the early 1800s?

_____

_____

_____

_____

_____

SOURCE 2: INDUSTRY IN THE NORTH

The "North" was the nation's first area to industrialize. In the early 1800s, it emerged as a center for manufacturing, shipbuilding, logging and small farms.

By the mid-1800s, the North had more factories, textile mills, and railroads than any other section of the country. A growing number of Northerners worked in factories and lived in large cities and towns. Coal was the major fuel used to power steam engines in these factories.

CHECKING YOUR UNDERSTANDING

What can you *infer* from Source 2 about the effect of the use of coal for industry on the North's environment?

_____

_____

_____

_____

_____

SOURCE 3: LARGEST CITIES IN THE U.S. IN 1820

Rank	Place	State	Population	Section
1	New York City	New York	123,706	North
2	Philadelphia	Pennsylvania	63,802	North
3	Baltimore	Maryland	62,738	North
4	New Orleans	Louisiana	27,176	South
5	Charleston	South Carolina	24,728	South
6	Washington	D.C.	13,247	South
7	Salem	Massachusetts	12,731	North

CHECKING YOUR UNDERSTANDING

What can you *infer* from Source 3 about the location of large cities in the United States in the 1820s?

_____

_____

_____

THE SOUTH

The South was largely agricultural. The South enjoyed long, hot summers and had rich, fertile soil in its river valleys. It provided excellent conditions for growing cotton.

SOURCE 4: THE GROWTH OF "KING COTTON"

The South's coastal marshes and long growing season favored the growth of such crops as cotton and tobacco. These crops were grown for sale in the North and to foreign markets, usually in Europe. Cotton represented the economic backbone of the South's economy. The textile (*clothing*) factories of the North and Britain depended on raw cotton raised on Southern plantations.

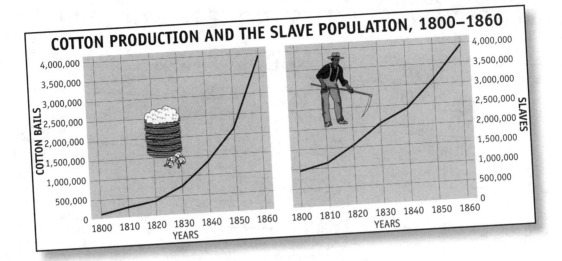

COTTON PRODUCTION AND THE SLAVE POPULATION, 1800–1860

CHECKING YOUR UNDERSTANDING

What can you *infer* from Source 4 about the relationship between cotton production and the number of slaves in the South?

_____

_____

_____

_____

SOURCE 5: COMPARING THE NORTH AND SOUTH

The mounting demand for cotton led to a growing call for more slave labor. Southern states failed to expand their industries, or to develop their transportation systems. In general, the South failed to develop as many cities, factories, or railroads as in the North.

Item	North	South
Railroad Mileage	72% of the nation's track	28% of the nation's track
Value of Exports	68% of the nation's exports	32% of the nation's exports
Factories	85% of the nation's factories	15% of the nation's factories
Farms	16% of the nation's farms	84% of the nation's farms
Iron/Steel Production	92% of iron/steel production	8% of iron/steel production

CHECKING YOUR UNDERSTANDING

What can you *infer* from Source 5 about the effect on the South of its dependence on growing cotton?

_____

_____

_____

_____

THE WEST

In the early 1800s, the Ohio River was the great highway of North America. Tens of thousands of people used it to move westward into the interior of the continent. The region's rich, fertile soil and inexpensive land attracted many farmers. Wagon trains carried immigrants into the West in ever growing numbers.

What was then known as the West is known today as the "Midwest." This region became the nation's "**bread basket**" since it grew most of the food crops Americans ate. Wheat, easy to grow and ship to market, became the main crop. By 1810, one in ten Americans lived west of the Appalachians. By 1815, Cincinnati's population was 4,000, while farther west, Louisville and St. Louis had half that figure. By 1840, more than a third of all Americans lived in this "First West."

SOURCE 6: IMAGES OF THE WEST

As settlers pushed west, various images began to illustrate Western lifestyles. They showed settlers moving west and taming the wilderness. This painting depicts America in the early 1800s.

This image shows settlers moving westward in the 1850s.

CHECKING YOUR UNDERSTANDING

What can you *infer* from the images in Source 6 about life in different parts of the West?

_____

_____

_____

_____

_____

EXPRESS YOURSELF

Using information from the six sources you have just examined, write an essay explaining how geography affected the lives of people in different sections of the United States in the early 1800s.

Name _____

MAKING CONNECTIONS

INTERPRETING A PRODUCT MAP

Maps provide a variety of information. Below is a **product map**. It shows where different products are made in an Ohio today. On a product map, picture symbols are used to stand for agriculture and mineral products and where they are located.

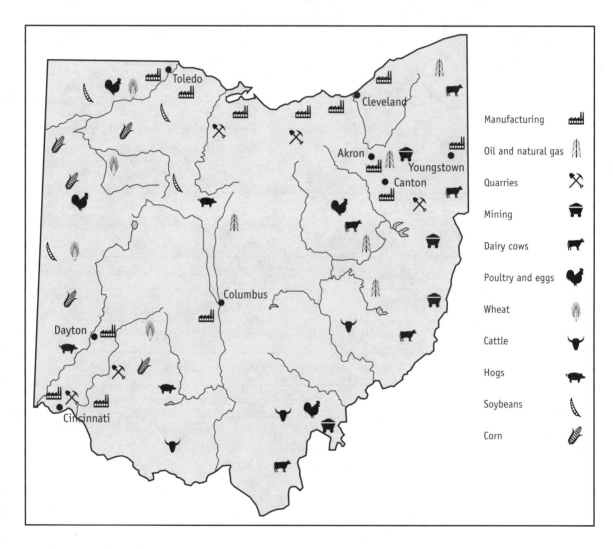

Manufacturing	
Oil and natural gas	
Quarries	
Mining	
Dairy cows	
Poultry and eggs	
Wheat	
Cattle	
Hogs	
Soybeans	
Corn	

Name _____

Based on the product map of Ohio, answer the following questions:

- List two crops grown in Ohio.

    1 _____

    2 _____

- Name two animals raised in Ohio.

    1 _____

    2 _____

- Which two places in Ohio can minerals be found?

    1 _____

    2 _____

The legend on a product map explains what each symbol represents. For example, the legend tells us that each small ear of corn [🌽] indicates an area where corn is grown. Answer the following questions based on the product map:

- What does [🐄] represent? _____

- What does [🏭] represent? _____

- Name an Ohio city located near where wheat is grown. _____

- What symbol on the map is used for mining? _____

- How is a product map different from a physical map? _____

    _____

    _____

- Based on this product map, what inferences can you make about how the geography of Ohio influences the lifestyle of its people.

    _____

    _____

    _____

    _____

    _____

STUDY CARDS

The North

What inferences can you make about how the geography of the North influenced the lifestyles of its people in the early 1800s?

_____

_____

_____

_____

The South

What inferences can you make about how the geography of the South influenced the lifestyles of its people in the early 1800s?

_____

_____

_____

_____

The West

What inferences can you make about how the geography of the West influenced the lifestyles of its people in the early 1800s?

_____

_____

_____

_____

Name _____

LEARNING WITH GRAPHIC ORGANIZERS

Directions: Complete the graphic organizer below by explaining the physical characteristics of the United States before 1860.

The North

_____
_____
_____
_____
_____
_____

The South

_____
_____
_____
_____
_____
_____

The United States in the Early 1800s

The West

_____
_____
_____
_____
_____
_____

ACTIVITY 1E

WHAT ARE THE CONSEQUENCES OF MODIFYING THE ENVIRONMENT?

■ People have modified the environment since prehistoric times. There are both positive and negative consequences for modifying the environment in Ohio and the United States.

The **environment** consists of the air, land and water around us. It includes the plants and animals living there. People have **modified**, or changed, the environment since prehistoric times. In this activity, you will consider the positive and negative effects that come with modifying the environment.

KEY TERMS

- Environment
- Modified
- Wetlands
- Dams

- Soil Erosion
- Fertilizer
- Pesticide
- Herbicide

- Algae
- Bar Graph
- Vertical Axis
- Horizontal Axis

People modify the environment to make their lives better. However, modifying the environment often brings with it negative consequences. Let's look at some examples of changes people have made to their environment, and evaluate if the negative consequences of these changes outweighed the positive ones, or if the opposite was true.

HOW PEOPLE MODIFY THE ENVIRONMENT

DESTRUCTION OF WETLANDS

When settlers first moved to Ohio, they found large areas of shallow water and soggy soil known as **wetlands**. These wetlands included swamps, marshes, and bogs. They were home to hundreds of different types of waterfowl, fish, mammals, and insects.

Wetlands are important to the environment. They act as giant natural sponges that slow the flow of water, reducing the damage that might be caused by flooding. Wetlands also help to prevent soil erosion. They protect water qual-

ity by trapping nutrients and blocking pollutants. Wetlands are especially important when they supply water to rivers and lakes used by people for drinking, swimming, fishing and other recreational purposes.

In the 1600s, more than 220 million acres of wetlands existed in the United States. However, by the 1980s over half of those wetland acres had been destroyed. They were drained and converted to farming, commercial, or residential use. The draining of wetlands made more soil available to farmers to grow crops to feed an ever expanding American population.

Today, fewer than one-tenth of Ohio's original wetlands remain. As more and more settlers moved into the Ohio Country, most of its wetlands were drained and filled to create farmland. From the 1780s to the 1980s, about five

million acres of Ohio wetlands were reduced to only 483,000 acres.

CHECKING YOUR UNDERSTANDING

- Do the benefits of wetland destruction outweigh its disadvantages?

  _____

  _____

  _____

- What suggestions do you have about dealing with wetland destruction?

  _____

  _____

  _____

BUILDING DAMS

Another way in which the people of Ohio have modified their environment is by building dams. A **dam** is a barrier constructed across a river or stream. The primary reason a dam is built is to prevent flooding. Settlers first began building dams in Ohio in the 1800s. A combination of materials are used to create a dam, including timber, rock, concrete, earth, and steel. In Ohio, most dams are constructed of earth.

Dams are useful in a number of ways. Dams provide people with clean, reliable energy that does not contribute to pollution. Although the cost of building a dam can be high, once built it is inexpensive to operate. The electricity generated by dams is often the least expensive form of electricity.

The Hoover Dam in Westerville, Ohio.

Dams also help to store water for irrigation in the summer and during times of drought. Dams permit some desert areas to be farmed because they supply water to farmers. Dams also assist in supplying water for drinking needs.

Dams can sometimes bring about serious problems. They often cause **soil erosion**, a washing away of the land. Dams also can hold back the natural sediment (*matter, like dirt, that settles to the bottom*) that flows in a river, preventing that sediment from traveling downstream. Large dams may bring about the extinction of fish and other water species. Dams also lead to the disappearance of birds, the loss of forests, wetlands and farmland, and the erosion of coastal areas.

At the time it was first built, Grand Lake St. Marys was the world's largest man-made reservoir.

The oldest dams in Ohio were built more than 150 years ago to create a water supply for canals. Early dams in Ohio included the Buckeye Lake and Grand Lake St. Marys, built between 1837 and 1841 to hold water for canals. Today, Ohio's more than 4,000 dams hold drinking water, prevent floods, and control the flow of water across the state.

CHECKING YOUR UNDERSTANDING

- Do the positive consequences of building dams outweigh their disadvantages?

  _____

  _____

  _____

- What suggestions do you have for the construction of dams?

  _____

  _____

  _____

CUTTING DOWN FORESTS

When settlers first arrived in the 1780s, Ohio was covered by forests. Ninety-five percent of Ohio was forest land. Ohio's forests were then gradually cleared. Settlers cut down trees to build farm homes, fences, and towns. The rich soil on the forest floors made the land ideal for farming. By 1900, only one-tenth of Ohio was still forest land.

Cabin made by cutting down trees.

Ohio's forests provide a great benefit to its citizens. Forests are important to city and rural residents alike. Ohio's forests provide such benefits as homes for wildlife, playgrounds for outdoorsmen, and views for sightseers, as well as filtering our air and water. Ohio's forests are the foundation of a multi-billion dollar wood industry. Ohioans grow some of the finest hardwood trees in the world. Concerned about this disappear-

Indian Trails Park, along the Ashtabula River in northeastern Ohio

ing natural resource, Ohioans passed laws to protect their woodlands. As people began moving from farms to cities in the 1930s, state agencies planted new trees, turning some farms back into woodlands.

Today, nearly one-third of Ohio is again forestland. Many of the state's forest recreation areas are found in the southeastern part of the state. For example, Brush Creek State Forest is at the southern end of Ohio.

CHECKING YOUR UNDERSTANDING

- Do the benefits outweigh the disadvantages of cutting down forests?

  _____

  _____

  _____

- What suggestions do you have about the cutting down of forests?

  _____

  _____

  _____

FARMING TODAY

When settlers first came to Ohio, they turned its wetlands and forests into farms for growing crops and raising animals. In the twentieth century, Ohio farmers were helped to increase their crop yields by the use of fertilizers, herbicides, and pesticides.

- **Fertilizers** are chemicals that are added to the soil to help crops grow.
- **Pesticides** are poisons sprayed on plants to either prevent weeds or kill insects and other pests that eat the crop.
- **Herbicides** are poisons used to kill unwanted plants, like weeds.

Americans use 75 million pounds of pesticides each year to ward off bugs from vegetables and plants. Use of chemical pesticides and fertilizers is common by Ohio farmers as well as by homeowners throughout the nation for use on their lawns and gardens. Use of such chemicals helps farmers and gardeners to enrich the soil and prevent insects from eating their crops.

Millions of pounds of chemicals are sprayed on crops each year.

However, use of these chemicals comes at a cost to the environment. These chemicals often run-off into nearby waterways, polluting streams, rivers, ponds, lakes and coastal areas.

When excess nutrients from fertilizer run off into a waterway, they cause **algae** (*a plant-like life form, including seaweed*) to grow. This algae sometimes makes waterways impassable. When the algae dies, it sinks to the bottom of the waterway and decomposes. When this occurs, it removes oxygen from the water, killing fish and other water animals. However, without the use of chemical fertilizers, Ohio farms would be much less productive. Pesticides also cause a problem because they are absorbed by plants and can end up in your food.

CHECKING YOUR UNDERSTANDING

- Do the benefits of using chemical fertilizers, pesticides, and herbicides outweigh the disadvantages?

  _____

  _____

  _____

- What suggestions do you have concerning the use of chemicals by farmers?

  _____

  _____

  _____

TOWNS AND TRANSPORTATION

One of the greatest changes to Ohio's landscape has been the building of towns, cities and modern transportation systems. Over the years, Ohioans dramatically changed their state's geography by building canals, roads, railroad lines and highways.

For the past 200 years, Ohio cities have increased in size. As Ohio's population expanded, Ohioans constructed new towns and larger cities. Increasing trade also led to the rise of towns and cities, especially along Lake Erie and Ohio's major rivers, canals, roads, and railroads.

Located between the Northeast and the Midwest, Ohio became a major transportation hub. As Ohio established itself as the industrial heartland of North America, many new transportation connections were built. However, this increase in highways, roadways, and canals has also come at a cost.

As new highways and roadways were built, increased traffic raised the number of pollutants pumped into the atmosphere. As the pollution of the nation's air increased, more people faced breathing problems and other health issues. In addition, some of the new roadways in Ohio threatened to cover important historical and archaeological sites.

Today, greater attention is paid to these problems by the state government of Ohio. There are growing demands for more public transportation. There is a rising fear that building more highways and roadways will only lead to a society that is ever more dependent on the automobile. Such a dependence will result in building more distant suburbs, decaying inner cities, and a greater reliance on foreign oil.

CHECKING YOUR UNDERSTANDING

- Do the benefits of building more cities and highways outweigh the disadvantages?

  _____

  _____

  _____

  _____

  _____

- What suggestions do you have concerning the growth of cities and highways?

  _____

  _____

  _____

  _____

Name _____

Activity 1E: The Consequences of Modifying the Environment   **57**

MAKING CONNECTIONS

HOW TO MAKE A BAR GRAPH

There are many ways to show information in order to make it easier to understand. One way is a **bar graph**, which allows you to communicate information visually. A bar graph is made up of parallel bars of different lengths. Bar graphs are often used to compare two or more things.

■ You need to provide a title for your graph. The title tells you what information is presented in the graph. Usually the title of the graph will be the same title as on the chart or a summary of the introduction to the chart's information.

■ Decide which measurements will be used for your bars. These measurements are usually shown along the vertical or horizontal axis.

• The **vertical axis** runs along the left-hand side of the bar graph. It is used to measure the length or the height of the bars. The scale of the vertical axis is determined by the data. If the value of a bar falls between two lines, you need to approximate where the correct value would lie.

• The **horizontal axis** runs along the bottom of the graph and often identifies what each bar represents. Label each bar in the center of the bar.

■ To find specific information on the graph, you need to examine each of these features.

There are websites that allow you to construct your bar graph online: (1) www.onlinecharttoool.com; (2) www.chartgo.com; (3) http://nces.ed.gov/nceskids/graphing/classic/bar.asp. There are several parts to a bar graph. Each part plays an important role in helping to present the information.

In 2011, pollution in the United States came from a variety of sources. The chart below indicates the sources of this pollution.

Sources of Pollution	Activities Causing Pollution	Amount of Pollution
Transportation	Cars, trucks, railroads	45%
Production of Energy	Burning coal, making electricity	20%
Industries and manufacturing	Making products in factories	14%
Farming and other agriculture	Raising crops and livestock	7%
Other Sources	—	14%

Now use this information to construct a bar graph on the following page.

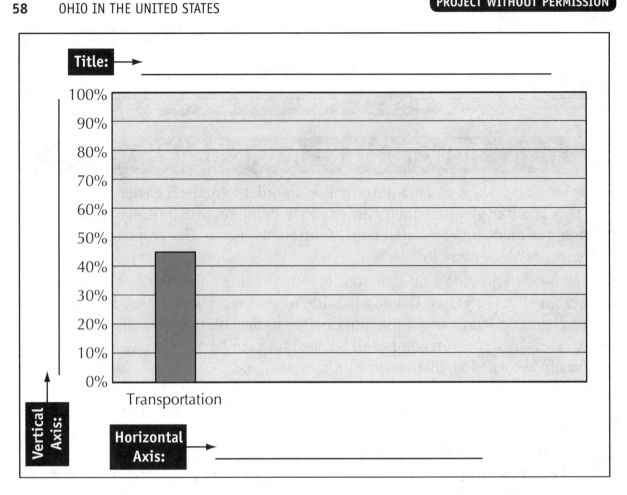

Title: ⟶ _____

Vertical Axis:

Transportation

Horizontal Axis: ⟶ _____

STUDY CARDS

Wetlands

- What are the positive effects of wetlands on the environment?

  _____

  _____

  _____

- What are the negative effects of wetlands on the environment?

  _____

  _____

Dams

• What are the positive effects of dams on the environment?

_____

_____

• What are the negative effects of dams on the environment?

_____

_____

_____

Forests

• What are the positive effects of forests on the environment?

_____

_____

• What are the negative effects of forests on the environment?

_____

_____

_____

Fertilizers, Pesticides, and Herbicides

• What are fertilizers? _____

_____

• What are pesticides? _____

_____

• What are herbicides? _____

_____

_____

 **LEARNING WITH GRAPHIC ORGANIZERS**

Directions: Complete the graphic organizer below by explaining how people modify their environment in each of these instances.

Wetlands:
_____
_____
_____
_____

Dams:
_____
_____
_____

Forests:
_____
_____
_____

**How People Modify
Their Environment**

Chemicals:
_____
_____
_____
_____

Transportation Systems:
_____
_____
_____
_____

EXPRESS YOURSELF

Ohio's environment is undergoing many changes. These changes include changes to Ohio's wetlands, dams, forests, agriculture, and transportation systems.

Choose *two* of the changes mentioned above. For each change you select, describe both a positive and negative effect of that change on Ohio's environment.

ACTIVITY 1F

WHAT GENERALIZATION CAN YOU MAKE ABOUT OHIO'S CULTURAL DIVERSITY?

■ The population of the United States has changed over time, becoming more diverse (e.g., racial, ethnic, linguistic, religious). Ohio's population has become increasingly reflective of the cultural diversity of the United States.

In this activity, you will learn about some of the groups that have made Ohio their home. After completing this activity, you will be able to describe these different groups that have settled in Ohio and explain some reasons why they came here.

KEY TERMS

- ■ Generalization
- ■ Culture
- ■ Cultural Diversity
- ■ Linguistic
- ■ Great Potato Famine
- ■ Pennsylvania Dutch
- ■ Segregation
- ■ Great Migration
- ■ Multicultural Fair

Generalizations are powerful organizing tools. They allow us to summarize large amounts of information. In this activity, you will learn how generalizations are formed. You will also practice making some of your own generalizations.

WHAT IS A GENERALIZATION?

Let's begin by examining the following list:

- ■ Marietta is located on the Ohio River.
- ■ Cleveland is located on the shores of Lake Erie.
- ■ Toledo is located on the Maumee River.

Cleveland is located along Lake Erie.

It may be hard to remember all of these separate facts. However, if you look at them as a group, you might see a pattern. These three facts have something in common. This pattern may actually be more important than any one specific fact.

CHECKING YOUR UNDERSTANDING

Can you find what these three facts have in common? _____

_____

HOW GENERALIZATIONS ARE FORMED

Each of these *cities is located near a large body of water*. This **general statement** describes what all of these specific examples have in common. When a general statement identifies a common pattern, it is known as a **generalization**. Let's see how this generalization might be presented in a diagram:

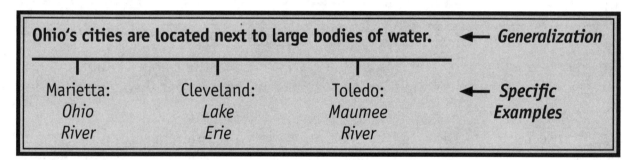

Ohio's cities are located next to large bodies of water. ← *Generalization*

| Marietta: | Cleveland: | Toledo: | ← *Specific Examples* |
| *Ohio River* | *Lake Erie* | *Maumee River* | |

A generalization shows what several facts have in common. It can also help us to make predictions. From this generalization, you might predict that if you select another city, it will also be located next to a large body of water.

Although generalizations are useful tools, you should be careful in using them. For example, is our generalization really true for *all* cities? For example, does it apply to Canton, another city in Ohio. A map will show that the city of Canton is actually **not** located next to a large body of water. This means we must modify (*change*) our original generalization.

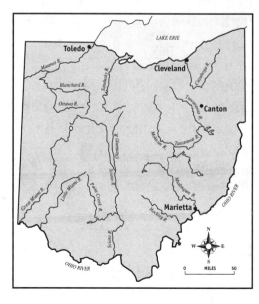

Based on this new fact, we can say that many, but not all, Ohio cities are located next to large bodies of water. Let's see how this new generalization looks in a "diagram":

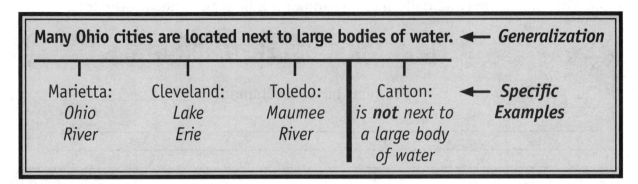

Many Ohio cities are located next to large bodies of water. ← *Generalization*

| Marietta: *Ohio River* | Cleveland: *Lake Erie* | Toledo: *Maumee River* | Canton: *is **not** next to a large body of water* ← ***Specific Examples*** |

When you are asked to judge if a generalization is true, you must find specific facts and examples that support it. Remember, generalizations are always subject to change as new information is learned.

MAKING YOUR OWN GENERALIZATIONS ABOUT OHIO'S CULTURAL DIVERSITY

How good would you be at forming your own generalizations about Ohio's cultural diversity? Read the following four case studies and make your own generalization from them.

Diverse means to show a great deal of variety or differences. **Culture** refers to a people's way of life and includes language, traditions, customs, and beliefs. **Cultural diversity** means to have many different cultures living together. Ohio's population shows great cultural diversity because of the different groups that have settled here. These groups have different racial, ethnic, linguistic, and religious backgrounds. **Linguistic** refers to language. A linguistic group speaks its own language. Often ethnicity and language are tied together. Arab Americans and French Americans, for example, are both linguistic as well as ethnic groups.

THE GERMAN AMERICANS

WHO THEY WERE

Germany is a country in the center of Europe. Before 1871, Germany was made up of several smaller independent states. Despite its lack of political unity, Germans shared a common culture and language — one of the world's major languages.

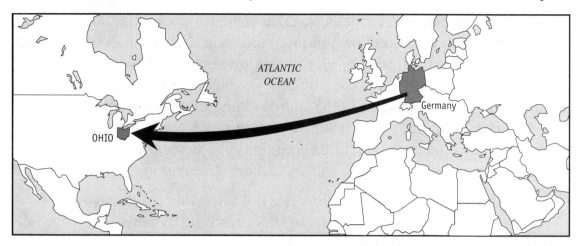

WHY THEY CAME

Even before Ohio officially became a state, Germans were among the first settlers to Ohio, many migrating from Pennsylvania in the late 1700s. Starting in the 1830s, large numbers of Germans in Europe began leaving their homeland and came to America. Some Germans came for political reasons. A revolution for greater democracy in Germany failed in 1848–1849, leading some Germans to flee.

German immigrants boarding a steamer in Germany to come to America.

Even more immigrants came from Germany in the following years for economic opportunities. Germany's population was growing rapidly. There was not enough land or jobs to satisfy the needs of many German families. With the arrival of railroads and steamships, the price of travel to the United States became cheaper. Many Germans packed their bags and took a chance in coming to America. Once immigrants successfully settled in an area, they often invited their relatives from Germany to join them. Between 1830 and 1880, more than one-quarter of all immigrants to the United States were German.

CULTURAL PRACTICES AND CONTRIBUTIONS

Germans settled both in Ohio's cities and in the countryside. There they found new opportunities in both industry and agriculture. Many German immigrants were skilled craftsmen.

They worked as farmers, carpenters, cigar makers, machinists and tailors. Others sought jobs as day laborers or building steamboats. Cincinnati was considered the "heart" of German migration. German immigrants in Cincinnati established their own community — "Over the Rhine" — which published newspapers in the German language. Cleveland and other large Ohio cities also received large numbers of German immigrants. By 1865, Columbus was one-third German. Today **German Village**, remains as a restored community of homes south of Columbus. It was built between 1840 and 1860, and was where German immigrants once lived.

With such a large German population, it is not surprising that there are large number of German-American organizations in Ohio. Each June, German Village holds a special *Haus* (*house*) and *Garten* (*garden*) Tour.

German immigrants had a strong impact on Ohio. German communities created hundreds of private schools that influenced American education. They introduced **kindergartens** to the United States. Germans also placed a heavy emphasis on sports programs. German excellence in music led many Ohio communities to organize singing festivals, orchestras and bands.

German workers brought different skills with them to Ohio. They were talented in carpentry, baking, and famous for brewing good beer. Each year many German communities in Ohio hold *Oktoberfests* to celebrate their beer-making skills. Although there are fewer German immigrants coming to Ohio in the twenty-first century, German culture and institutions continue to thrive.

CHECKING YOUR UNDERSTANDING

1 Why did German immigrants come to America? _____

_____

_____

2 Where did many of the German immigrants to Ohio settle? _____

_____

3 Describe a practice or skill of German Americans that has contributed to Ohio's cultural diversity.

_____

_____

THE IRISH AMERICANS

WHO THEY WERE

Irish immigrants came to Ohio from Ireland, a country in northwest Europe. Although most Irish were Catholics, Ireland was ruled by its Protestant neighbor, England.

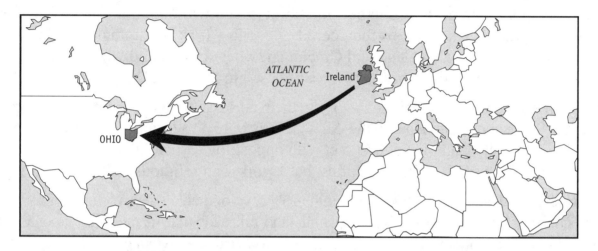

WHY THEY CAME

Irish immigrants were attracted to America as a land of economic opportunity. Large numbers of Irish settled in Ohio. The Irish accounted for one-fifth of the immigrants to Ohio before 1850. In these years, many Irish men came to America to work digging the Miami and Erie Canal, or to lay railroad tracks. Desperate to feed their families, Irish immigrants often took unskilled jobs that were dangerous

Irish immigrants prepare to travel to America.

and had low pay. Canal diggers were paid only 30 cents a day. Many of them died before they reached the age of 30.

The largest number of Irish immigrants came to Ohio after the **Great Potato Famine**. Irish farmers generally had to pay high rents to use small plots of land. Often these plots were barely able to produce enough food for a farmer and his family. Many Irish families depended on potatoes as their main food. A typical Irish family ate seven to fifteen pounds of potatoes each week. In 1845 and 1846, a disease turned the potatoes black and destroyed most of the Irish potato crop.

More than a million Irish starved to death. Unable to pay the rents on their lands, many sought to immigrate. Almost two million emigrated to America. Even after the famine, immigrants from Ireland continued coming to America to join their relatives and to seek economic opportunities.

CULTURAL PRACTICES AND CONTRIBUTIONS

Many Irish immigrants hoped to become farmers. But without money to buy land or tools, they took whatever jobs they could find. Most Irish immigrants to Ohio settled in cities such as Cleveland and Cincinnati, where they found work as unskilled laborers. They worked in dock yards, foundries, and factories.

Irish immigrants spoke English, giving them an advantage over some other immigrants. Since most Ohioans in the early 1800s were Protestant, Irish immigrants, who were usually Catholic, at first met with opposition and prejudice. The Irish had strong traditions of close-knit families, hard work, and religious faith.

Irish Americans played a key role in Ohio's development. They worked to improve its economy by helping to build the canals and railroads that made Ohio a center of transportation and industry. Later, Irish Americans became active in politics and government. Irish-American clergy made important contributions as teachers and educators.

CHECKING YOUR UNDERSTANDING

1 Why did Irish immigrants come to America? _____

_____

2 Where did many of the Irish immigrants to Ohio settle? _____

_____

_____

3 Describe a practice or skill Irish Americans have contributed to Ohio's cultural diversity.

_____

_____

_____

_____

THE AMISH

WHO THEY WERE

The **Amish** are a Protestant religious group that traces its roots back to Switzerland in the1600s. In Europe, they were persecuted for their unique beliefs.

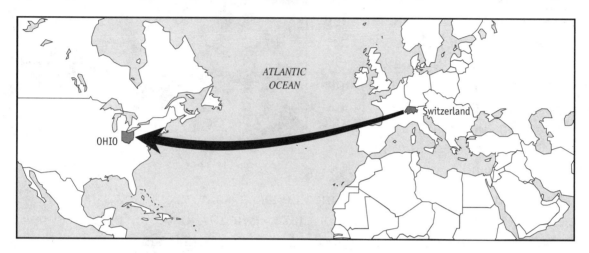

WHY THEY CAME

Facing persecution in Europe for their religious beliefs, the Amish decided to move to the American colonies. In 1727, the Amish first came to Pennsylvania. Later, many Amish settlers moved to Northern Ohio. Today, Ohio is home to the world's largest Amish population — about 45,000 people — scattered among 33 Amish settlements and 258 Amish congregations.

CULTURAL PRACTICES AND CONTRIBUTIONS

The Amish strive for humility, thrift, and simplicity. Amish parents teach their children to be obedient and to yield to the needs of family and community. Each Amish community is separate and independent: there is no central Amish government. The Amish reject many modern conveniences. Amish communities forbid the use of automobiles, electricity, telephones or televisions. They dress simply, without adornment. Men wear beards and shaven upper lips, while women wear a prayer cap.

The Amish speak a type of German called "**Pennsylvania Dutch**" (*Deutsch*). English is learned at school. Amish schools are often one-room buildings with Amish teachers. Schooling ends at the eighth grade, although many Amish children receive further instruction in their homes after graduation.

The Amish see work as an important way to build character. Much of their work is done in small groups. Such work often turns into a celebration. The Amish like to cook meals, build barns, cut firewood and even make quilts in groups.

Children are cared for by all the members of the family, creating strong ties with all their relatives. Family members care for the elderly when they are no longer able to care for themselves.

Amish life styles are dictated by both written and spoken rules. They rely on a horse and buggy (*small carriage*) for their transportation, and horses and mules for field work. They worship at home. Their unique religious beliefs and emphasis on simple living has cut them off from the outside world. Amish communities encourage this separation to keep alive their traditional values and beliefs.

The Amish use horses and buggies instead of modern conveniences like automobiles.

The Amish pay federal and state income taxes, sales taxes, real estate taxes, and property taxes. In fact, they pay school taxes twice — once for public school and once again for their own Amish schools. The Amish emphasis on hard work, community and craftsmanship has contributed to their cultural uniqueness. Amish handicrafts, such as quilts and homemade jams, are highly prized. Amish shops sell dry goods, furniture, shoes, and wholesale food items. Some Amish communities have opened family-style restaurants to travelers, helping encourage tourism in Ohio.

CHECKING YOUR UNDERSTANDING

1 Why did Amish immigrants come to the United States? _____
_____

2 Where did many of the Amish settle? _____
_____

3 Describe an Amish tradition or practice that has contributed to Ohio's cultural diversity.

_____

_____

_____

_____

THE AFRICAN AMERICANS

WHO THEY WERE

People from Africa were first brought to the Americas by force as slaves. Although slavery ended after the Civil War, African Americans continued to face prejudice and hardships, especially in Southern states. Southern states introduced a policy of racial **segregation** (*separation of the races by law*). African Americans were forced to use separate schools and other public facilities. In general, African Americans in the South lived in poor economic conditions with little hope of improvement.

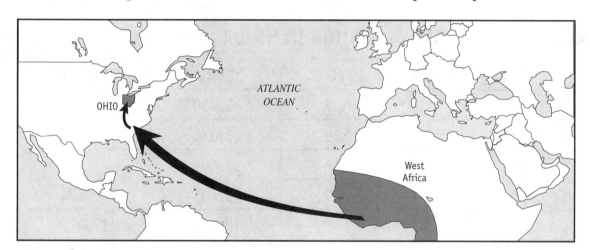

WHY THEY CAME

The ancestors of most of today's African Americans were forcibly taken to North America as enslaved people. They were captured on the West Coast of Africa and put on slave ships to cross the Atlantic Ocean for the voyage to the Americas. These enslaved Africans were treated so harshly that many of them failed to survive the brutal voyage. Slaves were chained and crammed together below the deck, where sitting or standing room was limited. The air below deck was so stifling that some suffocated. Others tried to starve themselves or to jump over board. When the slaves reached the Americas, they were sold off in auctions without regard to keeping families together.

Because of its role as an anti-slavery state, Ohio was a final destination for many escaped slaves. "Free Blacks" have lived in Ohio since American independence, but large numbers of African Americans only began migrating to Ohio from the South during World War I (1914–1918). During that war, Ohio's factories focused on producing war goods. Workers were needed to replace those fighting overseas.

Most African Americans settled in industrial cities such as Cleveland, Youngstown, Toledo and Akron, where jobs were plentiful. Between 1915 and 1970, more than six million African Americans left the South for cities across the Northeast and Midwest.

This movement of thousands of African Americans from the South northward in search of a better life has become known as the **Great Migration**.

During the Great Migration African Americans came to Ohio in search of jobs.

AFRICAN-AMERICAN POPULATION IN MAJOR OHIO CITIES, 1910–1930

City	1910	1920	1930
Akron	657	5,580	11,080
Cincinnati	19,639	30,079	47,818
Cleveland	8,448	34,451	71,899
Columbus	12,739	22,181	32,774
Dayton	4,842	9,025	17,077
Toledo	1,877	5,691	13,260
Youngstown	1,936	6,662	14,522

CULTURAL PRACTICES AND CONTRIBUTIONS

Even after their arrival, most African Americans faced many problems. Most African Americans in Ohio settled in segregated communities. They were often forced to live in overcrowded neighborhoods. Many Ohioans refused to hire them. Many schools refused to admit African-American students. African Americans responded by looking to their own traditions. They formed close-knit communities in which everyone helped each other out. Often, African-American churches played a key role in community life.

African Americans also played a major role in the fight against racial discrimination during the **Civil Rights Movement** of the 1950s and 1960s. In 1968, Cleveland voters elected **Carl B. Stokes** as the first African-American mayor of a large American city.

Carl Stokes

Ohio's African-American residents have also made important contributions in the arts and sports. Poet **Paul Lawrence Dunbar**, artist **Robert Duncanson**, architect **P. Ross Berry**, Nobel prize writer **Toni Morrison**, and Olympic gold medalist **Jesse Owens** were all African Americans from Ohio. Today, African Americans are leading players on many of Ohio's professional sports teams.

CHECKING YOUR UNDERSTANDING

1   Why did African Americans come to America? _____

_____

_____

2   Where did many of the African Americans to Ohio settle? _____

_____

3   Describe a practice or achievement that African Americans have contributed to Ohio's cultural diversity.

_____

_____

_____

Now that you have read about four of the groups that came to Ohio, let's see if you can create a generalization about what you have read. To help you get an idea, here is one generalization that can be created from these passages for these four groups:

People came to Ohio as a land of opportunity.	← *Generalization*
German Americans Irish Americans Amish Americans African Americans	← *Specific Examples*

What generalization can you make about the four groups in Ohio that you just read about? Use the space below to create your own generalization.

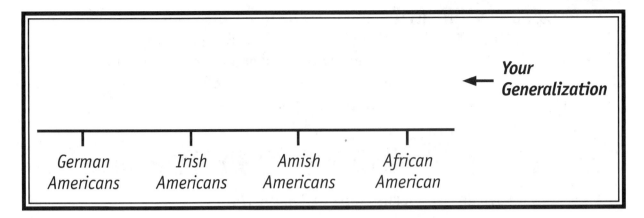

IDENTIFYING THE COUNTRY OF ORIGIN OF RECENT IMMIGRANTS TO OHIO

In this activity, you examined various groups that have immigrated to Ohio in the past. Today, Ohio remains a final destination for a variety of immigrants from all over the world.

In 2010, out of every 100 people living in the United States, 13 were from a foreign land. Although the number of foreign-born residents is smaller in Ohio than in the United States as a whole, foreign-born residents accounted for about 4 out of every 100 residents in Ohio. The largest foreign-born population in Ohio is from Asia (38%). Other areas from which groups have migrated to Ohio include Africa (12%), Europe (25%), South America, Central America, and Mexico (21%), and North America — Canada, Bermuda, Greenland (4%).

In 2011, the top three countries of origin for the foreign-born in Ohio were Mexico (11%), India (10%), and China (7%). Similarly, these same three countries provided the most immigrants to the United States.

On the blank map on the next page:

(A) Locate and write in the names of the continents mentioned above.

(B) Locate and write in the names of the three countries of origin of foreign-born Ohioans mentioned above.

You might find it helpful to use an atlas to help you find some of these places.

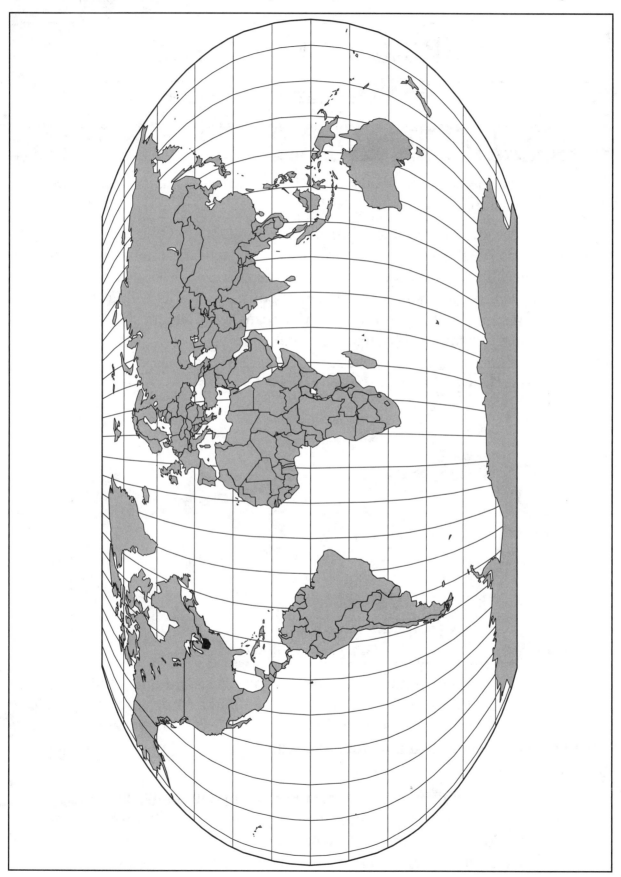

MAKING CONNECTIONS

HOLDING A MULTICULTURAL FAIR

Besides the groups you have already studied in this activity, many other groups have immigrated to Ohio.

In recent decades, increasing numbers of immigrants to Ohio have come from Latin America, Asia, and Africa. As might be expected, these newcomers to Ohio have brought with them their own cultural practices and products. For example, Mexicans have brought their taste for such foods as *tacos*, as well as salsa music. Vietnamese immigrants have introduced Americans to Vietnamese foods, the Buddhist religion, and traditional Vietnamese handicrafts.

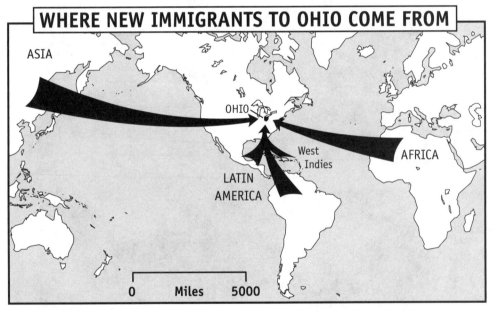

There are many ways you can learn more about these and other cultural groups now living in Ohio. One of the most fun ways is to hold a **Multicultural Fair**. Your teacher should divide your class into several teams. Each team should represent a different cultural group living in your community. Do not choose your own ethnic group for your team.

On the day of the fair, each team should create a booth in the classroom for the multicultural fair. Booths should be decorated to reflect the cultures they represent. Each team should collect or make some of the items listed below. Your teacher will award points to each team based on each of the following categories:

■ **Foods (20 points).** Display recipes and pictures of typical ethnic foods. They should be the foods for which the group is best known.

■ **Customs and Traditions (20 points).** Display posters or pictures showing some of the unique customs and practices of the group you represent.

■ **Music (15 points).** Bring tapes, CDs, or records of music popular with members of that group.

■ **Dance (15 points).** Perform some of the group's traditional dances.

■ **Holidays (15 points).** Display pictures illustrating holidays and other festive occasions the group celebrates.

■ **Costumes (15 points).** Display pictures, drawings or photographs of people dressed in traditional costumes of the group.

A Chinese immigrant spins dough while at work in his noodle shop.

STUDY CARDS

German Americans

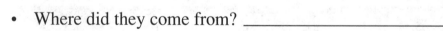

- Where did they come from? _____

- Why did they come to America? _____

  _____

- Name a contribution of German Americans to Ohio's cultural diversity:

  _____

  _____

  _____

Irish Americans

- Where did they come from? _____

- Why did they come to America? _____

  _____

- Name a contribution of Irish Americans to Ohio's cultural diversity:

  _____

  _____

  _____

The Amish

- Where did they come from? _____

- Why did they come to America? _____

  _____

- Name a contribution of the Amish to Ohio's cultural diversity:

  _____

  _____

  _____

African Americans

- Where did they come from? _____

- Why did they come to America? _____

  _____

- Name a contribution of African Americans to Ohio's cultural diversity:

  _____

  _____

  _____

EXPRESS YOURSELF

How different is life in Ohio for someone who was born in a foreign land? The simplest way to find out is to ask someone. Speak to an adult relative, neighbor or family friend who has immigrated to the United States from a foreign country.

■ Ask this person to describe the changes he or she has witnessed in the community.

■ Ask this person how everyday life in his or her country differs from life in Ohio. In particular, ask about the foods this person eats, and the traditions he or she enjoys.

Use the sheet below to record his or her responses:

Person Interviewed: _____

Where Born: _____   When immigrated: _____

ACTIVITY
1G

HOW CLOSELY DO OHIOANS REFLECT THE CULTURAL DIVERSITY OF THE UNITED STATES?

■ The population of the United States has changed over time, becoming more diverse (e.g., racial, ethnic, linguistic, religious). Ohio's population has become increasingly reflective of the cultural diversity of the United States.

Do you like pizza, tacos or egg rolls? Each of these foods was brought to Ohio by a different cultural group. A **cultural group** is a group of people who have a common way of life. They share the same traditions, customs and beliefs. Different cultural groups have introduced a variety of ideas and products to Ohio. In this activity, you will learn about the cultural groups that live in Ohio. You will also investigate how closely the people of Ohio reflect the cultural diversity of the United States.

KEY TERMS

- Cultural Group
- Cultural Diversity
- Thesis

- Foreign Born
- "New Immigrants"
- Race

- Ethnic Group
- Religion
- Amish

WHAT IS CULTURAL DIVERSITY?

What is **cultural diversity**? The United States is made up of many people with different cultural backgrounds. In a culturally diverse society such as ours, each group brings its own traditions, customs, and beliefs. Living in a culturally diverse society allows us to develop an understanding of the views of people from different backgrounds.

WRITNG A REPORT ON OHIO'S DIVERSITY

The United States is a culturally diverse nation of people with differing backgrounds. But how closely do the people of Ohio reflect our nation's cultural diversity? To find out, you will examine different data. Then you will write a report on what you have found.

SELECTING YOUR FOCUS

A **report** is an oral presentation or a written paper that gives information about a topic. Its purpose is to communicate information. To write a report, you gather ideas and facts from a variety of sources. Then you write about what you have learned. The first step is to select a **topic**. The topic is the main subject of the report. In this report, your topic is the cultural diversity of Ohio and the United States.

Once you have selected your topic, you need to think of a thesis. A **thesis** is the main argument you present in a report. In this report, your thesis would be your answer to the question: *Do the people of Ohio reflect the cultural diversity of the United States?* Remember, everything in your report should relate in some way to this thesis.

GATHERING INFORMATION

Next, you need to gather information about your topic. This process is called **research** because you are *searching* for information about your topic. To write a report you might look at reference books, such as textbooks, encyclopedias and almanacs. You might also look at newspapers, magazines, books, and the Internet. For this report, all of the information you need will be presented on the next pages.

THE PEOPLE OF OHIO

Ohio's population grew slowly during the colonial period, reaching 45,365 persons in 1800. After Ohio became a state in 1803, settlers flocked to Ohio. By 1810, the state's population had grown to 230,760, five times what it had been less than a decade before. The next paragraph provides some facts about Ohio's population.

By 1830, Ohio's population had risen to 937,903. That was an increase of 892,538 in 30 years. In 1860, Ohio's population was 2,339,511. That was an increase of 1,401,608 in 30 years. Thirty years later, Ohio's population was 3,672,329, an increase of 1,332,818 people. By 1920, Ohio's population stood at 5,759,394, an increase in 30 years of 2,087,065. By 1950, there were 9,946,627 people living in Ohio, an increase of 4,187,233 people in 30 years. In 1980, Ohio's population reached 10,797,630, an increase of 851,003 people in 30 years. By 2010, Ohio had a population of 11,536,504, an increase of 738,874 people in 30 years.

An immigrant family arrives in Ohio.

Sometimes having so many numbers in the same paragraph makes it difficult to get a sense of what is taking place. Let's turn these words into another format by constructing a table. The row line of this table has already been done for you

TABLE 1: OHIO'S POPULATION, 1800–2010

Year	Ohio's Population	Increase in Population
1800	45,365	—

CHECKING YOUR UNDERSTANDING

What trend do see regarding the population of Ohio from 1800 to 2010?

_____

_____

_____

OHIO'S FOREIGN-BORN POPULATION

People who live in the United States but were born in another country are "**foreign born**." Even before the American Revolution, Ohio's population included many foreign-born immigrants.

The vast majority of immigrants to Ohio before 1850 were from Germany and Ireland. By the mid-1800s, about half of all immigrants in Ohio were from Germany. Irish immigrants to Ohio also came in large numbers. The majority of these immigrants came to Ohio seeking better jobs. Most settled in Ohio's cities, where economic opportunities were greatest.

Existing patterns of immigration to the United States began to change in the 1880s. The spread of railroads and larger steamships made the voyage to America more affordable for many Europeans. Most of these "**New Immigrants**" to the United States came from Southern and Eastern Europe. The "New Immigrants" were often poor, spoke little or no English, and dressed differently from earlier immigrants.

Early immigrants to Ohio found jobs working on railroads or in factories.

Many of the "New Immigrants" who settled in Ohio in these years came from Spain, Italy and Greece. Most of them settled in Ohio's largest cities. In general, the "New Immigrants" were not welcomed to Ohio. Their religious and cultural differences were often viewed with suspicion and distrust. Many believed these foreigners would take jobs from American-born citizens.

Even today, immigration to Ohio continues to be a major source of new residents. In the years between 2000 and 2011, the foreign-born population of Ohio increased from 339,000 to 456,000. This was an increase of about 34 percent. Between 2000 and 2011, the foreign-born population in the United States grew from over 31,100,000 to 40,350,000, an increase of almost 30 percent. The size of Ohio's foreign-born population in 2011 was 19th out of the 50 states.

TABLE 2: FOREIGN-BORN POPULATION OF U.S. AND OHIO

Year	Percent of the U.S. Population	Percent of Ohio's Population
1990	8%*	2%
2000	12%	3%
2011	14%	4%
2012	13%	4%

* Remember, that 8% means 8 out of every 100 people.

TABLE 3: U.S. CITIZENSHIP STATUS OF FOREIGN-BORN RESIDENTS

Year	United States	Ohio
2000	40 out of every 100 foreign-born are U.S. citizens (40%)	50 out of every 100 foreign-born are U.S. citizens (50%)
2011	45 out of every 100 foreign-born are U.S. citizens (45%)	50 out of every 100 foreign-born are U.S. citizens (50%)

CHECKING YOUR UNDERSTANDING

- In what ways are the foreign-born populations of the United States and Ohio similar? _____

_____

- In what ways are the foreign-born population of the United States and Ohio different? _____

_____

PLACE OF ORIGIN

According to figures provided by the U.S. government, Hispanic Americans are the fasting growing minority group in the nation. The number of Hispanic Americans in the United States is expected to nearly triple between 2010 and 2050.

Asian Americans make up the third largest minority group and the second fastest growing population in the United States today.

In 2008, the national government reported that the number of Asian Americans in the United States accounted for 5% of the nation's population (*5 out of every 100 Americans*). It is now predicted that the Asian population in the nation will increase to 9% of the U.S. population by 2050.

In 2008, it was reported that Ohio's three largest immigrant groups were from Mexico, India, and China. Today, the largest share of foreign-born population in Ohio are from Asia.

TABLE 4: FOREIGN-BORN POPULATION OF U.S. & OHIO

Country	Percent of Foreign Born in the U.S. of this Nationality	Percent of Foreign Born in Ohio of this Nationality
Mexico	30%*	11%
India	5%	10%
China	5%	7%

* This means 30 out of every 100.

CHECKING YOUR UNDERSTANDING

• How are the origins of immigrants in the United States and Ohio similar?

_____

_____

_____

• How are the origins of immigrants in the United States and Ohio different?

_____

_____

_____

WRITING YOUR REPORT

The table below shows data for Ohio and the United States today.

OHIO AND U.S. POPULATION TODAY

Category	Ohio	United States
Population in 2012	11,544,225	313,914,040
Persons 65+	15% (15 out of every 100 people)	14% (14 out of every 100 people)
White	83% (83 out of every 100 people)	78% (78 out of every 100 people)
African American	12% (12 out of every 100 people)	13% (13 out of every 100 people)
Asian	2% (2 out of every 100 people)	5% (5 out of every 100 people)
Hispanic / Latino	3% (3 out of every 100 people)	17% (17 out of every 100 people)

Now that you have examined the data for Ohio and the United States, you need to decide if the people of Ohio reflect the nation's cultural diversity. Consider what conclusion you wish to make from all of the information you have examined. Use that information to support your thesis statement with logical, well-supported, conclusions. Be sure that everything you include in your report relates in some way to your thesis — the main point that you are trying to make.

Name _____

Activity 1G: How Do Ohioans Reflect the Nation's Cultural Diversity?   **87**

<table>
<tr><td></td><td></td></tr>
<tr><td></td><td></td></tr>
<tr><td></td><td></td></tr>
<tr><td></td><td></td></tr>
<tr><td></td><td></td></tr>
<tr><td></td><td></td></tr>
<tr><td></td><td></td></tr>
<tr><td></td><td></td></tr>
</table>

MAKING CONNECTIONS

HOW WOULD YOU CATEGORIZE YOURSELF?

In this *Making Connections*, you will learn some of the ways Ohioans and Americans identify themselves. First, let's see how you "group" yourself:

- What is your race? _____
- What is your ethnic group? _____
- What is your religion? _____

Did you group yourself correctly? The answer depends on how you define these words. Each of these terms — **race**, **ethnicity**, **religion** — are concepts. A **concept** gives a name to things that, although different, have something in common. For example, the idea of a "bird" is a concept. It applies to many different creatures: eagles, blue jays, ducks, and chickens. However, all of these animals share a common characteristic — they all have feathers.

duck

blue jay

eagle   chicken

You have probably heard people use words such as race, ethnic group and religion. Let's take a closer look at each of these terms and see what they mean.

RACE

Human beings from different parts of the world have developed physical characteristics that are sometimes used to identify where they are from. For example, people whose ancestors are from Northern Europe often have a light skin color; people whose ancestors are from West Africa often have a dark skin color.

A **race** is a group of people identified by certain characteristics based on where their ancestors came from, such as Europe, Africa, East Asia, the Pacific Islands, or the Americas. Today, many Americans actually have mixed racial backgrounds: their parents or grandparents belonged to different races. The United States is a diverse society, made up of people from many different races.

ETHNICITY

Members of **ethnic groups** share a similar culture, such as the same family background, language and race. In the United States, the country where people's ancestors came from often forms the basis of their ethnic identity. For instance, just over ten percent of Ohioans trace their ancestors back to Ireland. Known as Irish Americans, they share common traditions and practices such as celebrating St. Patrick's Day. These common ways of doing things are called cultural practices.

Polish Ohioans at a parade honoring their ethnic heritage.

One of Ohio's most important features is the diversity of its ethnic groups. Different ethnic groups have brought many different foods, clothes, ideas, and traditions to Ohio. The racial and ethnic makeup of Ohio has changed greatly since 2000. Asians and Hispanics are now the fastest-growing ethnic groups in nearly three-quarters of Ohio's 88 counties. The number of Asians in Ohio has increased the most in 45 of its counties, while Hispanics grew fastest in 20 of its counties.

RELIGION

A third way that people group themselves is by **religion**. Most religions have certain characteristics in common:

A belief in one God or several gods	**A set of customs and practices**	**An organization, such as a church, synagogue, or mosque**

Religion has played a key role in Ohio since its earliest history. Ohio's first English-speaking settlers were Protestants. Many later immigrants were Catholics from Poland, Germany, and other places.

Mennonite and Amish settlers came to Ohio from Pennsylvania. Ohio's Amish and Mennonites communities are the largest in the world. The largest Amish settlements are found in Holmes County, Ohio, where nearly half the residents there are Amish.

The Amish are the fastest growing religious group in North America.

Today, religious diversity in Ohio continues to grow. In the 1920s and 1930s, Muslims began settling in cities in Ohio, especially Toledo and Cleveland. Jews and Muslims make up Ohio's largest non-Christian groups.

At the start of this *Making Connections* you were asked to "group" yourself. Now that you have learned something about the ways in which people group themselves, would you change how you categorized yourself?

- ■ What is your race? _____
- ■ What is your ethnic group? _____
- ■ What is your religion? _____

STUDY CARDS

Cultural Diversity

- What is cultural diversity?

  _____

  _____

  _____

- Provide an example of cultural diversity:

  _____

  _____

The People of the United States

Describe the kinds of ethnic, religious and cultural groups that live in the United States.

_____

_____

_____

_____

_____

The People of Ohio

Describe the kinds of ethnic, religious and cultural groups that live in Ohio.

_____

_____

_____

_____

_____

EXPRESS YOURSELF

Some experts have stated that the make-up of Ohio's population is becoming increasingly like the make-up of the population of the United States.

Do you agree with this statement? If so, explain why. If not, explain why not.

ACTIVITY 1H

WHAT HAS BEEN THE IMPACT OF OHIO'S LOCATION AND TRANSPORTATION SYSTEMS?

■ Ohio's location in the United States and its transportation systems continue to influence the movement of people, products and ideas.

In this activity, you will learn about Ohio's roads, canals, railroads, highways, and air travel. After completing this activity, you will see how Ohio's central location and transportation systems have influenced the movement of people, products and ideas.

KEY TERMS

- ■ **National Road**
- ■ **"Gateway to the West"**
- ■ **B.F. Goodrich**
- ■ **John D. Rockefeller**
- ■ **Standard Oil of Ohio**
- ■ **Road Map**

The Governor of Ohio has announced a state contest to promote Ohio's transportation systems. Your teacher has decided that your class should participate in the contest. Here are the rules of the contest:

CONTEST RULES

- Any student living in Ohio can submit a design for a travel brochure.
- The focus of the travel brochure should be the benefits of Ohio's central location and its transportation systems.
- The travel brochure should present information about Ohio's early roads, canals, railroads, highways, and air travel.
- Brochures should be either two or three pages. All brochures must have at least one drawing, photograph, or illustration. Each brochure must include a map showing some of the locations mentioned in the brochure.
- Contestants must also submit an essay explaining how Ohio's central location and transportation systems continue to influence the movement of people, products, and ideas in the United States.
- The best brochure in each class will be submitted to the Governor's Office.

Your teacher passes out to each student a group of pages with all the information about Ohio that students will need to create their travel brochure.

OHIO'S CENTRAL LOCATION

Early travel on the Ohio River was usually done on flatboats.

Ohio's central location places the state in a unique position in the United States. Even in colonial times, the Ohio River was recognized for its importance as a waterway. Without roads and before the invention of trains, the Ohio River provided the safest and easiest way to travel to the West. The Ohio River was seen as the major route into the interior part of North America. Settlers from the Northeast headed to the Ohio River to board barges and flatboats. They could travel the length of the river faster than they could go the same distance on foot or by wagon.

Ohio was the first territory in the West to be admitted to the Union as a state. Ohio's pathway from a territory to state pointed the way for all future states to

follow. Ohio became the "**Gateway to the West**." Ohio's location served to connect the eastern and western parts of the United States.

Today, Ohio's geographic location continues to be an important part of its economic growth. Ohio is within 600 miles of 60 percent of all U.S. and Canadian manufacturing. The state continues to link the Northeast to the Midwestern part of the nation. People and goods pass through the state between these two regions.

PAGE 1

CHECKING YOUR UNDERSTANDING

How did Ohio's location make the state an important gateway to the West?

_____

_____

_____

EARLY ROADS

In the early nineteenth century, Ohio's untamed landscape made travel very difficult. Cities were connected by roads that were little more than dirt trails. Only a few roads were covered with logs or planks. Most short travel was done by walking. For longer trips, people rode on horse-drawn wagons.

In 1802, the federal government promised Ohioans a road connecting them to areas east of the Appalachians. The government began construction of the **National Road** to fulfill that pledge. Trees were cut, stumps were pulled out, and brush was cleared. In some areas, entire hills were leveled and rocks and debris were hauled away to build the first paved road to cross the Appalachian Mountains. To cover the cost of maintaining the 228 miles of the National Road, Ohio began collecting tolls along the road.

The National Road greatly advanced transportation, linking the frontier with the East Coast. Thousands of travelers took the road heading west to settle the lands of the Ohio River Valley. All along its path, the National Road saw cities begin

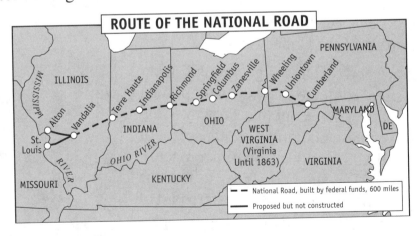

ROUTE OF THE NATIONAL ROAD

- - - National Road, built by federal funds, 600 miles
────── Proposed but not constructed

to grow and prosper. Later, as canals and railroads grew in importance, traffic along the National Road declined. Today a highway, U.S. Route 40, follows the path of the original National Road.

PAGE 2

CHECKING YOUR UNDERSTANDING

What role did Ohio's early roads play in the state's development?

_____

_____

OHIO'S CANALS

Even with the National Road, Ohio suffered from the absence of a good transportation system for the first two decades of statehood. Ohioans had difficulty getting their products to eastern markets. Although the National Road was completed, there were toll stations that travelers needed to pay along the roadway. This made travel along the road too expensive for most Ohioans.

In 1817, the opportunity to connect Ohio with eastern markets became a reality when New York broke ground on a canal connecting Lake Erie with the Hudson River and New York City. In 1822, Ohio set aside funds to build its first canal in an attempt to bring a modern transportation system to the state. Their goal was to create a waterway connecting the Ohio River with Lake Erie.

Ohio's canals directly affected the lives of its residents. Built between 1825 and 1847, these canals provided Ohioans with a new less expensive transportation system. The canals opened new markets for Ohio's agricultural and industrial products. They also helped to attract thousands of

The Ohio and Erie Canal as it looked in 1902

immigrants to the state. The canals transformed Ohio from an isolated frontier region to an area with a growing economy.

At its height, Ohio's canal system included about 1,000 miles of canals. But starting in 1855, the spread of railroads began to challenge Ohio's canal system. Travel on railroads was faster and easier than along the canal system. Today, only a few of the canals remain as reminders of Ohio's first attempt at a modern transportation system.

PAGE 3

CHECKING YOUR UNDERSTANDING

What role did canals play in the development of Ohio's economy?

_____

_____

_____

_____

THE RAILROADS IN OHIO

The first railroad locomotive was introduced when a steam engine was placed on a wheeled wagon that moved along a track. The invention of the railroad revolutionized land transportation.

Ohio Works of the Carnegie Steel Co., Youngstown, Ohio around 1910.

Throughout the later 1800s, Ohio's industrial growth was closely tied to the expansion of the railroads. Railroads affected almost every aspect of life in Ohio. They connected raw materials to factories, and connected factories to consumers across the nation. Railroad construction also stimulated Ohio's iron, steel, and coal industries.

Railroads promoted the settlement of the Western frontier. They brought settlers across Ohio to the farmlands of the Midwest. They linked Ohio farms to markets in the East. Moving goods by train was cheaper than using roads and faster than canal transportation.

As early as the mid-1820s, Ohioans began railroad construction to reduce travel time and to make shipping products easier. Track could be laid almost anywhere, including areas where canals could not be built. Ohio lay between the major East Coast cities and the cities on the Great Lakes and in the West. Many of Ohio's early railroads connected cities that lacked access to a canal.

PAGE 4

Name _____

Ohioans also demanded a better way of transporting people and products from northern to southern Ohio. The earliest railroads in Ohio were local ones. By 1853, 22 railroad companies were operating in Ohio.

Railroads remained the main method of transportation in Ohio for more than a century. Only after World War II (1939–1945) did trucks and automobiles take away much of the railroads' business. The greater use of automobiles took many railroad passengers off of the trains. The final blow to train travel came when airplanes presented an even faster alternative to trains.

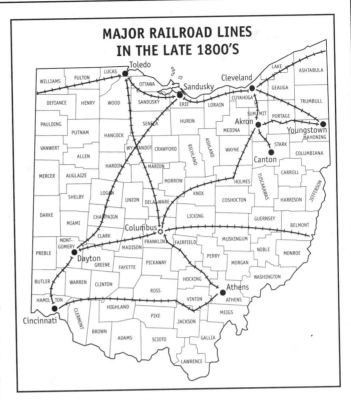

MAJOR RAILROAD LINES IN THE LATE 1800'S

PAGE 5

CHECKING YOUR UNDERSTANDING

What role did railroads play in the growth of Ohio's economy?

_____

_____

HIGHWAYS COME TO OHIO

In 1956, Congress passed the Federal Highway Act. This act created the largest public works project in American history up to that time. This act paid for the construction of thousands of miles of interstate highways, connecting the different regions of the nation. The highways also resulted in many economic benefits for America. It connected cities all across America, becoming the link for interstate commerce to this day.

With 49,000 miles of highway lanes, Ohio today boasts the seventh largest highway system in the nation. The highways of Ohio carry the fifth largest amount of traffic by vehicle miles and the third largest in the value of its commercial goods. Ohio also has the second largest number of bridges in the nation.

Ohio's interstate highway system has greatly contributed to the economic growth and quality of life in Ohio. The interstates and other super-highways continue to contribute to Ohio's economic growth and quality of life. The interstate highway system has given Ohioans the ability to move easily to any destination within their communities and to travel inexpensively throughout the nation.

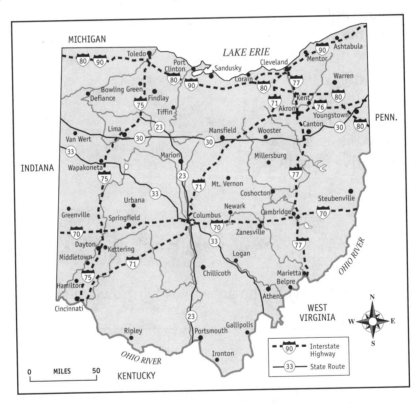

PAGE 6

CHECKING YOUR UNDERSTANDING

What role did highways play in the growth of Ohio's economy?

_____

_____

AIR TRAVEL

Ohio could be considered the birthplace of air travel. The first successful flight of a powered airplane was conducted by two brothers from Dayton, Ohio: Orville and Wilbur Wright. The first air travel was dangerous, and there were numerous crashes. Americans viewed flying as something exciting to watch, but not something that average people would do themselves.

After World War I (1914–1918), there were many advances in airplane design. These made flying much safer. Planes came to be used for military and commercial purposes. They were used to carry passengers and freight.

Aviation is very important to Ohio and its economy. With 175 airports, aviation contributes over $10 billion in economic activity to the state's economy.

About 142,000 jobs are connected with aviation in Ohio. Two of the top reasons a business selects a location for expansion is the closeness of commercial aviation, and local community airports. The Cleveland-Hopkins International

United States Navy Blue Angels perform at an airshow in Ohio.

Airport serves almost 12 million passengers every year. The Port Columbus International Airport is another important airport in Ohio.

Ohio, the birthplace of manned-flight, is also home to 26 astronauts. The Armstrong Air and Space Museum is located in Ohio. It is named after **Neil Armstrong**, the Ohioan who became the first person to set foot on the moon.

PAGE 7

CHECKING YOUR UNDERSTANDING

How is air travel important to Ohio's economic well-being?

_____

_____

_____

THE IMPACT OF LOCATION AND TRANSPORTATION ON OHIO

Because of its central location and the excellence of its transportation systems, Ohio has long been a center of industry and manufacturing. Heavy industry grew quickly in Ohio in the years after the Civil War. Because of its location on Lake Erie, Ohio was able to use iron and coal from nearby states. This helped Ohio to become a major center for making steel, iron, machinery, tools, and other metal products. Cleveland, Lorain, and Sandusky produced iron. Youngstown was a center for steel. Dayton became known for manufacturing cash registers. Toledo excelled at making glass products. Cincinnati became home to **Proctor & Gamble**, a multinational maker of personal care products, household cleaning goods, laundry detergents, prescription drugs and disposable diapers.

In 1870, **Benjamin F. Goodrich** opened a rubber manufacturing plant in Akron. Akron quickly became known as the "Capital of the Rubber Industry." Ohio was also an important source of oil. **John D. Rockefeller** founded the **Standard Oil Company of Ohio** in the 1870s. Rockefeller opened Ohio's first oil refinery. His company refined the crude oil coming out of the ground, turning it into useful products such as kerosene for lamps and gasoline for cars. Rockefeller's company soon became the world's largest oil company.

BP Tower in Cleveland, one of many large Ohio corporations.

Today, Ohio continues to be home to many important national and multinational corporations, major banks, insurance companies and retail stores. People around the world buy and use goods made by Ohioans. These include chemical, rubber and agricultural products. Ohioans also manufacture trucks and cut stone products. Fifty-seven of the largest companies in the United States are based in Ohio. Ohio is also home to nine major banks. Six of the America's largest insurance companies are headquartered in Ohio.

COMPLETING YOUR BROCHURE

Now that you have read about Ohio's central location and transportation systems, it is time for you to create your brochure. Here is a checklist for your brochure:

❏ Does your brochure have at least two to three pages?
❏ Does your brochure contain illustrations?
❏ Does your brochure describe each type of transportation system?
❏ Does your brochure include how people used that type of transportation when it was first used?
❏ Does your brochure explain what transportation is still used in Ohio today?

In the space below, create an outline or plan for your brochure. Indicate where you will have your introduction, illustrations, and what type of transportation systems you will show on each page.

PAGE 1

PAGE 2

PAGE 3

MAKING CONNECTIONS

WRITING YOUR ESSAY

The second part of the Governor's contest asks participants to write an essay. In this *Making Connections*, you will write an essay about what you learned in researching your brochure. Use the space below to describe how Ohio's transportation systems continue to influence the movement of people, products and ideas in the United States. You may want to conduct additional research on the Internet or in your school library before writing your essay.

Name _____

Activity 1H: Impact of Ohio's Location and Transportation Systems   **103**

After you complete your essay and travel brochure, your teacher will decide which essay and brochure are best. Those should be sent to the Governor's office. Who knows, maybe one of your ideas will find its way into being a part of Ohio's next official travel brochure!

STUDY CARDS

Ohio's Location

How is Ohio's central location beneficial to its economy?

_____

_____

_____

_____

_____

_____

Ohio's Canal System

What effect has Ohio's system of canals had on its economy?

_____

_____

_____

_____

_____

_____

Ohio's Railroad System

What impact did the expansion of railroads have on Ohio's economy?

_____

_____

_____

_____

_____

_____

Air Travel in Ohio

Why is air travel so important to Ohio's economic well-being?

_____

_____

_____

_____

_____

_____

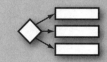

LEARNING WITH GRAPHIC ORGANIZERS

Directions: Complete the graphic organizer below by explaining Ohio's impact on the movement of people, products, and ideas in the United States.

Central Location:

_____
_____
_____
_____
_____
_____

Roads and Canals:

_____
_____
_____
_____
_____
_____
_____

How Ohio's location, roads, canals, railroads and air travel influenced the movement of people, ideas and products.

Railroads:

_____
_____
_____
_____
_____
_____

Air Travel:

_____
_____
_____
_____
_____
_____

EXPRESS YOURSELF

Ohio's transportation systems include its waterways, roads, canals, railroads, highways, and air travel. Throughout history, these transportation systems greatly affected the lifestyles of Ohioans. For example, the Ohio and Erie Canal linked Ohio to New York as well as to New Orleans and the Gulf of Mexico. This connection stimulated westward expansion and the growth of a national economy.

Choose any two methods of transportation mentioned above. For each one chosen, explain one way it has changed and how it has altered the lifestyle of Ohioans.

Name _____

UNIT 2

HISTORY

Paleo Indians of Ohio hunting for game to eat.

The "Battle of Lake Erie" with Oliver Perry (standing) in lifeboat.

People escaping slavery along Ohio's Underground Railroad.

History is the study of the past, how people once lived, and what they did. Just as your own memories tell you who you are, each society looks to its history for a sense of its identity. Seeing the results of past actions can often help us to make future choices. In this unit, you will learn about the early history of Ohio.

ACTIVITY 2A

HOW DO YOU MAKE A TIMELINE?

■ The order of significant events in Ohio and the United States can be shown on a timeline.

In this activity you will gain a sense of time — the past, the present and the future. You will learn how to make timelines.

KEY TERMS

■ Timeline
■ Chronological Order
■ BC (or BCE)

■ AD (or CE)
■ Decade
■ Century

■ Millennium
■ Illustrated Timeline
■ Search Engine

Think of the activities you completed this morning before you came to school. Imagine placing them along a line to make a diagram:

Woke Up	Brushed My Teeth		Got Dressed	Ate My Breakfast		Left for School
7:00	7:10		7:30	7:40		8:10

This type of diagram is known as a **timeline**. Historians often use timelines to show the connections between events.

TIMELINES AND THEIR MAIN PARTS

A **timeline** shows events in the order in which they happened. This is called **chronological order.** A timeline can cover a short period or up to several thousand years. To understand any timeline, you must examine its main parts: is **title**, **events** and **dates**.

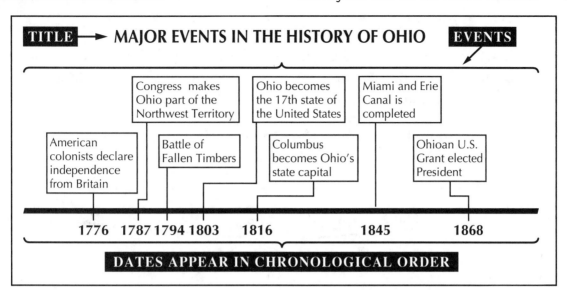

TITLE

The title of the timeline tells you its overall topic. In the timeline above, the title tells you that it shows some of the main events in the history of Ohio.

EVENTS

Each event on a timeline should be related to the timeline's title. For instance, if a timeline had the title "American Settlement of Ohio," The Battle of Fallen Timbers could appear as an event. Columbus' voyages should not appear, however, since Columbus never explored or settled in Ohio.

CHECKING YOUR UNDERSTANDING

The timeline above has seven important events in the history of Ohio.

Select **two** of the events on the timeline. Explain why they are important enough to include on a timeline of major events in the history of Ohio.

1 _____

_____

_____

2 _____

_____

_____

DIVISION BETWEEN BC AND AD

Dates in many parts of the world are based on when it is believed Jesus was born. These dates are divided into BC and AD. Sometimes BC is shown as BCE — before the Common Era. AD may be shown as CE — the Common Era. As time passes:

- BC dates go from higher numbers (500 BC to lower numbers (200 BC)
- AD dates go from lower (100) to higher numbers (2014).

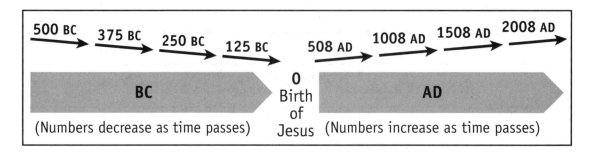

HOW TO DESIGN YOUR OWN TIMELINE

On a timeline, the earliest event usually appears at the far left. The rest of the events are placed to the right of it in the order in which they occurred. The space between events on the timeline shows the amount of time that has passed between those events. A longer space indicates the passage of a longer period of time.

In the timeline below, every 1¼ inches on the timeline represents the passage of one year of time.

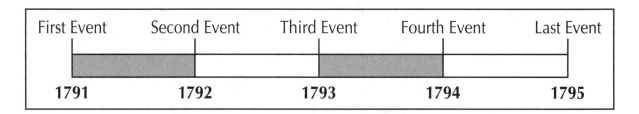

Sometimes timelines are drawn up and down (*vertically*) instead of left to right (*horizontally*). In that case, the earliest event is usually placed at the bottom of the time-line. The rest of the events are placed above the first event in the order in which they occurred.

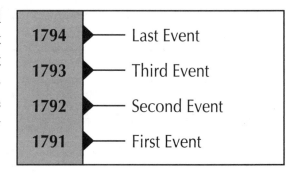

PERIODS OF TIME

To understand timelines, you must also know about time periods. For short periods of time, you can divide a timeline into one-year intervals. For example:

For longer periods of time, you might divide a timeline into decades. A **decade** is a period of ten years. For example, the following timeline shows a span of six decades:

An even longer period of time is a **century**. A century is a period of 100 years. A **millennium** spans 1,000 years. The following timeline shows six centuries of time.

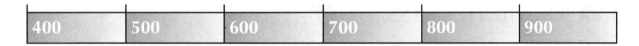

Now you try it. Fill in the timeline below by putting in the years 1300 to 1800, dividing the timeline by century:

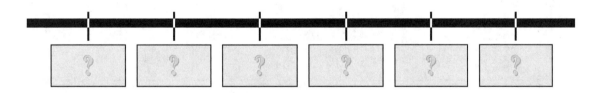

How we identify centuries may seem confusing at first. The "21st century" means the 100 years from 2001 to 2100. The present decade, therefore, belongs to the 21st century. Let's see why:

1–100	First Century	201–300	Third Century
101–200	Second Century	301–400	Fourth Century

CHECKING YOUR UNDERSTANDING

1 The numbering of centuries can be confusing. Explain why the numbering of centuries creates confusion.

_____

_____

_____

_____

2 Which century was 701–800? _____

3 Which century was 1501–1600? _____

4 What was the last century, 1901–2000, called? _____

5 What is this century called? _____

MEASURING THE PASSAGE OF TIME

To measure the number of years from one date to another, subtract the smaller date from the larger date. Suppose the year is 2015. How long ago was 1500? By subtracting 1500 from 2015, we arrive at 515 years ago.

2015	(2015 years since the birth of Jesus)
–1500	(1500 years since the birth of Jesus)
515	years ago

MAKE YOUR OWN TIMELINE

Let's practice making a timeline for this unit. In this unit, you will explore the birth of the United States as well as the early history of Ohio before the Civil War. On the space on the next page, you should make a timeline with this title:

KEY EVENTS IN UNITED STATES AND OHIO HISTORY, 1763–1860

As you go through the rest of this unit, you will learn about a number of important events. As you learn about each new event, add it to your timeline. To get started with this timeline, begin by adding the following three events to the timeline:

■ End of The French and Indian War (1763)
■ The Boston Massacre (1770)
■ The Boston Tea Party (1773)

KEY EVENTS IN UNITED STATES AND OHIO HISTORY, 1763–1860

Ohio History

U.S. History

MAKING CONNECTIONS

CREATING AN ILLUSTRATED TIMELINE

An **illustrated timeline** is one with pictures that show some its events. A graphic organizer can also be illustrated. In this part of the activity, you will complete an illustrated graphic organizer showing major changes in communication, industrialization, and transportation.

You will find the Internet is an invaluable tool for finding information. For example, to find a picture of a nineteenth-century communication device, you might use a major **search engine** like **Google**, **Yahoo**, **AOL**, or **Bing**. Complete the chart by finding a picture for each empty box. Print the picture, cut it out and paste it in place.

CHANGES IN THE WAY AMERICAN PEOPLE
COMMUNICATE, WORK, AND TRAVEL

	Communication	Industrialization	Transportation
17th Century	?	?	
18th Century	?		?
19th Century	?	?	
20th Century		?	?

Name _____

STUDY CARDS

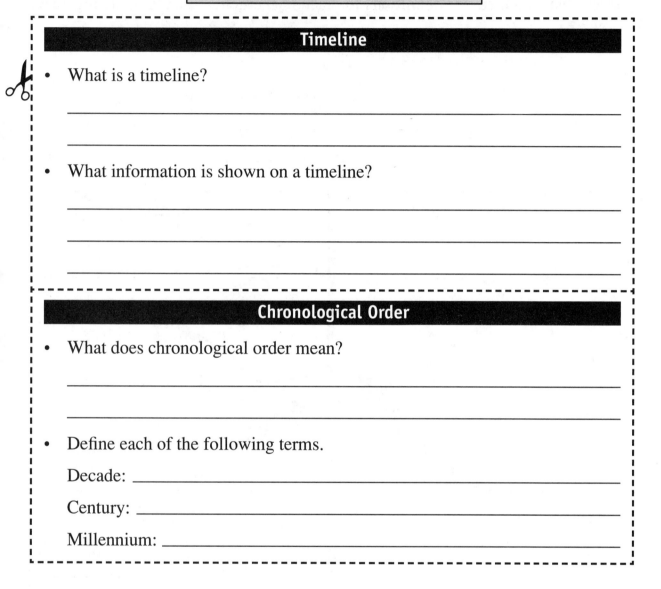

Timeline

- What is a timeline?

  _____

  _____

- What information is shown on a timeline?

  _____

  _____

  _____

Chronological Order

- What does chronological order mean?

  _____

  _____

- Define each of the following terms.

  Decade: _____

  Century: _____

  Millennium: _____

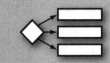 

LEARNING WITH GRAPHIC ORGANIZERS

Directions: Complete the definitions for each of the items in the graphic organizer below.

Title:

_____

_____

_____

Chronological Order:

_____

_____

_____

Events:

_____

_____

_____

Timelines

BC/AD:

_____

_____

_____

Century:

_____

_____

_____

Decade:

_____

_____

_____

Name _____

HOW CAN YOU USE PRIMARY AND SECONDARY SOURCES TO CREATE A NARRATIVE?

■ Primary and secondary sources can be used to create historical narratives.

In this activity, you will learn how to use primary and secondary sources to reconstruct a historical event. A source is a thing that provides information. You will also learn what a historical narrative (*story*) is and how to create one from a variety of sources.

KEY TERMS

- History
- Historian
- Hypothesis

- Primary Source
- Artifacts
- Secondary Source

- Historical Narrative
- Boston Tea Party
- Flashback

WHAT IS HISTORY?

History is what happened in the past. It refers both to the past events themselves and to the study of those events. **Historians** are people who study the past. They help us to uncover the past and to answer questions about the importance of past events, their causes, and effects. Historians help us to make connections between the world as it once was with how the world is today.

THE IMPORTANCE OF HISTORY

Just as your own life would be confusing if you had no memory of who you were or what you had done, each society looks to its history for a sense of identity. History helps a society remember what it is and where it is going. A knowledge of history gives us insight and provides a guide for our future actions.

THE VARIETIES OF HISTORY

There are many varieties of history. Some historians study politics, affairs between nations, and wars; others study past economies; still others study the history of the arts, culture, family life, or ideas. Some historians recount a series of related events; some study one country; while others a whole civilization. All historians develop **hypotheses** (*educated guesses*) about some aspect of the past.

CHECKING YOUR UNDERSTANDING

Identify two reasons why you think the study of history is important:

1 _____

_____

2 _____

_____

PRIMARY AND SECONDARY SOURCES

Every historian begins with some question about the past. For example, how were women treated during the American Revolution? What were the lives of slaves like in the South? What caused the Civil War? Once a historian has come up with a historical question, he or she next gathers sources of information to answer that question. The sources gathered are of two kinds:

PRIMARY SOURCES

Primary sources are original records of an event under investigation. They are records of the event as it is first described. They include eyewitness reports, official records from the time of the event, letters sent by people involved in the event, diaries, photographs, oral (*spoken*) histories and surviving **artifacts** (*objects*). Even a work of fiction, such as a story or poem, may be a primary source if it reveals how people felt about things at the time that it was written.

An ancient Indian stone scraper tool

All historical knowledge about past events can be traced back to primary sources. However, just because a document or artifact is a primary source, this does not mean it is true or without prejudice (*biased*).

SECONDARY SOURCES

Secondary sources are the writings and interpretations (*explanations*) of later writers who have reviewed the information in primary sources. They provide a second-hand account of information. Secondary sources, like textbooks and encyclopedia articles, often contain convenient summaries of information found in primary sources. Secondary sources frequently tell the writer's interpretation or point of view.

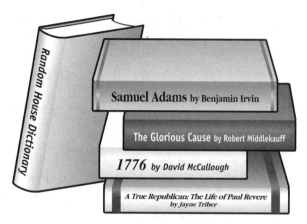

Historical sources can present many difficulties. Primary sources are sometimes incomplete, and a historian can never know exactly what happened before. History, therefore, depends on the interpretation of surviving sources. This can be very tricky.

Being a historian is like being a detective. When a historian discovers a particular record, he or she must interpret it. Is the document really what it seems to be? For example, is it really old or is it a recent fake? Because historians often disagree about the interpretation of sources, there are many conflicting views on what actually took place in the past.

Being an historian is similar to being a detective.

SELECTING AND INTERPRETING SIGNIFICANT FACTS

Of the thousands of facts, which are important for telling the story of a past event? In deciding which facts to include, historians must make judgments about what is important. Others might not agree with their judgments. You must be able to evaluate (*judge*) how well-informed these judgments are.

History, therefore, poses problems both in interpreting documents and in deciding which facts are important. These problems often lead to historical **controversies** (*disputes*). What you find in your history textbook, including this book, is just a summary of key points about which some historians have agreed.

CHECKING YOUR UNDERSTANDING

Suppose you find a website on the Internet about ancient Indians who lived in Ohio. Which of these items on the website are primary or secondary sources?

Website Item	Type?	Explain Your Answer
Pictures by a modern artist showing how Ohio looked in the 1700s.	☐ Primary ☑ Secondary	It is secondary because it was a modern artist (now)
Indian tools used during Ohio's early history.	☑ Primary ☐ Secondary	It was primary because the tools were used during the event.
Copies of arrow heads sold by modern merchants to tourists.	☐ Primary ☑ Secondary	The weren't real from the event they werer were just copys.
Pottery unearthed near an ancient Ohio Indian settlement.	☑ Primary ☐ Secondary	It was a primary source because it was used during that event.

DECIDING WHICH SOURCES ARE PRIMARY AND WHICH ARE SECONDARY

How well do you understand the difference between primary and secondary sources? Imagine that you are researching the question: Why did the 13 British colonies declare their independence from Great Britain? Look over the following sources. Indicate if you think each is a primary or secondary source.

1   Declaration of Independence

☑ Primary Source   ☐ Secondary Source

Explain your answer.

It is a primary source because it happened right then

2 A nineteenth-century painting of Paul Revere, warning the American colonists that British soldiers are coming.

❏ Primary Source   ☑ Secondary Source

Explain your answer.

It is a secondary source because it's happening now,

3 Money used in the colony of North Carolina.

❏ Primary Source   ☑ Secondary Source

Explain your answer.

It is a secondary source because it is happening NOW!

WHAT IS A HISTORICAL NARRATIVE?

Telling stories is part of our daily lives. It is one of the ways we communicate with others. For example, if you came home from school, a friend asks you: "How was your day?" When you describe the events that took place, you are actually telling the story of what you did.

Suppose you wanted to write the story of your life. To help you tell the story, list three primary or secondary sources that you would use in writing this story. For

example, one possible primary source you could use is a birth certificate issued by the state in which you were born. Now, list three other sources you would use:

1 _____

2 _____

3 _____

See if you can use these sources to write a **narrative**. For example, your birth certificate tells when you were born. You might begin your narrative with this event: "I was born on (date you were born). It was stormy night." Look at the other sources you listed above. Use these to create a narrative about your life in the space below.

MAKING CONNECTIONS

WRITING A HISTORICAL NARRATIVE

Just as the narrative above tells the story of your life, a **historical narrative** tells the story of a historical event. At the heart of every historical event is a story, just like the story of your life. You have to tell where the event took place; who was involved in the event; what happened; why it happened; and what were the effects of the event. Now let's see how well you have learned about narratives. Your next task will be to write your own historical narrative using six documents.

In the next few pages, you will be provided with six sources. Some of them are primary sources and some are secondary sources. You will use those sources to write your own historical narrative about a historic event — the Boston Tea Party.

SOURCE #1

The first source is from a textbook, *The Story of America*, by John A. Garraty.

The Boston Tea Party took place on a bright, cold, moonlit evening on December 16, 1773. The dispute was staged against King George III and the British government. A group of Massachusetts Patriots protested against the importing of tea granted by Parliament to the East India Company.

A large group of colonists disguised themselves as Native American Indians. The colonists took 342 chests of tea in a midnight raid and threw them into Boston Harbor. In only three hours, more than 100 colonists emptied the tea into the harbor. The chests held more than 45 tons of tea. In today's dollars, it would be worth nearly $1,000,000.

CHECKING YOUR UNDERSTANDING

- Is this a primary or secondary source? _secondary SOURCES_
- What information did you learn about the Boston Tea Party?

I learned that chests held 45 tons of tea

_____

_____

_____

SOURCE #2

Below is part of a journal entry written by John Cook, a British soldier stationed in Boston during the Boston Tea Party.

Boston, December 17th, 1773

How can these colonists act so dishonorably? When I went to the harbor this morning I noticed chests of tea floating in the water. I soon learned that all the tea that had arrived yesterday had been thrown into the water! I cannot understand why these colonists show us such hostility. We protect them from the Indians and French. Governing them across a distant ocean costs us a large sum of money. T'is only fair that they pay for these services in the form of taxes. Our empire is the most powerful in the world. Should not the colonists be overjoyed to receive the benefits of our protection? Instead, they complain, throw rocks at us, refuse to buy our goods, or even throw them into the harbor. I truly hope the colonists come to their senses soon ...."

CHECKING YOUR UNDERSTANDING

- Is this a primary or secondary source? _____

- How did this British soldier see the events that took place in Boston Harbor?

  _____

  _____

  _____

- How did his background and position influence his views of this event?

  _____

  _____

  _____

SOURCE #3

The following is a printed sheet of paper known as a **broadside**. In the eighteenth century, broadsides were put up on walls or popular gathering areas as posters to announce an event. This broadside appeared around Boston after the arrival of tea ships from Great Britain.

> Monday Morning, December 27, 1773.
> THE Tea-Ship being arrived, every Inhabitant who wishes to preserve the Liberty of America, is defired to meet at the STATE-HOUSE, This Morning, precisely at TEN o'Clock, to advise what is beft to be done on this alarming Crifis.

Monday Morning, December 27, 1773. The Tea-Ship being arrived, every inhabitant who wishes to preserve the Liberty of America, is desired to meet at the State-House, this morning, precisely at TEN o'Clock, to advise what is best to be done on this alarming crisis.

CHECKING YOUR UNDERSTANDING

- Is this a primary or secondary source? _____

- Who do you think was responsible for printing this broadside?

  _____

  _____

- What additional information did you learn about the Boston Tea Party from this broadside?

  _____

  _____

  _____

  _____

SOURCE #4

The letter below was written by George Hewes, a shoemaker who lived in Boston. The letter is written to his wife. Hewes was one of the men who disguised himself as an "Indian" and boarded the tea ships that night. According to Hewes, it took three hours for him and the others to dump the tea chests into Boston harbor. In his letter, Hewes describes how the colonists made their way to the ships:

It was now evening, and I immediately dressed myself in the costume of an Indian. I carried with me a small hatchet, which we called a tomahawk, and a club. After having painted my face and hands with coal dust in the shop of a blacksmith, I went to the harbor where the ships lay that contained the tea. When I first appeared in the street after being disguised, I fell in with others who were dressed, equipped and painted as I was. We all marched to the ship that was our target.

CHECKING YOUR UNDERSTANDING

- Is this a primary or secondary source? _____

- What does this letter tell you about the Boston Tea Party that night?

_____

_____

_____

_____

_____

_____

_____

Name _____

SOURCE #5

Below is a modern artist's view of what the scene looked like at midnight when the Boston Tea Party took place.

CHECKING YOUR UNDERSTANDING

- Is this a primary or secondary source? _____

- What does this source tell you about the Boston Tea Party?

_____

_____

_____

_____

_____

SOURCE #6

Here is a copy of a newspaper published in London, England shortly after the Boston Tea Party took place.

THE MORNING CHRONICLE

Volume   VXIII

December 28, 1773

BOSTON COLONISTS DESTROY TEA

Following the horrible incident of some misguided Boston colonists, the leaders of the British government are meeting today. Many in the King's government are calling for strong action against these colonists.

Chiefly responsible for this incident is Samuel Adams, who is said to control the Boston mobs. He is said to use this uprising for his own personal gain and glory. Also involved is the businessman John Hancock. He is described as a rich merchant and landowner who threatens the King's policies.

Members of the King's government are furious over this act. They are considering a series of laws to force the Massachusetts colonists to pay for the tea. The act will provide that no ship can enter or leave Boston Harbor until the colonists have paid for the tea they destroyed.

A second act is also being considered by Parliament. This act would transfer all trials of British soldiers and royal officials accused of a serious crime to courts outside of Massachusetts.

CHECKING YOUR UNDERSTANDING

- Is this a primary or secondary source? _____

- How is the reaction of this newspaper different from colonial accounts?

  _____

  _____

- What does this source tell you about the effect of the Boston Tea Party in London?

  _____

  _____

  _____

MAKING CONNECTIONS

WRITING A HISTORICAL NARRATIVE

Now that you have read these six sources, you are ready to write your own historical narrative about the Boston Tea Party. The simplest way to start may be to look over what you have written about each source in the *Checking Your Understanding*. Next, think about what your narrative should tell.

You might want to explain the motives of the people involved: what made them take the actions that they did? You should be sure to describe how the events unfolded. Describe each part of the story in the order in which it occurred.

For example, you can select an important historical character to tell your narrative. Through that character your reader will experience the historical event. Another form your narrative may take is to use flashbacks. In a **flashback** you start in the present and recall events that took place in the past. Lastly, do not be afraid to use dialogue between the people in your story. This is an entertaining way to tell your story.

EXPRESS YOURSELF

Try to write an introduction that will immediately grab your reader's attention. Your story should probably have a *beginning*, *middle* and *end* showing how the story unfolds. However, you can also be different. You can bypass the traditional way of writing history and begin in the middle or the end of the story and use flashbacks to earlier events to tell your story.

STUDY CARDS

Primary Source

- What is a primary source? _____

_____

_____

- List three examples of a primary source.

    1. _____

    2. _____

    3. _____

Secondary Source

- What is a secondary source? _____

_____

_____

- List three examples of a secondary source.

    1. _____

    2. _____

    3. _____

LEARNING WITH GRAPHIC ORGANIZERS

Directions: Complete the following graphic organizers by describing examples of primary and secondary sources.

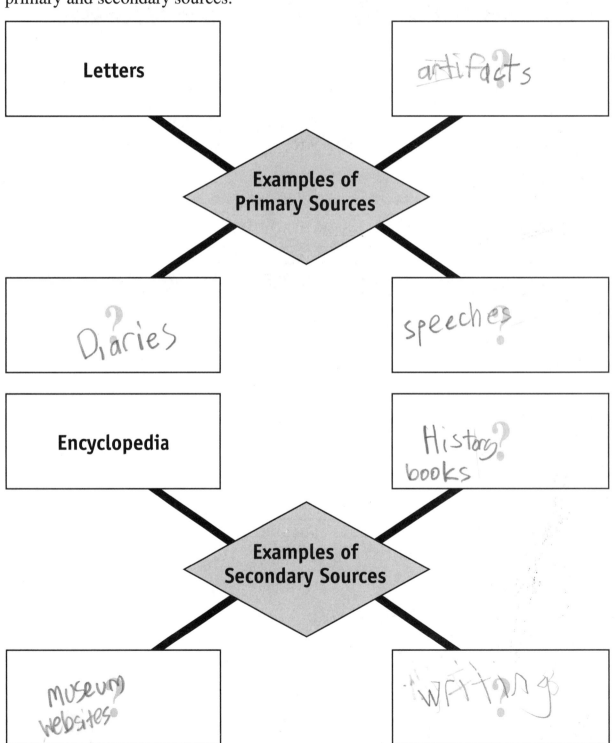

Letters

artifacts

Examples of Primary Sources

Diaries

speeches

Encyclopedia

History books

Examples of Secondary Sources

museum websites

writing

EXPRESS YOURSELF

In this activity, you used primary and secondary sources to create a historical narrative about the Boston Tea Party. Although the American Revolution is long since over, protest movements continue to be a part of modern America. Search the Internet, magazines, or newspapers for a story about a present-day protest movement in which people demonstrate their unhappiness with a current government policy.

■ Identify a primary or secondary source that you used for your response.

■ Describe the event in which people are demonstrating against a current government policy that they disagree with.

■ Explain how these actions are similar in some ways to the protests that took place in Boston in 1773.

ACTIVITY 2C

HOW WOULD YOU EDIT THIS ARTICLE?

■ Various groups of people have lived in Ohio over time including prehistoric and historic American Indians .... Interactions among these groups have resulted in both cooperation and conflict.

In this activity, you will edit an article about the Prehistoric Indians who once lived in Ohio for your school magazine. After completing this activity, you will be able to describe the earliest settlements in Ohio and some of the practices of Ohio's first people.

KEY TERMS

- Fact
- Accurate
- Opinion
- Prehistoric Indians
- Prehistory
- Culture
- Archaeologist
- Paleo Indians
- Hunter Gatherers
- Mound Builders
- Adena / Hopewell
- Fort Ancient People

This year's issue of your school's student magazine will focus on the American Indians who once lived in Ohio. The magazine's editor, the person who puts the magazine together, has just given you your first assignment.

"Here is an article by one of our students," the editor says. "I would like you to make sure it contains only facts. I don't want any opinions in this article!"

FACT AND OPINION STATEMENTS

A statement of **fact** is something that can be checked for accuracy. Something is **accurate** if it is true.

You can check a statement's accuracy by looking at other sources to see if they agree that it is correct. For example:

Correct	*Incorrect*
Columbus is the capital of Ohio.	Cleveland is the capital of Ohio.

An **opinion** is a statement of personal belief. It is not a statement that is true or false. An opinion *cannot* be checked for accuracy. There are three types of opinion statements:

- Opinions of personal taste express a person's feelings. For example, "Ohio is the best state to live in." People from another state might feel their state is better.

- Opinions about the future make a prediction. For example, "I think John Smith will win the election for mayor."

- Opinions that are made when there is not enough information to state a fact. For example, "The Fort Ancient Indians probably built the Great Serpent Mound. I am interested in how the groups described in the article cooperated or engaged in conflict."

"Recognizing opinions is just part of your assignment," the editor continues. "I also need you to check the accuracy of factual statements. Finally, I would like to know what you think is the most interesting thing in this article."

Here is a note from the editor along with the article you are asked to read:

EDITOR'S INSTRUCTIONS: Read the following paragraphs, and:
1. Copy any sentence with an opinion.
2. Pick one of the sentences you copied. Why do you think it is an opinion?
3. Copy two factual statements.
4. Check to see if these statements are accurate.

THE FIRST OHIOANS

At least 20,000 years ago, hunters from Asia crossed a narrow land bridge that once connected Asia to North America. It was not really a bridge but more of an area made up of several hundreds of square miles. These peoples followed animal herds as they moved across North America.

Traveling in small fur-and-skin lined canoes, small bands of people paddled along the shores of this land bridge. They followed the herds of animals they hunted, and never settled in any one place for very long. The lands they crossed were breathtaking in their beauty. It is believed that the earliest people to live in Ohio were American Indians. Later other groups settled in Ohio.

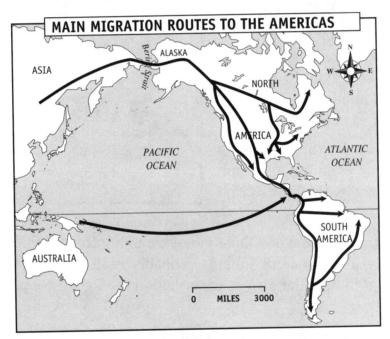

MAIN MIGRATION ROUTES TO THE AMERICAS

ASIA · ALASKA · Bering Strait · NORTH · AMERICA · PACIFIC OCEAN · ATLANTIC OCEAN · AUSTRALIA · SOUTH AMERICA · 0   MILES   3000

PAGE 1

CHECKING YOUR UNDERSTANDING

Why is so much information about how the first people came to North America often considered to be more opinion than fact?

_____

_____

_____

Name _____

THE PREHISTORIC INDIANS OF OHIO

Prehistory is the period of time before the development of written records. **Culture** is a people's way of life, including their customs, products, and beliefs.

Archaeologists study prehistoric and ancient cultures by looking at the objects people left behind. The earliest tribes in Ohio are known as **Prehistoric Indians**. By studying pieces of stone, pottery and other remains, archaeologists can piece together a great deal of information about the Prehistoric Indians who once lived in Ohio.

Archaeologists at work in a grassy field along the Ohio River.

PALEO INDIANS (12,000-7,000 B.C.)

The oldest of these peoples, the **Paleo Indians**, lived in Ohio between 12,000 and 15,000 years ago. The Paleo Indians made tools of wood, stone, and bone. They wore animal skins and furs, and knew how to make fire. They were primarily hunter-gatherers. A **hunter-gatherer** society is one in which most of the food people obtain comes from wild plants and animals.

Groups of Paleo Indians cooperated with each other in many ways. They would often form small groups to hunt large mastodons, mammoths, bison, and smaller animals. They also gathered berries, seeds, and roots to eat. Parents would teach their children which plants they could eat.

The Paleo Indians were hunter-gatherers.

Some Paleo Indians would drive large animals into a trap or into a group of hunters with large spears. Anyone was free to join or leave the group any time they wished. Life must have been very hard for those Paleo Indians hunting such large animals.

Without permanent settlements, the Paleo Indians were constantly on the move. Members of their tribe worked together to take apart their tents made of wooden poles and covered in bark. When they arrived at their next location, tribal members worked with each other to erect and establish a new settlement.

PAGE 2

ARCHAIC INDIANS (8000 TO 1000 B.C.)

The **Archaic Indians** lived in Ohio about 10,000 years ago. Like the Paleo Indians, they lived by hunting and gathering plants. As the climate changed, mastodons, mammoths and other giant mammals died out. Archaic Indians hunted smaller animals, fished, and ate a wider variety of plants than the

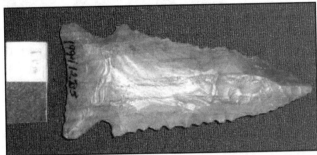
Archaeologists have found arrow heads of animal bone from the Archaic Period

Paleo Indians. Archaeologists believe the Archaic Indians knew how to make baskets, pottery and objects out of copper. They passed this knowledge from one group to another. Archaic Indians must have been much smarter than the Paleo Indians.

THE MOUND BUILDERS OF THE WOODLAND PERIOD

The next Indians to live in Ohio are known as the **Mound Builders**. They built small hills or mounds of earth over places where they buried their dead or held religious ceremonies. The Mound Builders are also known as the Woodland Indians because at this time Ohio was covered by great forests. The Adena and Hopewell peoples were both Woodland Indians.

PAGE 3

CHECKING YOUR UNDERSTANDING

1   What is an archaeologist? _____

_____

2   What might explain why some Prehistoric Indians built mounds?

_____

_____

_____

_____

THE ADENA

The **Adena Indians** settled in the Ohio River Valley. The Adena were also mainly hunters and gatherers. However, they kept gardens where they grew sunflowers, squash, and other plants. The Adena were master craftsmen. Adena craftsmen handed down their skills by teaching others. They obtained mica and copper from other areas to make jewelry and other objects. Archaeologists do not know if they received these materials through travel or trade with other groups. I think travel is more likely. Archaeologists are unsure what happened to the Adena. Since the Adena had no system of writing, they left few traces of their lives and culture.

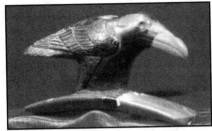

This Adena pipe, shaped like a raven, was discovered by archaeologists.

THE HOPEWELL

The **Hopewell** culture arose out of the Adena about 2,000 years ago. It is not clear if the Adena and Hopewell peoples engaged in conflict against each other. Settlements of Hopewell Indians were found throughout the Ohio River and Mississippi River Valleys. The Hopewell, like the Adena, were mound builders. Many of their mounds were surrounded by **embankments** (*earthen walls*).

The Hopewell built their mounds for many purposes. Building these mounds required the cooperation of the entire community. Some mounds covered the remains of wooden buildings where ceremonies once took place. Families came to bury their dead and to make offerings of objects made of mica, copper, and obsidian (*a black mineral-like glass*). These earthen works were also used for community feats and rites of passages, such as marriage or a young boy passing into manhood.

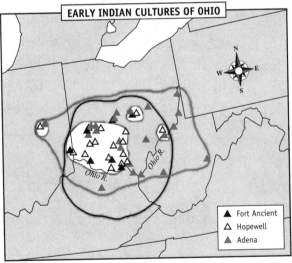

EARLY INDIAN CULTURES OF OHIO

Ohio R.

▲ Fort Ancient
△ Hopewell
▲ Adena

Besides building mounds, the Hopewell worked with each other to hunt, garden, and gather food. Like the Adena, they grew sunflowers and other plants. The Hopewell were happier than the Adena. However, their civilization also failed to last.

LATE PREHISTORIC INDIANS: THE FORT ANCIENT INDIANS (1000 TO 1750)

The growing of **maize** (*corn*) slowly spread from Mexico northwards, until it reached Ohio about 1,000 years ago. Knowledge of growing this plant provides another example of cooperation among Indian groups.

The Great Serpent Mound is one of the largest and most famous prehistoric structures.

This gave rise to the **Fort Ancient** culture. These people continued the traditions of the earlier mound builders. They built immense walls of earth at Fort Ancient using wood, shells, and bones to move the dirt.

Archaeologists believe that the Fort Ancient Indians also built the Great Serpent Mound in Peebles, Ohio. This giant mound is in the shape of a giant snake. The Fort Ancient Indians were hunters and gatherers as well as farmers.

Archaeologists have found arrowheads, revealing that the Fort Ancient Indians used bows and arrows. The bow and arrow was probably the greatest invention of prehistoric times. They not only used arrows for hunting, but may have also engaged in warfare against neighboring peoples. Probably they fought over land for setting up camp or planting, or over territories for hunting.

When Europeans first began to arrive, these Indians cooperated with them. The Europeans often traded their goods in exchange for animal fur pelts (*skins*). Animal fur was highly sought after in Europe as a sign of wealth and importance.

PAGE 5

CHECKING YOUR UNDERSTANDING

1   What evidence is there of cooperation among different Indian groups?

_____

_____

2   What evidence is there of conflict between these American Indian groups?

_____

_____

REVIEWING AND CHECKING THE ARTICLE

Now it is time to report back to your editor. Remember that you must tell your editor whether the article was completely factual or if it contained some opinions. You should also tell the editor what you found most interesting in the article.

Dear Editor,

I have reviewed the article, I found that the article contained several opinions. Two examples are:

_____

_____

_____

_____

_____

The most interesting thing I learned from your article was

_____

_____

_____

_____

Sincerely,

_____

Later you meet your editor. The editor reminds you that you were supposed to do one more thing — to check the **accuracy** of the article. Remember, a **factual statement** is **accurate** if it is true and correct. Since it would take too long to check every fact in the article, the editor had asked you to check **two** factual statements.

You can use a history book, encyclopedia, or the Internet to check the accuracy of these two factual statements.

Factual Statements Selected	The Source Used	Statement is:
(1) _____ _____		❏ Accurate ❏ Not Accurate
(2) _____ _____		❏ Accurate ❏ Not Accurate

MAKING CONNECTIONS

A VISIT TO AN OHIO MUSEUM OR HISTORIC SITE

One way to learn more about the Prehistoric Indians of Ohio is to visit a **museum** or **historic site**. Ohio has a number of locations where you can still see the remains of the mound builders. For example:

■ **The Museum at Fort Ancient** in Oregonia (513-932-4421) has indoor and outdoor exhibits focusing on 15,000 years of American Indian history in Ohio. At the museum is a huge monument to the technological ability of the earliest people's of prehistoric North America. The monument was built by dumping thousands of baskets of soil one on top of another.

■ **Mound City Group-Hopewell Culture National Historical Park** in Chillicothe (704-774-1126). The site is operated by the National Park Service. The site contains mounds from the Hopewell Indians who used it exclusively for burials. The group also includes other sites in the region — High Bank Works, Hopeton Earthworks, and Hopewell Mound Group.

Mound City, Chillicothe, Ohio

Name _____

■ **Miamisburg Mound** in Miamisburg, is located in the southeast part of the state. It is the largest cone-shaped earthwork in Ohio and possibly in the United States. The shapes of the mounds and the types of burials found here indicate that the Miamisburg Mound was the work of the Adena Indians. Once an ancient Indian burial ground, today it is the most well-known historical site in Miamisburg.

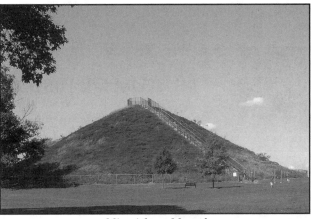
Miamisburg Mound

■ **Seip Mound** is found in Ross County (800-686-1535) about two miles east of Bainbridge. Seip Mound is the central mound of a group of geometric earthworks. The Mound measures 240 feet long, 130 feet wide, and 30 feet high. It is believed that the Hopewell Indians built Seip Mound for burials, based on artifacts found with bodies at the site.

■ **The Serpent Mound** in Adams County (937-587-2796) lies on a plateau overlooking the valley of Brush Creek. Nearly a quarter of a mile long, it is the largest example of an uncoiling serpent form in the United States. It stretches 1,348 feed over the ground, and is beautifully preserved. The mound is the largest mound of its kind in the world. Although there are burial mounds nearby, the mound was not constructed for burial purposes. The mound does not contain any human bones or remains.

The Serpent Mound in Adams County.

To learn more about the Prehistoric Indians of Ohio, you should visit a museum or historic site in your area. During your visit, select one object or artifact that you found about the Prehistoric Indians from the museum's collection. Then write a brief description about it.

To help guide your understanding of what to look for, use the worksheet below:

MUSEUM OR HISTORIC SITE WORKSHEET

Name of Museum Visited: _____

Name of the Object: _____

Description of the Object:

❧ Shape _____

❧ Colors _____

❧ Design _____

❧ Condition _____

❧ What is it made of? _____

❧ How old is it? _____

What was the object used for?

_____
_____
_____
_____
_____
_____
_____
_____
_____
_____

Your Drawing or Photograph
of the Object:

Name _____

Activity 2C: How Would You Edit this Article?   **145**

STUDY CARDS

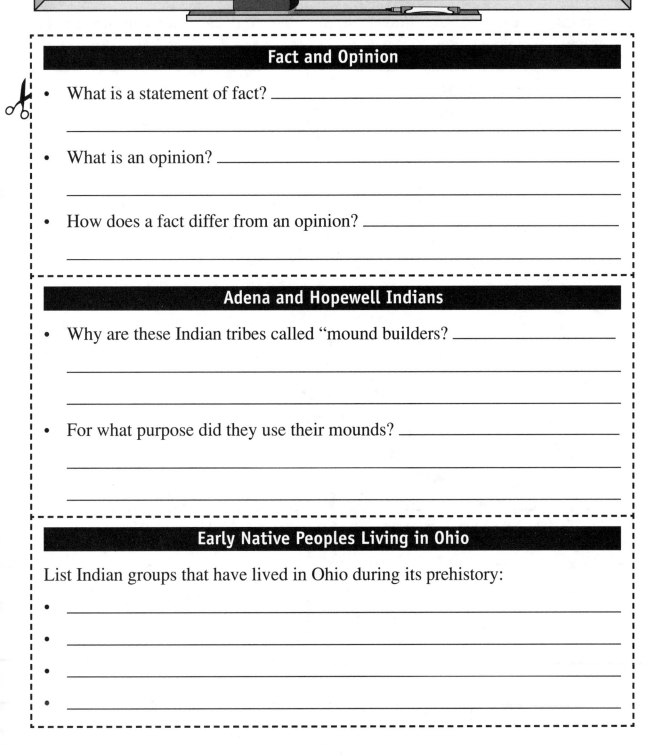

Fact and Opinion

- What is a statement of fact? _____

    _____

- What is an opinion? _____

    _____

- How does a fact differ from an opinion? _____

    _____

Adena and Hopewell Indians

- Why are these Indian tribes called "mound builders? _____

    _____

    _____

- For what purpose did they use their mounds? _____

    _____

    _____

Early Native Peoples Living in Ohio

List Indian groups that have lived in Ohio during its prehistory:

- _____

- _____

- _____

- _____

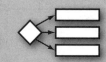

LEARNING WITH GRAPHIC ORGANIZERS

Directions: Complete a description of each of the American Indian groups listed in the graphic organizer below.

Paelo Indians:
_____
_____
_____

Archaic Indians:
_____
_____
_____

The First Ohioans

The Mound Builders

Adena:
_____
_____
_____

Hopewell:
_____
_____
_____

Fort Ancient Indians:
_____
_____
_____

Name _____

ACTIVITY 2D

HOW WERE OHIO'S HISTORIC INDIAN TRIBES ALIKE AND DIFFERENT?

■ Various groups of people have lived in Ohio over time including prehistoric and historic American Indians, migrating settlers and immigrants. Interactions among these groups have resulted in both cooperation and conflict.

In this activity, you will read about the Historic Indian tribes living in Ohio when the first Europeans arrived. After completing this activity, you will be able to describe and compare the cultural practices of these Historic Indian tribes.

KEY TERMS

- ■ Culture
- ■ Algonquian Tribes
- ■ Wigwams
- ■ Canoes

- ■ Shawnee Indians
- ■ Delaware Indians
- ■ Ottawa Indians
- ■ Longhouse

- ■ Miami Indians
- ■ Iroquoian Indians
- ■ Ohio Seneca Indians
- ■ Wyandot Indians

As you know, the term **culture** describes a people's way of life. Culture includes how people get their food, make their homes, and dress. It also includes their religious beliefs, systems of government, language, literature and sports. Almost anything people do together is part of their culture.

Sometimes it is easier to understand how a culture is unique by comparing it to other cultures. One way to increase your understanding of American Indian cultures is to compare them. When you **compare** things, you identify how they are similar and different. Comparing helps you to appreciate the qualities of each thing.

Does the way these individuals dress tell us anything about their cultures?

In this activity, you will be given information about the Historic Indian tribes of Ohio when Europeans first came. Based on this information, you will be asked to decide which **two tribes** were most *alike* and which were *most different*.

Before you read about the tribes of Ohio, make a larger copy of the chart below. As you read, fill in the information called for in the chart. You will then use this information to decide which two tribes were most **alike** and which were most different.

COMPARING AMERICAN INDIAN CULTURES OF OHIO

Category	Shawnee	Delaware	Ottawa	Miami	Ohio Seneca	Wyandot
Language						
Food						
Shelter						
Clothing						
Family Roles						
Transportation						
Dances, Ceremonies and Beliefs						
Conflict/ Cooperation						

THE HISTORIC INDIANS OF OHIO

American Indians played an important role in shaping the history of Ohio. The first written descriptions of American Indians in the Ohio region come from French missionaries who entered the region in the late seventeenth and early eighteenth centuries. From these records, we know that six major American Indian groups lived in this area. These six groups were the **Shawnee**, **Delaware**, **Ottawa**, **Miami**, **Ohio Seneca**, and **Wyandot**.

Except for the Ohio Seneca and Wyandot, all these tribes spoke a form of the Algonquian language. The Wyandot and Ohio Seneca were related to the Iroquois, the other main group of American Indians in the Northeast Woodlands.

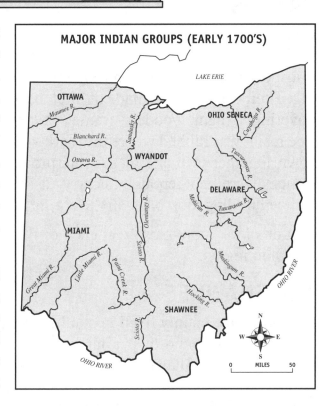

THE ALGONQUIAN TRIBES

The Algonquian tribes not only spoke related languages, they also shared similar traditions and lifestyles.

WIGWAMS

Most Algonquians lived in wigwams. These circular homes were made by bending tree branches into a dome-shaped frame. The dome was then covered with strips of birch bark sewn together with roots. Animal skins were used as beds. A hole in the center of the wigwam allowed smoke to escape.

This style of wigwam was common to many Algonquian tribes.

Some Algonquian tribes also made larger rectangular buildings like the "long-houses" of the Iroquois. Often these served as council buildings. Algonquian villages were sometimes surrounded by walls of sharpened, upright logs for protection.

CANOES

Canoes were an important part of Algonquian life. They were used as a means of transportation and to obtain food by fishing. Their canoes were made of birch bark covering a light wooden frame. Sticky tree resin was rubbed where the bark was sewn together to make them waterproof. Canoes were light enough to carry easily. Canoe building took place in the spring.

Algonquian Indians building a canoe.

Let's look more closely at each of the four Algonquian tribes that once lived in the Ohio region.

THE SHAWNEE

The **Shawnee** mainly lived in southern Ohio, but they were found over a large area. During summer, the Shawnee lived in villages of bark-covered longhouses. Each village had a large council house for meetings and religious ceremonies.

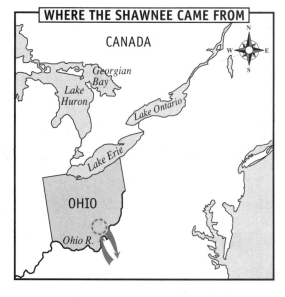

In the fall, the Shawnee separated into small hunting camps of extended families. Men did most of the hunting and fishing. They hunted deer, beaver, bear and other animals for their fur, skins and meat. The Shawnee grew corn, squash, beans, and other vegetables. The work in the fields was done by the women. They also took care of child raising and cooking.

Shawnee clothing was usually made from buckskin (*deer skin*). They wore buckskin moccasins on their feet and decorated their clothes with feathers and shells. Many important Shawnee ceremonies were tied to the growing cycle. The spring bread dance was performed at planting time; the green corn dance was conducted when crops ripened; and the autumn bread dance celebrated the harvest.

THE DELAWARE

The **Delaware** (or *Lenape*) tribe originally lived in New Jersey. When Dutch and English colonists came to North America, the Delaware fled westward. By 1700, many Delaware had settled in eastern Ohio.

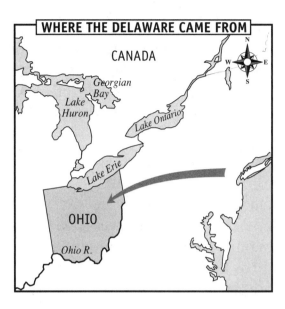

WHERE THE DELAWARE CAME FROM

Like most Algonquian tribes, the Delaware Indians lived in wigwams in villages near creeks and rivers. They also built longhouses for council meetings. The Delaware planted corn, beans, squash, tobacco and other products. Women did most of the work of farming. They gathered berries, nuts, and other wild plants from forests and meadows. Women also took care of the cooking and the raising of children.

Their clothing was made from buckskin and decorated with shell beads, feathers, and other ornaments. Delaware men did the hunting, fishing, and fighting. They killed deer and other mammals. They also hunted ducks and turkeys for their meat and feathers. To prevent spoiling, some fish and meats were dried with smoke before eating.

Skilled craftsmen, the Delaware were known for their expert boat-making. Living near the Great Lakes, travel by water was their main method of transportation. Their birch bark canoes were both strong and light-weight.

Delaware villages often contained a steambath (*sauna*) to help fight off sickness and purify members before religious ceremonies. Following a steambath, Delaware men painted their bodies, and women painted their faces with colored dyes. Delaware men usually removed all of the hair from their faces. Body tattooing was common to both men and women. Like other Indian tribes, the Delaware believed spirits ruled the world. After death, a person's spirit went to another world.

CHECKING YOUR UNDERSTANDING

1   Describe how a wigwam was constructed? _____

_____

2   What role did canoes play in Algonquian life? _____

_____

THE OTTAWA

The **Ottawa** originally lived in Canada along the Ottawa River. They moved into northern Ohio around 1740. They hunted, fished, and gathered wild rice like other Algonquian tribes living near the Great Lakes. They collected sap from trees to make maple syrup.

The Ottawa had a long tradition as a trading tribe. They traded woven mats and foods with other tribes for pottery and dyes. Paddling their canoes over great distances, the Ottawa became the middlemen between the French and other tribes in the region. They traded furs and food for guns and cooking utensils. The Ottawa believed that two great spirits — one good and one evil — fought for control of the world.

Unlike most Algonquian tribes, the Ottawa usually lived in **longhouses**. Their homes were more typical for Iroquoian-speaking tribes. Each longhouse measured 50 to 100 feet long. As many as ten families might share a longhouse. Like wigwams, longhouses were made of branches covered with tree bark. Holes in the roof allowed smoke to escape. Benches along the sides of the longhouse were used for sitting, eating and sleeping.

Inside a longhouse

THE MIAMI

The **Miami** Indians moved south to Ohio around 1700. The Miamis were independent and warlike. They quickly became the most powerful tribe in Ohio.

The Miamis often lived in villages of small oval houses with walls made of woven reeds. These dome-shaped **wigwams** were surrounded by fields of corn. They fished, hunted, and grew corn, beans and squash. The Miamis wore animal skins, leggings, and moccasins in winter. Earrings, nose rings and face paint was common. Tattooing of the body was common among both men and women.

The Miamis also did not believe in physical punishment. Children that disobeyed their parents were reprimanded instead of receiving a spanking. A favorite dance was the feather dance, in which performers imitated the movement of birds. The Miamis also introduced the use of the peace pipe. They often buried their dead in the ground under a pile of logs. They believed the sun was the creator of all things.

THE IROQUOIAN INDIANS OF OHIO

Two tribes in Ohio spoke Iroquoian languages rather than Algonquian. They were related to the Iroquois tribes of New York and Canada.

THE OHIO SENECA

The **Ohio Seneca** or Mingo Indians were a small tribe. They followed many Iroquois customs: they lived in longhouses and hunted, fished, and gathered plants. By 1760, the Seneca settled in Ohio. One of their villages was on the banks of the Scioto River, near modern-day Columbus.

WHERE THE OHIO SENECA CAME FROM

THE WYANDOT

The **Wyandots**, also known as the **Hurons**, originally lived in Canada. When other Iroquois tribes attacked the Wyandots, some moved to southern Ohio. Indians often changed relationships between tribes. One day they could be involved at war, while a few months later they would be cooperating with each other in an alliance against other tribes.

The Wyandots spoke a form of Iroquoian and lived in longhouses. Many of their customs and practices were similar to the Algonquians. The Wyandots fished in lakes and rivers in birch bark canoes. They used nets for fishing. Men hunted deer and other game. Their principal crops were corn, beans, and squash. They wore clothes made of buckskin.

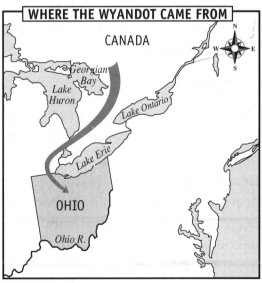

WHERE THE WYANDOT CAME FROM

The Wyandots were excellent fur traders. They settled in northern Ohio, where they controlled trade routes in this part of Ohio. Like the Ottawa, the Wyandots often acted as middlemen in trade between Europeans and other tribes.

CHECKING YOUR UNDERSTANDING

1 Describe life in a longhouse. _____

_____

2 What was the main difference between Algonquian and Iroquoian Indians?

_____

_____

3 In what way did the Wyandot resemble the Ottawa Indians? _____

_____

_____

_____

CONFLICT AND COOPERATION AMONG TRIBES OF OHIO

Information about the historic tribes of Ohio is incomplete. Most modern-day historians and archaeologists believe that the evidence points to both cooperation and conflict between the tribes.

CONFLICT

There is some evidence of conflict between the early tribes of Ohio. Tribes sometimes fought against each other. There is proof that Historic Indians in Ohio surrounded their villages with fences or earthen walls to protect themselves against attacks. Weapons have also been uncovered at burial sites throughout Ohio. This has led archaeologists to conclude that Indian tribes often fought each other. Tribes usually lived off the game they hunted and killed for their skins and food supply. Tribes also fought over the hunting rights to certain areas.

An Algonquian village. Note the fence surrounding the village

Some tribes practiced **rituals** (*customs*). A popular ritual for achieving manhood among Indian groups was to have a boy participate in making a raid against another tribe before being accepted as an adult. Some archaeologists even believe that conflict between tribes may have led to the decline of the Adena people. By the time of the arrival of Europeans, tribal traditions in warfare were well established.

COOPERATION

Cooperation was a valued behavior in many tribal communities since cooperation was necessary for survival of the family and group. Emphasis was put on maintaining agreement within the group. Most Indians placed the needs of the group over those of the individual. There is evidence of cooperation among Indians in hunting, settlement in villages, and farming. Cooperation also extended to the building of the burial mounds. Hundreds of tribal members were needed to construct the vast burial mounds.

CHOOSING THE TRIBES WITH THE GREATEST SIMILARITIES AND DIFFERENCES

You have just finished reading about the Historic Indians who once lived in Ohio. Now you are ready to decide which two tribes were most alike and which two were most different. Look over the chart you worked on earlier in this activity to help make your decision. Then answer each of these questions:

CHECKING YOUR UNDERSTANDING

1 Which two Ohio tribes were the most alike? Explain your answer.

_____

_____

_____

2 Which two Ohio tribes were the most different? Explain your answer.

_____

_____

_____

After everyone in the class has completed answering these two questions, class members should share and discuss their answers. Write several pairs of similar and different tribes on the chalkboard. Then have the class vote on one pair for each.

MAKING CONNECTIONS

USING THE INTERNET TO LEARN ABOUT OHIO'S TRIBES

Almost any kind of information you can think of is available on the Internet. You can locate a website with the information you are looking for by using a "search engine" like **America-On-Line (AOL)**, **Yahoo**, **Bing**, or **Google**.

Usually, the search engine will have a blank box on its "home page." This blank space is where you type in the subject you want to search for. Then you need to click the highlighted "search button" on the screen. Your computer will then search the entire Internet and create a list of websites for you to explore.

Quite often, your search will come back with hundreds of thousands of websites for you to search. This can be a bit overwhelming. If your search comes back with too many websites, you will need to narrow down your search. For example:

- If you enter the keyword "Ohio," your search would bring up tens of thousands of websites.

- If you narrowed your search to "Ohio Miami Indians" you will find far fewer websites to explore.

- Once you get it down to a more manageable, smaller list, simply double click your cursor on each website you want to view. Usually you will not have to search more than the first five or ten websites to locate what you are looking for.

Let's see how well you can find additional information about Ohio's six main American Indian tribes. For each tribe listed, find its website "address" and record one fact you learned from that website. The first tribe has been filled in for you:

Ohio's Indian Tribes	Website with the Information	Statement of Information from that website
Shawnee	www.tolatsga.org/shaw.html	Currently, there are more than 14,000 Shawnee in the United States. Most Shawnee now live in Oklahoma.
Delaware	www.	
Ottawa	www.	
Miami	www.	
Ohio Senaca	www.	
Wyandot (or *Huron*)	www.	

Another website with useful information about Ohio's Historic Indians is the **Ohio Historical Society's** website: www.ohiohistorycentral.org.

STUDY CARDS

Algonquian Tribes of Ohio

- Name two Algonquian tribes:

  1. _____   2. _____

- What were some of the customs of the Algonquian tribes?

  _____

  _____

  _____

Iroquoian Tribes of Ohio

- Name two Iroquoian tribes:

  1. _____   2. _____

- What were some of the customs of the Iroquoian tribes?

  _____

  _____

  _____

The Role of American Indian Women

List and describe four activities of women in American Indian societies.

1 _____

2 _____

3 _____

4 _____

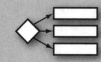

LEARNING WITH GRAPHIC ORGANIZERS

Directions: Complete the following graphic organizers by describing some important features of each Algonquian and Iroquoian tribe in Ohio.

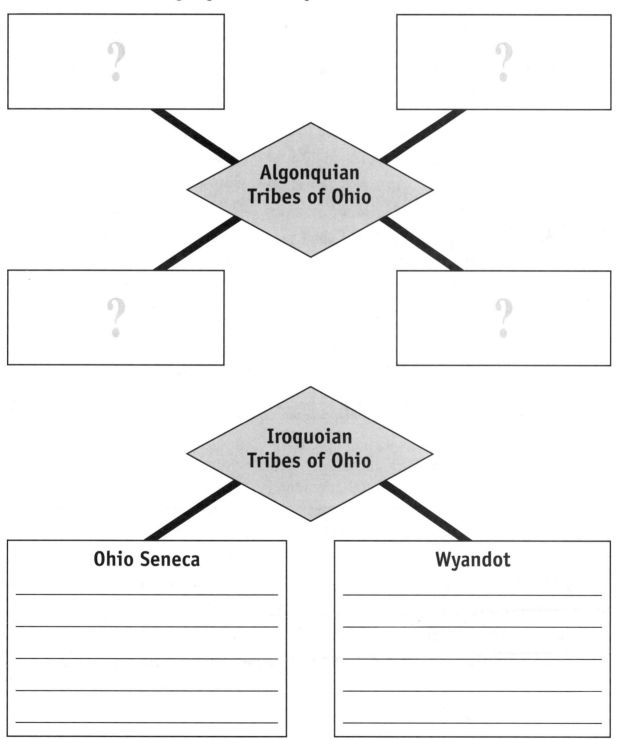

Algonquian Tribes of Ohio

Iroquoian Tribes of Ohio

Ohio Seneca

Wyandot

HOW WOULD YOU OUTLINE THE EARLY HISTORY OF THE BRITISH COLONIES?

■ Various groups of people have lived in Ohio over time including ... migrating settlers .... Interactions among these groups have resulted in both cooperation and conflict.

In this activity you will learn about the benefits of outlining what you read to better understand it. You will also learn about early European explorers to Ohio. Finally, you will find out how the English established thirteen colonies along the Atlantic coast.

KEY TERMS

- **Christopher Columbus**
- **Northwest Passage**
- **Samuel de Champlain**
- **René-Robert de La Salle**
- **New France**
- **New England Colonies**
- **Middle Atlantic Colonies**
- **Southern Colonies**
- **Plantation System**

THE ART OF OUTLINING

An **outline** is a brief plan in which a topic is divided into smaller parts. The purpose of an outline is to show how a topic and its parts are related. An outline can serve as a blueprint to help guide you through a reading.

I. Roman Numerals. Outlines go from the general to the specific. The major parts of an outline are given by a **Roman numerals** (I, II, III).

A. Capital Letters. If these topics need to be further divided, these sub-topics are identified by **capital letters** (A, B, C).

1. Arabic Numerals. If these sub-topics need to be even further divided, each smaller topic is given an **Arabic numeral** (1, 2, 3).

Let's look at how this process works. Assume you want to create a simple outline about your own life. It might be outlined as follows:

MY LIFE (Main Topic)

I. Early Childhood (Main Topic)
   A. Family (Sub-Topic)
      1. Parents ⎫
      2. Brothers and Sisters ⎬ (Part of Sub-Topic)
      3. Grandparents ⎭
   B. Friends (Sub-Topic)
   C. Neighborhood (Sub-Topic)
II. Elementary School Years (Main Topic)
   A. Kindergarten (Sub-Topic)
   B. Early Grades (Sub-Topic)
      1. Teachers ⎫
      2. Friends ⎬ (Part of Sub-Topic)

Notice that in this example, each smaller part helps us to understand a larger idea. For example, **Family**, **Friends** and **Neighborhood** helps us to understand the larger topic **Early Childhood**. At the same time, **Family** is subdivided into **Parents**, **Brothers** and **Sisters**, and **Grandparents**.

Now let us look at a passage about the early explorers who came to North America and Ohio. After you read the passages below, you will be asked to complete an outline.

EARLY EXPLORERS TO NORTH AMERICA

In the 1400s, Europeans wanted spices and other goods from Asia. Merchants used land routes that were long and dangerous. Some sought an all-water route to Asia. Some European rulers sent out explorers to find this route.

Christopher Columbus believed that Asia could be reached by sailing westward. In **1492**, Columbus set sail across the Atlantic Ocean.

Christopher Columbus

After two and a half months at sea, Columbus became the first European to land in the Americas. On Columbus' return to Spain, he reported to the King and Queen of Spain that he had found great wealth. Later, other Europeans sailed to what they called the "New World" in search of gold and other riches.

THE SEARCH FOR THE NORTHWEST PASSAGE

The dream of an all-water route to the spice trade in Asia encouraged later explorers to seek a shortcut through the newly found continent of North America. Some explorers believed they could succeed by sailing north. They went looking for what they called the **Northwest Passage**. The search for such a route motivated much of the European exploration of both coasts of North America.

Champlain explores the St. Lawrence River

Searching for the Northwest Passage, the French explorer and navigator **Samuel de Champlain** sailed up the St. Lawrence River. In 1608, he founded a fort at what is today the city of Quebec.

RENÉ-ROBERT DE LA SALLE

In **1669**, the French adventurer **René-Robert de La Salle** came to Ohio. He was exploring the region between Lake Erie and the Ohio River. He is believed to be the first European to enter the area. In 1671, La Salle claimed the entire region of Ohio for France.

The area around the Ohio River did not attract permanent settlers at first, but did attract French fur traders. In the late 1600s and early 1700s, Europeans were willing to pay high prices for furs to make clothing and hats. This made American beaver skins extremely valuable. The French traded their guns and other weapons with Indian tribes for beaver pelts (*skins*) and other furs.

René-Robert de La Salle

The French were soon followed by English settlers. Later waves of immigration to North America included the Scotch-Irish and Germans. As the area began to fill from settlers, many migrated into the Ohio Country from other colonies.

THE FRENCH AND ENGLISH IN OHIO

The French. Gradually, many tribes in the Ohio region gave up their traditional ways of life to sell furs to the French. French fur trappers, traders and American Indians generally lived peacefully together. Although the French failed to establish many large settlements in North America, they sought to lay claim to the Ohio River Valley in order to control this region.

Capt. George Washington led troops in the French and Indian War

The English. In contrast, the government of England encouraged settlers to start their own colonies. As English colonists moved into the region, they cut down forests to create farmlands and build towns. By 1700, there were thirteen English colonies all along the Atlantic coast from Georgia to Massachusetts.

CHECKING YOUR UNDERSTANDING

1 How did the search for a Northwest Passage influence settlement of North America?

_____

_____

_____

2 What role did René-Robert de La Salle play in the settlement of Ohio?

_____

_____

_____

3 How did the British differ from the French in the Ohio region?

_____

_____

_____

Here is what this passage might look like in outline form. Notice that some items have been omitted. Complete any omitted items in the outline.

EARLY EXPLORERS TO NORTH AMERICA

I. Christopher Columbus
   A. An Italian from Genoa, Italy
   B. Set sail in 1492 across the Atlantic Ocean
   C. He became the first European to land in the Americas

II. The Search for the Northwest Passage
   A. Explorers dreamed of an all-water route to Asia.

   B. *What would you put here?* _____

   C. *What would you put here?* _____

III. René-Robert de La Salle

   A. La Salle is believed to be the first European to enter Ohio.

   B. *What would you put here?* _____

   C. *What would you put here?* _____

IV. The French and English in Ohio
   A. The French

   1. *What would you put here?* _____

   B. The English

   1. *What would you put here?* _____

The next passage begins below. First read through these passages. Then complete the outline that follows.

DIFFERENCES EMERGE AMONG THE THIRTEEN COLONIES

By the mid-1730s, thirteen English colonies existed along the Atlantic coast. New patterns of life developed in three separate regions of the English colonies.

Differences were based on the physical characteristics of their environment, the origins of the colonists, and different ways of earning a living.

NEW ENGLAND COLONIES

The colonies of **New England** — Massachusetts, New Hampshire, Connecticut, and Rhode Island — had rocky soil and less fertile land. Since the New England Colonies were the farthest north, they had longer winters and a colder climate than the other colonies.

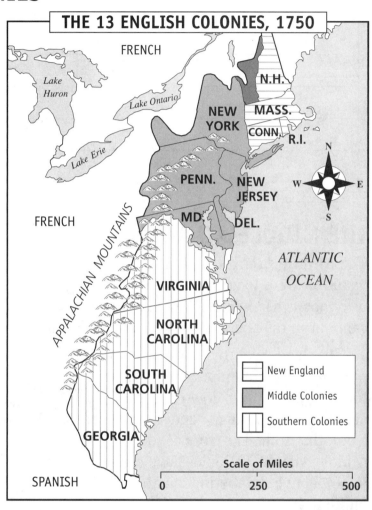

THE 13 ENGLISH COLONIES, 1750

FRENCH

Lake Huron

Lake Ontario

Lake Erie

N.H.

NEW YORK

MASS.

CONN.

R.I.

FRENCH

PENN.

NEW JERSEY

MD.

DEL.

APPALACHIAN MOUNTAINS

VIRGINIA

NORTH CAROLINA

SOUTH CAROLINA

GEORGIA

ATLANTIC OCEAN

New England

Middle Colonies

Southern Colonies

SPANISH

Scale of Miles

0   250   500

Many New Englanders had small farms where they grew crops for use by their family. Others used the forests in the region for lumber and building ships. Since there were few large tracts of fertile land, the main occupation was commerce and fishing. With these colonies located near the Atlantic Ocean, there was an abundance of whales and fish. As a result, large numbers of New Englanders became sailors, fishermen, and merchants. Whaling as an occupation was also important to the region.

Trading was another occupation important to New Englanders. They often owned and manned trading ships. These ships brought sugar from the West Indies to New England, where it was turned into rum. Rum was traded in Africa for slaves. New England merchants also carried sugar to England. In England, manufactured goods were bought for sale in New England.

Shipbuilding was a major occupation in the New England Colonies.

CHECKING YOUR UNDERSTANDING

How did the settlers in New England adapt to their physical environment?

_____

_____

_____

_____

_____

THE MIDDLE ATLANTIC COLONIES

The **Middle Atlantic Colonies** — New York, New Jersey, Delaware, and Pennsylvania — were located between New England and the Southern Colonies. Winters were not as harsh as in New England and summers were longer. Most of the settlers came from the Netherlands (*Holland*), Germany, Sweden, France, and Scotland.

The land had to be cleared to prepare it for planting. Settlers first focused on cutting down the trees and removing stones and stumps from the soil. The forests of the Middle Atlantic Colonies gave birth to an active lumbering and ship-building industry.

The Middle Atlantic Colonies were particularly well suited for small farms, and soon became known as the "**Bread Basket**." It was in the Middle Colonies that most of the food was grown in the colonies.

The first job of colonial farmers was to clear the land for planting.

A typical small farm was usually about 50 to 150 acres. They usually grew wheat, oats, barley, and rye. The fertile soil of the area even permitted large amounts of grain to be exported to Europe.

People were also attracted to a greater atmosphere of religious freedom. No single church or religion dominated the Middle Atlantic Colonies. These colonies had greater religious diversity than either New England or the South.

CHECKING YOUR UNDERSTANDING

Why were the Middle Atlantic Colonies known as the "Bread Basket"?

_____

_____

_____

_____

_____

THE SOUTHERN COLONIES

The **Southern Colonies** — Virginia, Maryland, North Carolina, South Carolina, and Georgia — had a warmer climate than other parts of Colonial America. The land was flat and the soil was well-suited to growing crops throughout the year. The fact these colonies were farther south meant that their growing season was longer. Resin, made from the sap of Southern pine trees, provided some of the best ship-building materials in the world.

As soon as the trees were cleared, farmers focused on planting crops.

Southerners were largely English, Scots, and Scotch-Irish settlers who came to America for economic reasons. In Europe, poor farmers could not afford to buy their own land.

Some Southerners developed plantations along major water routes. Under the **plantation system**, each plantation was a large-scale agricultural operation on which 20 or more slaves worked crops such as tobacco, cotton, rice and **indigo** (*a blue dye used to color fabrics*) for shipment to England in exchange for manufactured goods.

Large plantations, owned by rich families, depended on enslaved peoples from Africa as the main work force. In a rich plantation, the children were educated by teachers who taught the children at home. The children led easy lives, learning reading, writing, dancing, and music. Boys learned to ride horses and hunt.

Although not every farm in the South was a plantation, those that were needed a great deal of human labor.

The main crops planted on a plantation required a great amount of labor. A successful harvest depended on slaves working from sunrise to sunset. Overseers, slave supervisors, often whipped the slaves and punished them if they didn't like what they were doing.

Women usually worked the same hours as the men. Women were expected to return to the fields not long after giving birth to children. Children were expected to work as well. The harsh conditions of most slaves meant that many did not live long lives often died an early death. The great majority of whites did not live on plantations, and farmed their land on a smaller scale.

As the American colonies grew in population, their trade became increasingly important to Britain for its own economic well-being. Trade between Europe, Africa, and the Americas also helped disperse African slaves throughout the Western Hemisphere.

CHECKING YOUR UNDERSTANDING

How did the Southern plantation system make that region unique?

_____

_____

_____

_____

_____

_____

On the next page is an incomplete outline of the three regions of the British colonies. Complete the information in the outline that has been omitted. If you are not sure of a particular item in the outline, you should reread the text of the passage that deals with that part.

DIFFERENCES AMONG THE ENGLISH COLONIES

I. NEW ENGLAND COLONIES

A. Colonies in New England

1. _____

2. _____

3. _____

4. _____

B. Physical Geography

1. _____

2. _____

C. Economic Activities

1. _____

2. _____

II. MIDDLE ATLANTIC COLONIES

A. Colonies in the Middle Atlantic

1. _____

2. _____

3. _____

4. _____

B. Physical Geography

1. _____

2. _____

C. Economic Activities

1. _____

2. _____

CONTINUED

III. SOUTHERN COLONIES

    A. Colonies in the South

        1. _____

        2. _____

        3. _____

        4. _____

        5. _____

    B. Physical Geography

        1. _____

        2. _____

    C. Economic Activities

        1. _____

        2. _____

MAKING CONNECTIONS

COMPLETING A MAP OF COLONIAL AMERICA

An **historical map** shows the way an area was in the past. It is a great resource to help you learn about a place at a past point in time. The map on the next page provides an outline of the original thirteen English colonies. Using the Internet, your school or local library, research the locations need to answer the following:

■ **Names of Colonies:** Identify each of the thirteen British colonies by name.

■ **Regions:** Use different colored crayons or markers to show the three regions of Colonial America: New England, the Middle Atlantic Colonies, and the Southern Colonies.

■ **Spanish and French Territories:** Add other colors to show the areas claimed by Spain and France.

■ **Topography:** Identify the Appalachian Mountains, St. Lawrence River, Mississippi River, Lake Erie, Lake Ontario, and Long Island.

Name _Jarves Kinyuy_

Activity 2E: Outlining the Early History of the British Colonies   **171**

■ **Ports & Towns:** Identify these ports and towns: Savannah (Georgia), Charleston (S.C.), Raleigh (N.C.), James- town (VA), Williamsburg (VA), Baltimore (MD), Philadelphia (PA), New York (NY), Boston and Plymouth (MA).

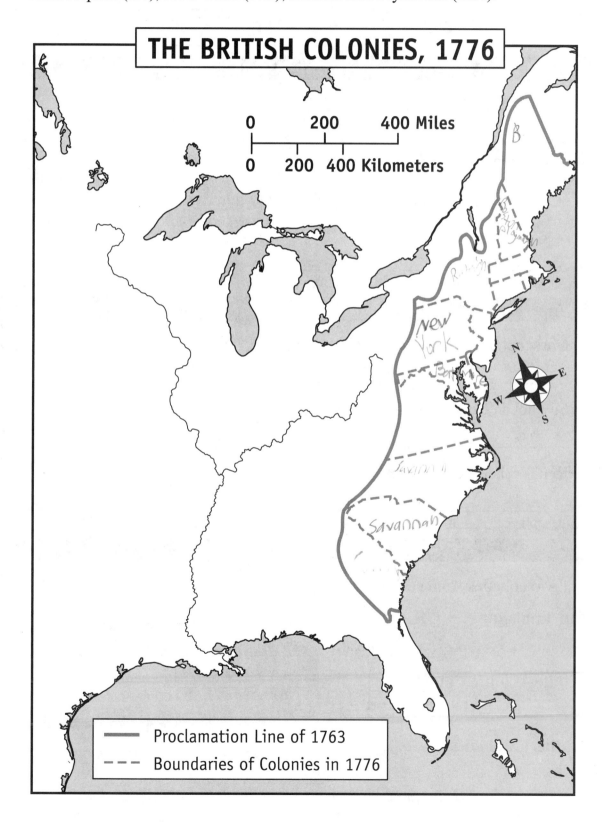

THE BRITISH COLONIES, 1776

0   200   400 Miles

0   200   400 Kilometers

——— Proclamation Line of 1763

– – – Boundaries of Colonies in 1776

STUDY CARDS

Northwest Passage

- What was the Northwest Passage?

  _____

  _____

- Why were European explorers so anxious to find the Northwest Passage?

  _____

  _____

Identify Each Explorer

- Christopher Columbus: _____

  _____

- Samuel de Champlain: _____

  _____

- René-Robert de La Salle: _____

  _____

The Thirteen British Colonies

List two colonies from each region:

New England:
1. _____
2. _____

Middle Atlantic Colonies:
1. _____
2. _____

Southern Colonies:
1. _____
2. _____

Occupations in the British Colonies

What were some of the major occupations in:

- **New England:** _____
  _____

- **Middle Atlantic Colonies:** _____
  _____

- **Southern Colonies:** _____
  _____

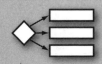 **LEARNING WITH GRAPHIC ORGANIZERS**

Directions: Complete the graphic organizer below by describing the area that each explorer found.

Christopher Columbus
_____
_____
_____

Samuel Chaplain
_____
_____
_____

Early Explorers to North America

René-Robert de La Salle
_____
_____
_____

Directions: Complete the graphic organizer summarizing the similarities and differences between the three regions. Parts of the first region have been completed for you.

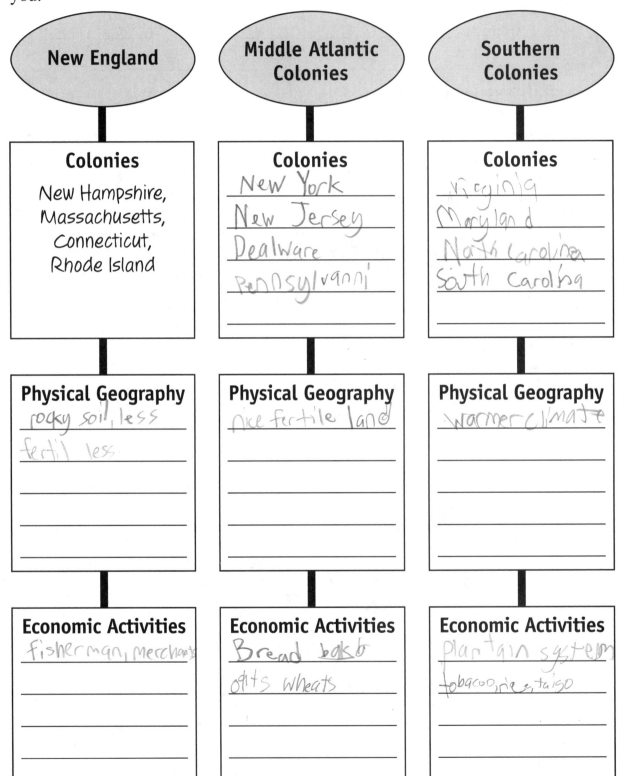

New England

Colonies

New Hampshire,
Massachusetts,
Connecticut,
Rhode Island

Physical Geography

rocky soil, less
fertil less

Economic Activities

fisherman, merchants

Middle Atlantic Colonies

Colonies

New York
New Jersey
Dealware
Pennsylvanni

Physical Geography

nice fertile land

Economic Activities

Bread basb
olits wheats

Southern Colonies

Colonies

Virginia
Maryland
North carolina
South Carolina

Physical Geography

warmer climate

Economic Activities

Plantain system
tobacco, rice, taiso

Name _____

ACTIVITY 2F

CAN YOU IDENTIFY CAUSES AND EFFECTS?

■ Various groups of people have lived in Ohio over time including ... American Indians, migrating settlers and immigrants. Interactions among these groups have resulted in both cooperation and conflict.

■ The 13 colonies came together around a common cause of liberty and justice, uniting to fight for independence during the American Revolution and to form a new nation.

In this activity you will learn about one of the most important events in American history — the American Revolution. You will learn how the French and Indian War set the stage for this struggle. Then you will learn how the colonists objected to the Proclamation Line of 1763. These disagreements eventually brought the colonists into armed conflict (*disagreement*) with Great Britain. This struggle finally pushed the colonists to declare their independence from England.

KEY TERMS

- Cause and Effect
- French and Indian War
- Chief Pontiac
- Proclamation Line:1763
- King George III

- Samuel Adams
- Stamp Act
- Boston Massacre
- Crispus Attucks
- Boston Tea Party

- American Revolution
- Lexington and Concord
- Declaration of Independ.
- George Rogers Clark
- Fort Laurens

IDENTIFYING CAUSE-AND-EFFECT

History consists of events that lead to still other events. Understanding how an event came about and its effects gives history much of its meaning.

CAUSES

A **cause** is what makes something happen. For example, by turning the switch of a light, you **cause** the light to go on.

EFFECTS

An **effect** is what happens because of something. An effect is the result of an event, action or development. For example, when you turn a light switch, the **effect** of your action is that the light goes on.

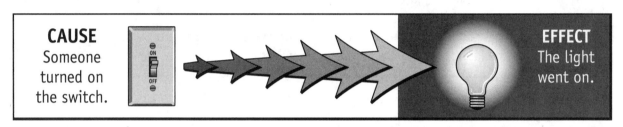

CAUSE
Someone turned on the switch.

EFFECT
The light went on.

Often, important developments in history have more than one cause. In this activity you will learn about some of the different causes that led to the American Revolutionary War.

THE FRENCH AND INDIAN WAR, 1754-1763

In the last activity, you learned how different groups sometimes come into conflict. One example of this was the struggle of European powers for control of Ohio, a land rich in natural resources and well suited to growing crops.

In the 1700s, France and Britain were competing for overseas trade and land. By the 1750s, the British claimed control of the Ohio River Valley, just across the Appalachians from the British colonies. Meanwhile, the French had built forts long the Great Lakes. They also claimed control of the Ohio River Valley, southwest of their settlements.

THE FRENCH AND INDIAN WAR, 1754–1763

FRENCH

ENGLISH

ENGLISH

OHIO RIVER VALLEY

War between Britain and France finally broke out in 1754. Because many Indian tribes sided with the French, the conflict became known in North America as the **French and Indian War**. French military bases were located in Quebec and Montreal, while the British had bases along the Hudson River. The area between them became the main battleground. In 1756, the war spread from North America to Europe.

Capt. George Washington led his troops in the French and Indian War.

A British force captured the French city of Quebec in 1759. This victory gave the British control of the St. Lawrence River. Under the terms of the peace treaty in 1763, France lost most of its colonial empire in North America, including Canada and all lands east of the Mississippi River. These lands now became British.

Conflict and Cooperation. Settlers and Indians cooperated at first. They communicated through **interpreters** (*people who could speak both languages*). The Indians welcomed trading with the colonists, but opposed colonial settlements in their territories. They strongly desired European goods, such as guns, gunpowder, musket balls, rum and cloth. The Indians were excellent hunters of beavers. They were willing to trade their beaver skins to Europeans in exchange for goods they wanted.

Indians trade their beaver furs with American settlers.

In general, the British colonists did not mix well with their Indian neighbors. The Indians in the Ohio River Valley wanted to live on their traditional lands and hunt on them. The goal of the British settlers was to farm and own the land. Most of the colonists also believed their way of life was far superior to the culture of the Indians. This brought the two groups into conflict.

In 1762, an Ottawa chief named **Pontiac** organized several local tribes in an attempt to drive out the British. **Pontiac's Rebellion** (*uprising*) threatened British control. Although the tribes managed to capture several forts in Michigan and Pennsylvania, the British soon recaptured them.

American Indians carry out an attack on a British fort.

Pontiac finally agreed to a peace treaty in 1766. Although his struggle against the British was unsuccessful, Chief Pontiac became a symbol of American Indian resistance.

CHECKING YOUR UNDERSTANDING

1 What was the main cause of the French and Indian War?

_____

_____

2 What were the effects of the British victory in the French and Indian War?

_____

_____

3 How did the British settlers and Indians both cooperate and come into conflict in the Ohio River Valley?

_____

_____

_____

_____

ORIGINS OF THE AMERICAN REVOLUTION

In 1763, North America was finally at peace. The British had defeated the French and the colonists had put down Pontiac's rebellion. Yet only 12 years later, the colonists would again be at war. To understand the reasons for this new conflict, it is important to remember that the colonists had inherited the rights of free Englishmen.

The colonists had also developed their own elected assemblies. By 1763, the colonists were already used to a large degree of self-government. After the British victory in the French and Indian War, the colonists felt safer and less in need of British military protection. They no longer had the French threat along their borders. But the colonists soon became involved in a series of new disputes with the British government.

PROCLAMATION LINE OF 1763

After the French and Indian War, many colonists hoped to move to the lands opened to them by the recent French defeat. Others hoped their children would find land there. The British government, on the other hand, was very concerned with maintaining peace with the Indians on these lands.

King George III issued a royal proclamation. To prevent further Indian attacks, he declared that the colonists could not settle west of the Appalachian Mountains. **The Proclamation Line of 1763** was greatly resented by the colonists who had hoped to settle on these western lands. They saw this as an unwelcome interference in their affairs.

The British also continued to keep some forts and an army in North America. American colonists saw these forts and troops as evidence of a British desire to continue to control them.

CHECKING YOUR UNDERSTANDING

Complete the cause-and-effect concept map below:

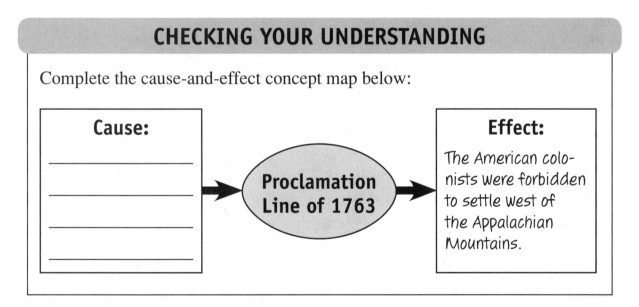

Cause:

_____
_____
_____
_____

Proclamation Line of 1763

Effect:
The American colonists were forbidden to settle west of the Appalachian Mountains.

THE DISPUTE OVER TAXATION

After the French and Indian War, Britain faced a large debt because of the large amount of money it had spent in fighting the war. It also cost money to station British troops in the 13 colonies and the West Indies.

In Britain, people already paid much higher taxes than the colonists. The British government therefore proposed (*suggested*) a series of new taxes on the colonists. These taxes were passed by Parliament without consulting the colonists. British leaders thought this was only just because the colonists were not paying their fair share towards their own defense. Since the colonists lived so far away from London, it seemed impossible for them to be consulted or to participate effectively in the British Parliament.

Taxation without Representation. Back in the colonies, wealthy merchants and landowners, used to acting in their colonial assemblies with little British interference, resented these new policies.

Samuel Adams and other colonists argued that the British government should not tax the colonists without their consent. These colonists cried out that "taxation without representation" was "tyranny" — a cruel use of power.

Colonists met to express their opposition to British taxes without their consent.

The Stamp Act. The first of these new British taxes was the **Stamp Act** (1765). This law stated that all newspapers, pamphlets (*booklets*), and legal documents had to be printed on paper with an official stamp on it. This was a form of tax since the British government had to be paid for the stamp. The colonists opposed this tax for being imposed on them without their permission. Colonists held meetings, **boycotted** (*refused to buy*) British goods, and even attacked some British officials in protest.

In Boston, Samuel Adams organized the colonists in a series of protests. Colonists sent petitions (*written requests*) to the king and Parliament stating their objections to the new taxes. These petitions argued that as Englishmen the colonists could only be taxed if they agreed to them.

The British repealed the Stamp Act, but then passed other taxes. New taxes were placed on glass, paper, and other goods.

A British tax collector is tied to a pole by an unruly crowd.

Name _____

CHECKING YOUR UNDERSTANDING

In this activity, you read about some of the British policies forced on the colonists in the years following the French and Indian War. Notice that in the illustration below, the signs being carried by colonists are blank. Suppose these colonists are demonstrating against British policies. Fill in the signs with phrases you think the colonists might have written.

THE BOSTON MASSACRE

More British soldiers were sent to the colonies to end the protests and to prevent further unrest. Their presence only added to the growing bitterness of the colonists. These soldiers were poorly paid. Many worked at part-time jobs to meet their basic needs. In so doing, they were taking away jobs needed by the colonists. Bad feelings reached a boiling point in 1770. A group of colonists in Boston teased the soldiers and threw snowballs. By accident, the soldiers fired, killing several protesters.

Paul Revere's depiction of British soldiers firing on colonists.

Crispus Attucks, a man of mixed African and American Indian ancestry, was the first colonist killed. Samuel Adams and other opponents of British policies called this incident the "**Boston Massacre**." They circulated pictures and used this tragedy to win public support against the British.

THE TEA DUTY AND THE BOSTON TEA PARTY

In response to colonial protests, the British canceled all of the new taxes except the duty on tea. As you learned in Activity 2B, a group of colonists disguised as Mohawk Indians then boarded three British ships in Boston Harbor in December 1773. They seized 45 tons of tea on the ships. The disguised colonists proceeded to dump the chests of tea into Boston Harbor in protest against the British tax.

Colonists disguised as American Indians dump tea overboard to protest the British tax on tea.

The "**Boston Tea Party**" brought a strong reaction from the British government. The British condemned the action of the colonists as treason. The British ordered Boston Harbor closed until the people of Boston had paid for the tea that had been dumped into the harbor.

Throughout the colonies, people reacted strongly to the British measures. Some colonists secretly began to arm themselves. In 1775, British soldiers and American colonists fired at each other at **Lexington and Concord** in Massachusetts. The American Revolution had begun!

CHECKING YOUR UNDERSTANDING

Complete the cause-and-effect concept map that follows:

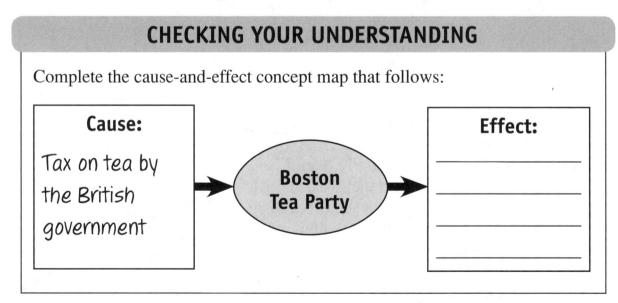

Cause:

Tax on tea by the British government

→ **Boston Tea Party** →

Effect:

_____
_____
_____
_____

THE STRUGGLE SPREADS

Representatives, already meeting in Philadelphia, agreed to join the rebellion in support of Massachusetts. They also created a colonial army. Many colonists began to feel they would be better off without British rule. After much debate, the colonists decided that they should declare their independence.

A **Declaration of Independence** was issued on **July 4, 1776**, explaining to the world the reasons why the American colonists were declaring independence. The Declaration of Independence explained the ideas that form the basis of our system of government.

The opening paragraph of the Declaration of Independence summarized the main argument of the colonists. They believed that a government should be based on the consent of the people it governed:

"We hold these truths to be self-evident, that all men are created equal, that they are endowed (given) by their Creator with certain unalienable rights, that among these are Life, Liberty and the pursuit of Happiness — That to secure these rights, Governments are instituted (created) among men, deriving (getting) their just powers from the consent (approval) of the governed, — That whenever any form of Government becomes destructive (works against) of these ends, it is the right of the People to alter or to abolish it, and to institute (establish) a new Government ...."

CHECKING YOUR UNDERSTANDING

Briefly summarize this paragraph in your own words. _____

_____

_____

_____

_____

OHIO IN THE AMERICAN REVOLUTION

At this time, Ohio was a frontier area populated by American Indians and a few settlers. During the Revolutionary War, the British hoped to hold onto their lands west of the Appalachian Mountains with the help of the Indians. British officials provided the Indians with guns and ammunition. They encouraged them to attack American settlers in the area.

In 1778, the colonists attacked the British in the west to put an end to these threats. General Washington sent **George Rogers Clark** along with 170 soldiers to conquer Ohio. Clark successfully conquered the lands northwest of the Mississippi River. He and his small force tricked the British into thinking he had a much larger number of soldiers with him. Clark and his soldiers helped to show the Indians in the region that their British protectors could no longer protect them.

The British surrender to Clark.

Fort Laurens, built in 1778, was the only fort in Ohio country during the American Revolution. The fort was intended to prevent American Indians, loyal to the British, from attacking settlers in Ohio. No major battles were fought in the Ohio Country. The fort was intended to be a jumping-off point for an attack against the British at Detroit. Conditions at the fort were so harsh during the winter that most of the American soldiers there had to be removed.

Fort Laurens

Learning of this, a handful of British soldiers and several hundred Indian warriors surrounded and attacked the fort. Their **siege** (*a military blockade of a fort or a city*) was finally lifted without capturing the fort. The fort was abandoned on August 2, 1779.

After two more years of fighting, General Washington, with French help, forced British General Cornwallis and his 8,000 soldiers to surrender in 1781. Although fighting would continue for a little while longer, this battle turned out to be the last major one of the war. When news reached London of the British army's surrender, the British government decided to recognize the loss of its colonies and negotiate a peace treaty.

CHECKING YOUR UNDERSTANDING

What role did Ohio play in the American Revolutionary War? _____

_____

_____

_____

_____

THE TREATY OF PARIS (1783)

In 1783, the **Treaty of Paris** was signed. A treaty is a formal agreement. It formally brought the American Revolutionary War to an end. Great Britain recognized the independence of the new country, the United States. The British gave all the land between the Mississippi River and the Atlantic Ocean, from the Great Lakes to the border with Florida, to the new United States. This settlement gave the new nation twice the land area of the former thirteen colonies.

A page of the Treaty of Paris.

The new American government was in great need of money. To raise cash, the new government sold off large pieces of land in Ohio. Many of the first Ohio settlers were veterans of the American Revolution. They were given land in Ohio as payment for their services in fighting the British during the war. After declaring their independence from Great Britain, each colony became an independent state.

FINDING CAUSES AND EFFECTS

Now that you have read about both the French and Indian War and the American Revolution, let's see if you can fill in your own cause-and-effect concept maps. In each of the concept maps below, provide the missing the information.

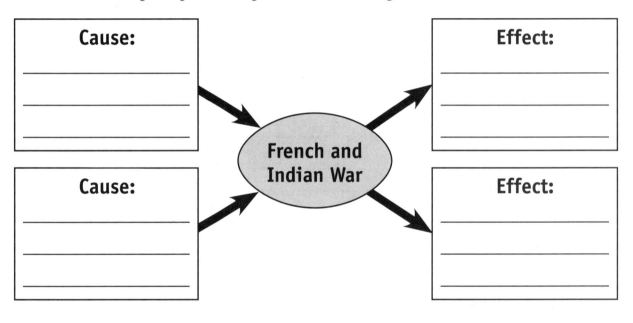

Cause:

Cause:

French and Indian War

Effect:

Effect:

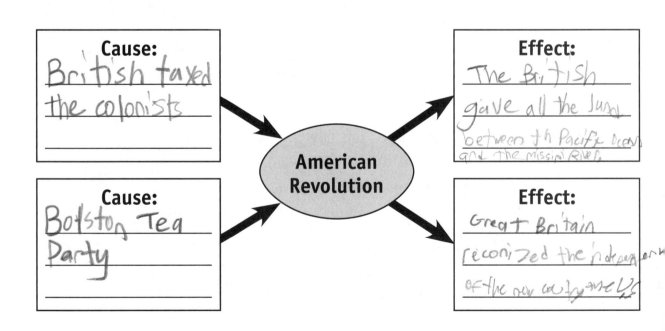

Cause:
British taxed the colonists

Cause:
Bofston Tea Party

American Revolution

Effect:
The British gave all the land between th Pacific Ocean and the missin River

Effect:
Great Britain reconized the indeplendent of the new coutry the US

MAKING CONNECTIONS

INTERPRETING A WORK OF ART

Photographs are especially useful for understanding the past. They show how people looked, dressed, and lived. A photograph can give us a feeling for an earlier time period. However, photography was only invented in the early 1800s. Historians rely on drawings and paintings for a glimpse of what life was like before that time.

Below is a famous painting, *Washington Crossing the Delaware*. It shows General George Washington and James Monroe (*holding flag*) crossing the Delaware River in December 1776 during the American Revolution. Although the crossing was at night during a bad storm, the artist has used symbolism in this painting:

■ General Washington is shown leading his men out of the darkness (right side) into the light of freedom (*left side*).

■ General Washington is shown in a superior way. For example, he is shown taller than anyone else in the painting. Washington would become the first President and represents strength and courage in this painting.

1   What other symbolism do you think the artist used in this painting?

_____

_____

_____

_____

2   This painting was created just before the start of the Civil War. The artist's goal was to inspire hope and courage in the American people. He wanted to motivate them to fight for their freedom and remind them of those who had given their lives to earn independence for the nation. Does his painting achieve this purpose? Explain your answer.

_____

_____

_____

_____

STUDY CARDS

French and Indian War

•   Which nations were involved in the war?

_____

_____

•   Why is the French and Indian War of such importance?

_____

_____

•   Who was chief Pontiac? _____

_____

Name _____

ACTIVITY 2G

HOW GOOD A LISTENER ARE YOU?

■ The Northwest Ordinance established a process for the creation of new states and specified democratic ideals to be incorporated in the states of the Northwest Territory.

In this activity you will listen to passages read aloud about the Northwest Ordinance. After completing this activity, you will be able to explain the terms of the Northwest Ordinance and to describe how Ohio became a state.

KEY TERMS

■ Articles of Confederation	■ Northwest Ordinance	■ Bill of Rights
■ Limited Government	■ Statehood	■ Ohio Constitution

PLAYING THE TELEPHONE GAME

When we listen, we try to pay close attention in order to understand what we hear. Just how good a listener are you? In this activity, you will have a chance to measure your listening skills by playing the "Telephone Game." Here are the rules:

■ Your teacher will divide the class into four groups. Your teacher will make up a sentence and whisper the sentence to one student in each group.

■ This student will then whisper what he or she has heard from the teacher to a second student in the group. The second student should write down the sentence he or she heard where no one else can see it.

■ The second student should now whisper the sentence to a third student in the group, who will also write it down. This procedure should continue until all the students in the group have listened to the sentence.

■ The last student in each group will write the sentence on the chalkboard. Then that student will read to the class what he or she has put on the chalkboard.

Compare what the last student in each group announced with what the teacher whispered to the first student in each group:

■ Were the two sentences the same? _____

■ If not, what might explain the differences between the two sentences?

_____

_____

If your class is like most groups, the last sentence was different from the sentences first whispered by your teacher. This shows that not everyone listened carefully. Yet listening, speaking and communicating are key skills in our modern society. This activity will help you to focus on improving your listening skills. Good listening requires the following steps as you prepare to listen:

■ **Get Ready to Listen.** Face the person who is about to speak. Remove anything that may block your view or hearing. Place your attention and focus on the speaker.

■ **Determine your Purpose.** Know why you are about to listen. Are you listening to obtain information, to solve a problem or to provide feedback? If so, you should have your pen or pencil ready and your notebook open. If you are listening for enjoyment, you usually do not need to take notes.

To practice listening, your teacher will divide your class into groups. Each group should use the passages in this activity to practice with. A different student in each group should read one of the passages aloud. The reader should begin with the title and questions at the start of the reading. The student who is doing the reading should read slowly, with pauses for paragraph breaks. Other students in the group should listen without looking at the passage. As they listen, the students in the group should jot down notes to discuss at the end of the reading.

NOTES FOR DISCUSSION

Notes during the reading:

1. What is the title of the reading?
2. List any words and ideas you want to discuss after the reading.

Notes after the reading:

1. How would you answer the questions you heard at the start of the reading?
2. Comment on how well the person has read. Do you have any helpful suggestions for improvement?

Use a copy of the following form when it is your turn to listen.

As this passage is read, listen for answers to the following qu

A. What were the Articles of Confederation?

B. What were the main features of the Northwest Ordinance?

C. How did the Constitution differ from the Articles of Confed

---

READING #1: THE NORTHWEST O___NANCE

Once the colonies declared their independence, ~~they became~~ ~~teen independent~~ states. Americans soon realized they needed some form of ___ional government. However, many Americans feared making a central govern___ that was too strong. In 1781, Americans created a weak national government in an ___eement known as the **Articles of Confederation**. The Articles of Confederation ___elped to establish the idea of **limited government** — that a government should h__e specific powers based on popular consent, and it should not act beyond the powe__ it is given.

ACHIEVEMENTS OF THE ARTICLES OF CONFEDERATION

Despite its shortcomings, the Articles of Confederation created a national government that had some important achievements. One achievement of the new government was negotiating a peace treaty with Great Britain. This treaty gave the "Northwest Territory" to the United States. The Northwest Territory stretched from the Appalachian Mountains westwards to the Mississippi River and from the Ohio River northwards to the Great Lakes. It included present-day Ohio.

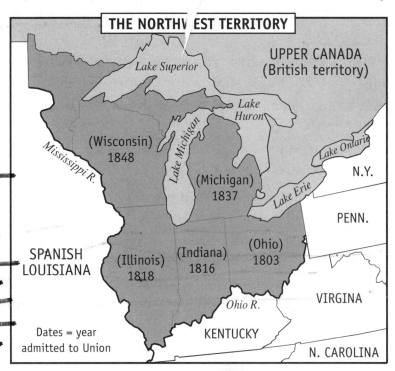

THE NORTHWEST TERRITORY

UPPER CANADA (British territory)

Lake Superior

Lake Huron

Lake Michigan

(Wisconsin) 1848

Mississippi R.

(Michigan) 1837

Lake Ontario

Lake Erie

N.Y.

PENN.

SPANISH LOUISIANA

(Illinois) 1818

(Indiana) 1816

(Ohio) 1803

Ohio R.

VIRGINA

Dates = year admitted to Union

KENTUCKY

N. CAROLINA

THE NORTHWEST ORDINANCE OF 1787

Another achievement of the new government was passing the **Northwest Ordinance of 1787**.

This "ordinance," or law, established steps for creating future states out of the Northwest Territory. Part of the language would be repeated in state constitutions over the next 100 years. The **Northwest Ordinance** divided the Northwest Territory into several smaller territories.

Three-Step Plan to Statehood. The Northwest Ordinance established a three-step plan for admitting states into the United States. First, a group of leaders would be appointed by Congress to govern the territory. Secondly, when a territory reached a population of 5,000 adults, its citizens could elect representatives to govern them. Finally, once the population reached 60,000 people, the territory could apply for admission as a state.

Voting Rights and Slavery. The Northwest Ordinance also dealt with many other important issues. Any male who owned fifty acres of property in the Northwest Territory was allowed to vote. Slavery was banned in the Northwest Territory, making the Ohio River a natural dividing line between free and slave states.

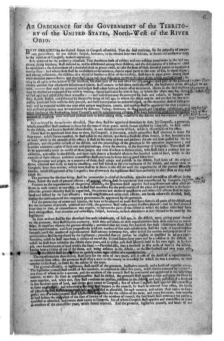

The Northwest Ordinance

Individual Rights. The Northwest Ordinance encouraged public education, and guaranteed individual rights to the people living in the territory. Many of the rights that would later become part of the U.S. Constitution and Bill of Rights were first found in the Northwest Ordinance. For example, people's freedom of religion, the right to a trial by a jury, the right to bail, and the right to enter into private contracts all first appeared in the Northwest Ordinance.

Effect on American Indians. The Northwest Ordinance also dealt with American Indians in the region. The Ordinance stated that Indian lands and other property would not be taken from them without their agreement. It also called for laws to be passed that would make sure that wrongs would not be carried out against the Indians. At the same time, the Northwest Ordinance established clear procedures, which helped to encourage westward expansion. This made clashes between Indians and settlers almost inevitable.

Conflicts With American Indians. Despite the attempt at cooperation in the Northwest Ordinance, most Indian tribes in Ohio opposed any treaty that took their land away. The Shawnee and Miami tribes opposed these provisions of the Northwest Ordinance. They refused to recognize any treaties with the United States. Disagreements between the U.S. government and these Indian tribes quickly developed into warfare. Tribes launched attacks on settlers moving into Ohio.

The U.S. government sent soldiers to protect the settlers. At first, the Indian tribes resisted with some success. They successfully destroyed two military forces, costing the lives of 800 soldiers. Eventually, the military forced the Indians of Ohio to give up most of their land. (*You will learn more about these conflicts in the next activity.*)

Conflicts arose between the Indians and Ohio settlers.

DISCONTENT WITH THE ARTICLES OF CONFEDERATION

Despite its achievements, there were serious problems with the new government created by the Articles of Confederation. In fact, there were so many problems that many American citizens demanded that the Articles of Confederation be changed.

In 1787, representatives from the states met in Philadelphia to write a new constitution. They quickly agreed that there was need

George Washington speaks to members of the Constitutional Convention of 1787.

for a much stronger national government. This stronger government would have a President, a Congress and a Supreme Court.

Delegates to the Constitutional Conventional also agreed that the new Constitution would only go into effect after nine of the thirteen states had approved it. By 1788, the U.S. Constitution was approved. Three years later, a **Bill of Rights** was added to the Constitution.

> The reader of these passages should act as discussion leader. Ask group members to discuss their answers to the questions at the start of this passage.

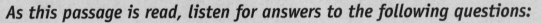

READING #2: STATEHOOD FOR OHIO

As this passage is read, listen for answers to the following questions:

A. How did Ohio become settled?

B. In what ways was Ohio's first constitution similar to the U.S. Constitution?

C. When did Ohio officially become a state?

AFTER THE AMERICAN REVOLUTION

During the Revolutionary War, the Continental Congress promised land as an incentive to those who volunteered to fight for their country. After the American Revolution, the new government decided to give away some of its western lands to veterans who had fought in the American Revolution as payment for their service. The first permanent settlement in Ohio was built in 1788.

Inauguration of the territorial government at Marietta.

   Men, women and children cleared the land, building homes, and constructing a fort. The settlers of this first community in Ohio named their settlement **Marietta**, in honor of the French queen, Marie Antoinette. Marietta was situated on two major rivers, making it an ideal location for trade. Marietta became the capital of the Northwest Territory.

EARLY SETTLERS POPULATE OHIO

Early settlers to Ohio found a land rich in vegetation. Almost ninety percent of the area was covered by forests.

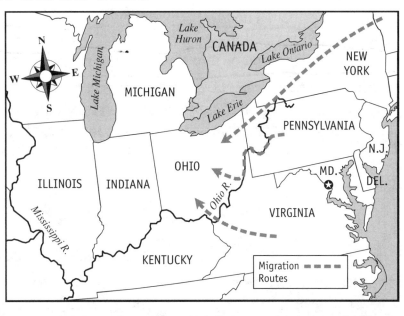

The main focus of the early settlers was survival. They made most of their own clothing and furniture, and grew all their own food. Some goods, such as salt, sugar, and tools, had to be purchased from merchants in neighboring states. Women usually cooked, washed clothes, sewed, and watched the children. Men's work mainly consisted of clearing and farming the land.

Thousands of settlers came to Ohio from Eastern states. The largest number came from the Middle Atlantic states, especially Pennsylvania. They usually settled along the Ohio River and other waterways. New Englanders settled in the northeastern part of the state. Southern newcomers to Ohio came mainly from Virginia, and usually settled in the western part of the state.

Immigrants from other countries were also attracted to Ohio. People of German heritage were among the earliest settlers in Ohio. Many overseas immigrants in the early 1800s also came from Ireland, Britain, France, Switzerland and Canada.

OHIO'S CONSTITUTION

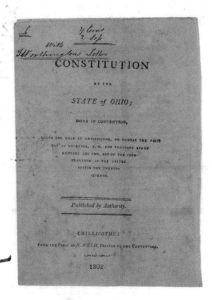

In 1802, a group of people living in Ohio met in Chillicothe to draw up a state constitution, modeled after the U.S. Constitution. Like the U.S. Constitution, Ohio had a chief executive, known as the governor. The governor served for a term of two years. Also, like the U.S. Constitution, Ohio's Constitution established a two-house legislature to decide on the state's laws. Unlike the U.S. Constitution, the Ohio Constitution prohibited slavery. Ohio's constitution provided that all white men could vote if they paid taxes or helped build and maintain the state's roads.

OHIO ACHIEVES STATEHOOD

In 1803, President Thomas Jefferson endorsed the U.S. Congress's decision to grant statehood to Ohio. Ohio was admitted to the United States as the nation's 17th state. Ohio became the first of five states to be formed out of the Northwest Territory.

> The reader of these passages should act as discussion leader. Ask group members to discuss their answers to the questions at the start of this passage.

MAKING CONNECTIONS

IDENTIFYING STATES OF THE NORTHWEST ORDINANCE

On the map below, locate the states that were created as a result of the Northwest Ordinance and label the surrounding lakes and rivers.

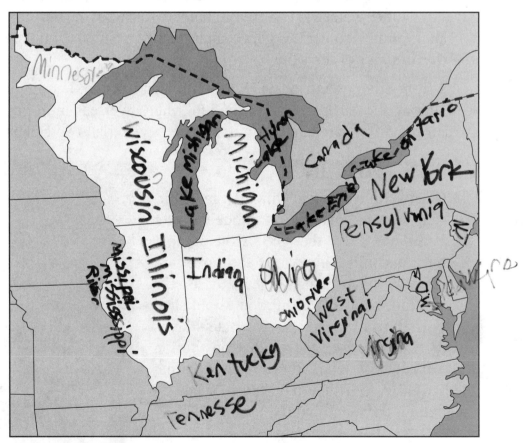

STUDY CARDS

Articles of Confederation

- What were the Articles of Confederation? _Weak national goverment that helped establish the idea of limited goverment_

- What were its achievements? _Negoshateing a peace treaty with great Britain. It gave "Northwest territory to the Us_

- What were its problems? _It gave "Northwes Territory To weak wanted a stronger goverment that lead to the Us constituation._

Protection of Freedoms in the Northwest Ordinance

List three freedoms protected by the Northwest Ordinance.

1 _____

_____

2 _____

_____

3 _____

_____

Effects of the Northwest Ordinance on American Indians

List the provisions of the Northwest Ordinance that dealt with the American Indians:

_____

_____

_____

_____

ACTIVITY

Directions: Complete the graphic organizer below by explaining the three steps necessary for a territory to become a state under the Northwest Ordinance.

1 _____
_____
_____
_____
_____

2 _____
_____
_____
_____
_____

Northwest Ordinance Plan for Statehood

3 _____
_____
_____
_____
_____

A concept map can often help you to see connections. What is a concept map?

A **concept map** is a diagram or illustration of ideas, examples, and facts. Seeing information organized in a diagram often helps you to relate details and to remember them for longer periods of time. In addition, a concept map is usually limited to the most important ideas and facts.

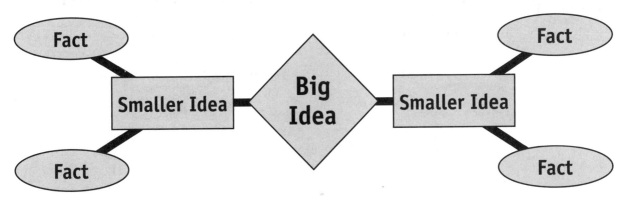

In this activity, you will complete several concept maps to demonstrate how well you have understood what you have read. This process will also help you to improve your long-term recall of this information. With this in mind, let's begin by reading the passages below. You will then be asked to create concept maps based on this information.

AMERICAN INDIANS AND SETTLERS

Almost as soon as the Declaration of Independence was signed in 1776, the colonists sought to deal with the American Indians.

INTERACTIONS DURING THE AMERICAN REVOLUTION

During the American Revolution, several attempts were made to persuade the American Indian tribes to remain **neutral** (*not take sides*) in the war. However, the British were more successful in winning the support of the Indians to their side. The Indians often distrusted the colonists. They saw the settlers moving west of the Appalachian Mountains and feared that they would eventually take over the lands they had lived on for centuries. On the other hand, the British promised to preserve and protect the tribal lands if a tribe supported the British cause.

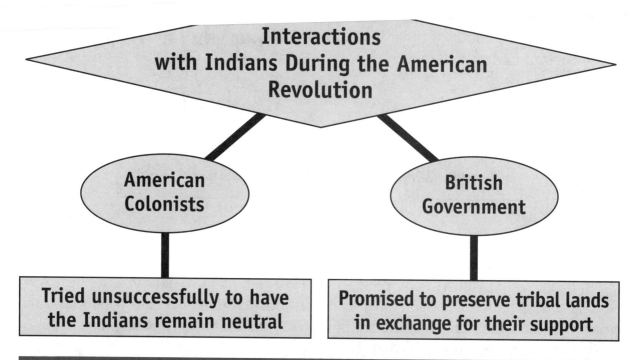

Interactions with Indians During the American Revolution

American Colonists

Tried unsuccessfully to have the Indians remain neutral

British Government

Promised to preserve tribal lands in exchange for their support

INTERACTIONS AFTER THE AMERICAN REVOLUTION

Even after the American Revolution, the British continued to supply some Indian tribes with weapons. The British sought to create an independent Indian nation in what is now the "Midwest" to act as a barrier between the United States and British colonists in Canada. The British also did not want to end their profitable fur trade in the Northwest Territory. The arrival of more settlers threatened that trade. Finally, the British feared American expansion would eventually threaten British possession of Canada.

The British continued supplying weapons to the Indians after the American Revolution.

On the other hand, the new U.S. government felt that many Indian tribes had given up the right to their lands by fighting on the side of the British. However, these Indians refused to give in to American demands to leave their traditional lands. The U.S. government formed by the Articles of Confederation lacked the military force needed to make the Indians leave.

Northwest Ordinance in 1787. With the passage of the Northwest Ordinance in 1787, the U.S. government tried to act more responsibly towards the American Indians in the Ohio River Valley. Under the provisions of the Northwest Ordinance, tribal rights to the land were recognized by the government. The ordinance further stated that any purchase of tribal lands needed to be done by agreement in a treaty.

The Northwest Ordinance

If you were to use the information in the last three paragraphs to make a concept map, here is what it might look like:

Interaction With
Indians After the American
Revolution

The British Viewpoint

The American Viewpoint

The British sought an independent Indian nation to act as a barrier between Canada and the United States

Americans felt some tribes had given up their lands in supporting the British

The British wanted to continue their profitable fur trade in the Northwest Territory

The national government lacked military force to make the Indians to leave the Ohio River Valley.

What would you put here? _____
_____
_____

What would you put here? _____
_____
_____

CONFLICTS BETWEEN THE AMERICAN INDIANS AND OHIO SETTLERS GROW

Despite attempts to deal with the American Indians peacefully, many of the tribes, especially those in the Ohio River Valley were not ready to surrender their lands. American Indian tribes, led by **Little Turtle** and the Shawnee Chief **Blue Jacket**, attacked the growing number of settlers in Ohio. In 1790 and 1791, Little Turtle defeated two American armies, killing hundreds of soldiers.

In 1792, President George Washington ordered **General Anthony Wayne** to go to Ohio. His orders were to protect American settlers against further Indian attacks. In 1794, Wayne led a large and well-trained force against the American Indians in northwest Ohio in one of the frontier wars.

Little Turtle

The **Battle of Fallen Timbers** took place in a forest where many trees had been toppled by a storm. Although the Indians used the fallen trees for cover, Wayne's army drove them from the battlefield. General Wayne defeated the Indians. A year later, most of these tribes agreed to give up their claims to lands in Ohio in the **Treaty of Greenville**. The treaty opened the way for thousands of new settlers to enter the Northwest Territory.

The Battle of Fallen Timbers

CHIEF TECUMSEH

Despite the signing of the Treaty of Greenville, not all Indian tribes agreed to leave Ohio. Even after Ohio achieved statehood, Indians continued to attack Ohio settlers. In 1806, a Shawnee chief named **Tecumseh** and his brother, known as the **Prophet**, began uniting different tribes. By 1811, more than twenty tribes were united by Tecumseh. He argued that all the Indian tribes should act together.

Tecumseh

Tecumseh and his brother believed that treaties would not protect them from the growing number of settlers. They believed they should not surrender any more of their lands. As news of their unhappiness spread, settlers in the Northwest Territory feared an attack by American Indians. American soldiers attacked first and defeated the Indians at the **Battle of Tippecanoe**. Tecumseh's brother was killed during the fighting in the battle. After their defeat the remaining tribes in Ohio were pushed off of their traditional homelands. The Indians' continuing hostility remained an unresolved issue that later contributed to the War of 1812.

Battle of Tippecanoe

CHECKING YOUR UNDERSTANDING

Briefly describe why Tecumseh and his brother were so distrustful of the American government.

_____

_____

_____

_____

THE WAR OF 1812

Since 1793, France and Britain had been almost continuously at war against each other. In 1812, their conflict finally spilled over into a new war between the United States and Britain.

MAIN CAUSES OF THE WAR

There were three unresolved issues that led to the outbreak of the War of 1812. First, British ships on the high seas were stopping American ships and seizing (*or impressing*) U.S. sailors into the British navy. The British claimed these sailors were deserters from the British navy. The Americans saw this as an excuse for the British to seize free Americans.

Secondly, there were still unresolved issues about the use of the Northwest Territory. You will recall, that disagreement over control of the Ohio River Valley had been one of the factors that had led to the French and Indian War. Occupation of the region continued to be a cause of conflict between Indian tribes and American settlers. The British government continued to allow its troops in Canada to supply American Indians in this region with weapons. American settlers believed the British were providing these weapons to help the Indians attack American settlements.

Thirdly, several young Congressmen thought the time was ripe to seize Canada from the British.

As a result of these reasons, President **James Madison** asked Congress to declare war on Britain in 1812.

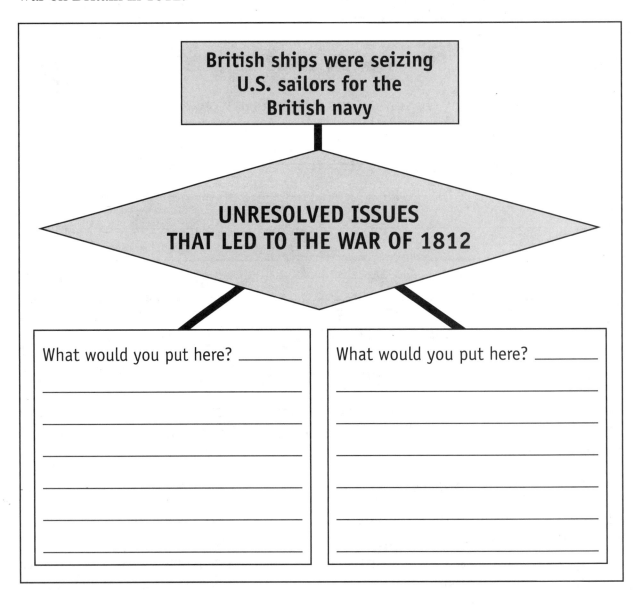

MAIN EVENTS OF THE WAR

American forces tried to invade Canada but were not successful. In 1812, **Fort Meigs** was built along the Maumee River in Ohio as a supply depot and staging area for the eventual invasion of Canada. The fort experienced two attacks by the British, but was able to resist them. Fort Meigs helped Americans to secure control of the Great Lakes region. The fort also prevented further invasions of Ohio by the British.

Fort Meigs's walls were made of 15-foot high logs buried into the ground.

Much of the fighting during the War of 1812 took place on the Great Lakes and in upstate New York. In 1813, British troops burned the American settlement at Buffalo, New York. To strike back at American attempts to conquer Canada, British troops temporarily occupied Washington, D.C. and burned down the White House. **Francis Scott Key** wrote the words to "The Star Spangled Banner," our national anthem, when the British were unable to take nearby Baltimore.

In 1813, American and British ships also clashed in the **Battle of Lake Erie**. The battle was fought on the side of the lake close to Ohio. Admiral **Oliver Perry** led a fleet of nine American ships to victory over six British warships. This victory left the United States in control of Lake Erie. It eliminated any chance that the British could resupply their soldiers in their fort at Detroit. The British were forced to abandon Detroit and retreat.

Admiral Perry during the Battle of Lake Erie.

Treaty Signed. In December 1814, a peace treaty was finally signed between Britain and the United States. This agreement left things much as they had been before the war. However, the British promised they would no longer search American ships for British deserters. Americans promised to respect British rule in Canada. Americans felt they had proved they could protect their independence.

The biggest battle of the war actually took place after the treaty was signed. Not knowing that peace had been agreed to, the British attacked New Orleans early in 1815, and were defeated by General Andrew Jackson.

IMPACT OF THE WAR OF 1812

IMPACT ON THE AMERICAN INDIANS

The War of 1812 turned out to be a major turning point for the American Indians in their attempts to stop new settlers from occupying their lands. After the War of 1812, the U.S. government entered into more than 200 treaties with Indian nations. Each treaty required Indian tribes to surrender their lands and to move to new lands west of the Mississippi River.

A key outcome of the War of 1812 was that Americans gave up their designs on Canada. In exchange, the British stopped encouraging American Indians to fight against new settlers in the area. Tecumseh's defeat in 1813 marked the beginning of the end for the American Indian nations in the Ohio region. Tecumseh was seriously wounded. When he died, Indian hopes of ever driving back the settlers died with him.

SHRINKING AMERICAN INDIAN LANDS IN OHIO

BEFORE 1785	1785	1795	1805	1817
Ohio was completely occupied by American Indian tribes.	In the Treaty of Fort McIntosh, tribes gave up large amounts of their land.	The Treaty of Greenville further limited tribal lands in Ohio.	The Treaty of Fort Industry took away even more tribal lands.	With the Treaty of Fort Meigs, tribes in Ohio were limited to a few reservations.

IMPACT ON THE UNITED STATES

The United States emerged from the war with worldwide respect for having resisted Great Britain. The morale of American citizens greatly increased. The United States had fought one of the greatest military powers in the world and had managed to survive. Oliver Perry became a national hero, and villages and towns were named after him. The Great Lakes became the shared property of British Canada and the United States. Ohio was safely secured, and its population and economy began to grow rapidly.

The Ohio River became a major route for settlers moving west. In 1800, Ohio's population was only 45,000. By 1850, Ohio's population had grown to more than two million people.

What goes here? _____	What goes here? _____
_____	_____
_____	_____
_____	_____
_____	_____

**Impact on
the United States**

**IMPACT OF
THE WAR OF 1812**

**Impact on
American Indians in Ohio**

What goes here? _____	What goes here? _____
_____	_____
_____	_____
_____	_____
_____	_____

MAKING CONNECTIONS

DETECTING BIAS IN A SOURCE

Every primary and secondary source is influenced in some way by the point of view of its author. A **bias** is a slanted point of view based on a person's pre-existing beliefs. Bias is a form of prejudice or opinion. For example, you might believe that the Cleveland Browns are the best football team in America. The team's record would likely show otherwise. Biases are often unsupported by the facts.

There are many factors that can contribute to an author's bias. An author may be biased because of his or her upbringing, experiences, social class, race, nationality, religion, beliefs, or gender.

Read the following two passages about the War of 1812. Then answer the questions that follows.

British cruisers have been in the practice of violating the American flag on the great seas, and carrying off persons sailing under it . . . The practice is more then affecting just British subjects alone. Under the excuse of searching for these persons, thousands of American citizens, under the safety of their national flag, have been taken from their country and from everything that is dear to them. They have been dragged on board ships of war of a foreign nation. They have been taken to the most distant lands, to risk their lives in the battles of their oppressors .... — President James Madison, June 1, 1812	His Royal Highness will never agree that in searching neutral merchant ships, the impressment of British seamen, when found, can be seen as a violation of a neutral country. Neither will the King admit that taking such seamen from their ships, can be considered by any neutral nation as a hostile act, or a cause of war. There is no right more clearly established, than the right of a ruler to the loyalty of his subjects, especially in times of war. — Prince Regent of Great Britain, *On the Causes of the War with America*, February 3, 1813

- What does President Madison see as the cause of War of 1812?

  _____

  _____

  _____

- What does the Prince Regent of Great Britain say about the right of British ships to search American ships?

  _____

  _____

  _____

- What biases influenced the explanations these speakers gave for the outbreak of the war?

  _____

  _____

  _____

STUDY CARDS

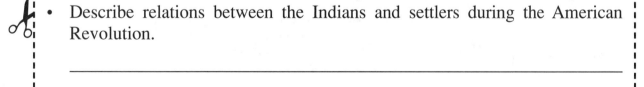

American Indians and Settlers

- Describe relations between the Indians and settlers during the American Revolution.

  _____

  _____

- Describe relations between the Indians and settlers after the American Revolution.

  _____

  _____

War with Native Americans

- Who were Little Turtle and Blue Jacket? _____

_____

- What role did General Wayne play in the Battle of Fallen Timbers?

_____

_____

- What role did Chief Tecumseh play in relations between Indians and settlers?

_____

_____

LEARNING WITH GRAPHIC ORGANIZERS

Directions: Complete the graphic organizer below by explaining the cause of the conflicts that existed between the American Indians and the Ohio settlers.

```
┌──────────────────────┐          ┌──────────────────────┐
│  _____    │          │  _____    │
│  _____    │          │  _____    │
│  _____    │          │  _____    │
└──────────────────────┘          └──────────────────────┘

┌──────────┐      ╱‾‾‾‾‾‾‾‾‾‾‾‾‾╲      ┌──────────┐
│          │     │  Conflicts Between │     │          │
│  Causes  │─────│ Indians and Settlers│────│ Effects  │
│          │     │  in the Ohio        │     │          │
└──────────┘      ╲  Territory  ╱      └──────────┘

┌──────────────────────┐          ┌──────────────────────┐
│  _____    │          │  _____    │
│  _____    │          │  _____    │
│  _____    │          │  _____    │
└──────────────────────┘          └──────────────────────┘
```

EXPRESS YOURSELF

Some historians believe that General Anthony Wayne played a key role in the growth of Ohio. Wayne's victory over the Indian tribes at the Battle of Fallen Timbers led to the treaty which ended Indian claims to Ohio and its surrounding lands.

Do you agree with these historians about the importance of General Wayne to the growth of Ohio? If so, explain why. If not, explain why not.

CAN YOU IDENTIFY THE MAIN IDEA AND SUPPORTING DETAILS OF A READING?

■ Sectional issues divided the United States after the War of 1812. Ohio played a key role in these issues, particularly with the antislavery movement and the Underground Railroad.

In this activity, you will learn about developments that took place in Ohio in the years leading up to the Civil War. You will learn how Ohioans tried to free enslaved people fleeing from the South. Finally, you will learn how to identify the main ideas and supporting details of a reading selection.

KEY TERMS

- Main Idea
- Supporting Details
- Sectionalism
- North / West / South
- "Bread Basket"

- Whitney's Cotton Gin
- "King Cotton"
- Plantation System
- Free Blacks
- Abolitionists

- Harriet Beecher Stowe
- Fugitive Slave Act
- Underground Railroad
- Levi Coffin
- John Rankin

WHAT DOES IT MEAN TO READ SOMETHING?

Have you ever thought about what you do when you read? When you read, you must figure out what words are created by the combination of different letters. Then you must try to understand the meaning of each group of words and how they relate.

This is just the starting point. Reading is much more than only understanding the process of words on a page.

A reader must also make sense of those words when they are put together. The reader must understand the ideas suggested by those words.

CHAIR

READER

A "reading passage" is a text made up of several paragraphs about a topic. When you read a passage, you should first try to determine its topic. Usually, the author has some basic message about the topic — known as the **main idea** of the reading. The rest of the reading provides ideas, facts, and other details that explain and illustrate the main idea. These are known as **supporting details**.

CHECKING YOUR UNDERSTANDING

What does it mean to read something? _____

_____

_____

_____

The passages in this activity are about issues that once divided Americans. As you read each passage, try to determine its main idea — the central message. Then identify the supporting details — the ideas, facts and examples that support that main idea.

SECTIONAL DIFFERENCES ARISE

Following the War of 1812, the United States quickly expanded westward. Westward expansion, population growth, and advances in technology led to important changes in patterns of settlement. The number of American towns and cities increased. Finally, the rise of industry increased differences between the main regions of the country.

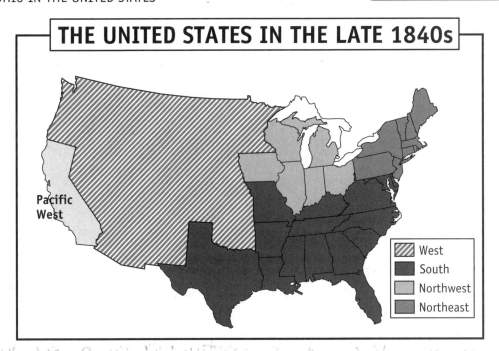

By the middle of the century, the three main regions of the country had developed their own distinctive ways of life. These regions were known at the time as "**sections**." These regional differences led to the rise of sectionalism. **Sectionalism** refers to the greater loyalty many Americans felt toward their own section rather than to the country as a whole.

THE NORTH

The **North** (*now called the Northeast*) was the first section to industrialize. As the North grew, it became a center for manufacturing, shipping and small farms. With industrialization, skilled craftsmen were replaced by unskilled workers in large factories. Gradually, the number of workers in Northern factories increased.

Large textile mills like this became common in Northern cities.

Northern cities also grew because of immigration to America. Between 1830 and 1880, more than one quarter of all immigrants to the United States were German. Many went to cities in the Northeast, like New York. Others settled in Midwestern states like Ohio, Michigan and Wisconsin.

As industries grew, inequalities between the rich and poor increased. The middle classes expanded. There were many new opportunities for merchants, bankers, sales clerks, and professionals. Workers and the poor were the chief victims of the new industrial society. They worked long hours for low wages and often faced unemployment.

Life in the countryside also changed. Instead of mainly growing food for themselves, Northern farmers began growing hay and raising cattle and pigs to sell wool, milk, and meat. As farm income declined, young farm people moved to the cities in search of better jobs. By 1860, half the population of the North were working at jobs in occupations other than farming.

Many young people left farm life for the city.

CHECKING YOUR UNDERSTANDING

Briefly describe life in the North in the mid-1800s. <ins>Life in the North expanding. People were getting better jobs. Farmers were leaving farm life and getting better jobs than just farming.</ins>

THE WEST

The Appalachian Mountains once stood as a barrier to settling lands farther west. However, the availability of cheap land, the construction of the National Road, and the building of canals opened the lands west of the Appalachians to settlers. Removal of the Americans Indians from the Northwest Territory to lands west of the Mississippi greatly increased settlement.

After the Erie Canal was built in 1825, Western farmers could send their crops up the Mississippi River to the Great Lakes, over the Erie Canal and down the Hudson River to New York City. Ohio and other Midwestern states became the main producers of wheat and corn. Farmers began using machines to work the land. The Midwest replaced the Northeast as the nation's "**Bread Basket**" — growing corn and wheat and grinding flour.

By the mid-1800s, the number of settlers moving to the West grew rapidly. The desire for land and new opportunities continued to fuel westward expansion. The region's rich soil attracted many farmers.

As settlers moved west toward the Pacific Ocean in their covered wagons, the West emerged as the nation's fastest growing section.

Ohio soon had more residents than Massachusetts. The attraction of the West was more than just farmland for settlers. There was also the attraction of timber, gold, silver and grazing lands. Settlers poured across the frontier to establish ranches, dig mines, and farm the land.

Settlers to the West set about clearing the land and preparing it to grow crops.

CHECKING YOUR UNDERSTANDING

Briefly describe how life in the West differed from life in the North.

The life in the West differed from life in the North because the jobs in the North were different from the South. The South focuse more on farming the the North focused on occupation jobs, "Bread Basket"

THE SOUTH

At the time of the Constitutional Convention, it appeared that slavery in the United States might soon die out. The prices of tobacco, rice, and indigo were falling, and planters in Virginia were introducing wheat, which did not require slave labor.

Impact of Whitney's Cotton Gin.
In 1792, Eli Whitney developed the **cotton gin** — a machine that combed through cotton and separated the seeds. With this new invention, it was possible for one machine to do the work of

Eli Whitney's Cotton Gin

fifty workers separating the seeds by hand. As a result, cotton growing became more profitable.

Over the next forty years, the **plantation system** spread throughout the South. Plantations became large agricultural businesses overseen by owners who used large labor forces made up of slave laborers. It was hard to satisfy the demand for cotton from the factories of the Northeast and England. Along the Atlantic Coastal Plain, plantation owners also used slave labor to grow cotton, rice, and tobacco for export to Northern cities and European markets.

Slaves toiling on a plantation.

Impact of Slavery on Southern States. "King Cotton" soon came to symbolize the South. An over-emphasis on growing cotton and other crops led some Southern states to ignore improvements in industry and transportation. Southern plantations often wore out the soil, fell into debt, and failed to develop new technologies. Although most Southern families did not own slaves, slavery had a great impact on the Southern economy. The South fell behind the North in the number of railroads, factories, and schools. Southern cities generally remained small and lacked industry.

THE LIFE OF A SLAVE

Slaves were generally owned by wealthy Southern landholders who grew crops, such as rice and sugar. Many slaves endured back-breaking work on plantations as field hands. Slaves were given tasks like plowing and gathering crops.

Living Conditions. Living conditions for slaves were usually primitive. Slave families generally lived in one-room cabins and ate simple, unbalanced meals of cornmeal, pork, and molasses. Slaves lacked clean living conditions or running water. A few slaves became skilled blacksmiths or carpenters and were hired out by their owners. Even then, their wages remained the property of their slave owners.

An African-American family under slavery.

Slaves were permitted to marry and could have children. This became the main source of new slaves. Slaves were denied basic human rights: they could be beaten or sold apart from their families at the whim of their owners.

Interior of a slave cabin showing the living conditions of these forced laborers.

Despite their horrible living and working conditions, many slaves held onto their rich African heritage through music, religion, and folklore. They also resisted slavery by not cooperating or escaping. In some cases, slaves openly rebelled. As a result, Southern states passed laws tightly controlling the activities of both slaves and free blacks.

Free Blacks. Most Northern states passed laws gradually eliminating slavery. Many Southern states passed laws making it possible for slave owners to free individual slaves. After the American Revolution, thousands of slaves were freed. By 1810, three-quarters of the African Americans in the North were free. Even free blacks, however, faced racial prejudice. Many worked in dockyards or craft shops in their own neighborhoods.

CHECKING YOUR UNDERSTANDING

How was life in the South different from the rest of the nation? <u>The</u>

<u>st South picked cotton called the Plantation System.</u>

_____

_____

_____

Now let's look more closely at what you have just read. In this reading passage, the main idea is stated in the title: "Sectional Differences Arise." The first paragraphs restated this general idea. The remaining paragraphs in the passage provide details to support this main idea.

Often, seeing ideas in a diagram can help you to understand them better. Look at the diagram that follows, which is based on the information in this passage:

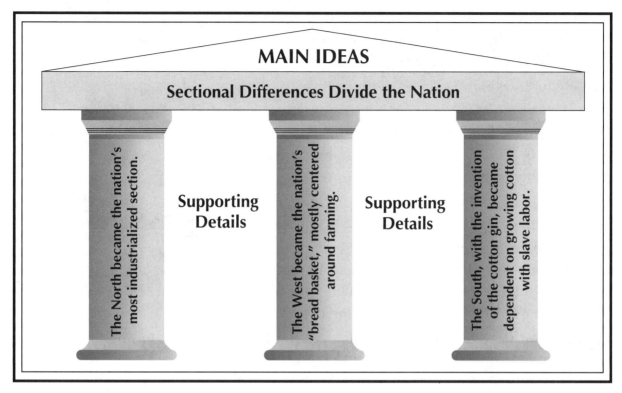

MAIN IDEAS

Sectional Differences Divide the Nation

The North became the nation's most industrialized section.

Supporting Details

The West became the nation's "bread basket," mostly centered around farming.

Supporting Details

The South, with the invention of the cotton gin, became dependent on growing cotton with slave labor.

OHIO AND THE ANTI-SLAVERY MOVEMENT

Many Southerners believed their way of life was threatened by those opposed to slavery in the North. Many Northerners feared the South wanted to spread slavery throughout the entire nation.

SLAVERY PROHIBITED IN OHIO

Ohio played an important role in ending slavery in the United States. Both the Northwest Ordinance and the Ohio State Constitution prohibited slavery in Ohio. The seeds of the anti-slavery movement in Ohio were planted by local antislavery newspapers. Quakers, a religious group, began publication of two newspapers in Ohio in the early 1800s. Ohio soon became a center of opposition to slavery.

TEN DOLLARS REWARD.

RUN AWAY on Friday the 26th of August 1774, from the subscriber, living in Middle-patent, North-Castle, Westchester county, and province of New-York,

A NEGRO MAN,

Named WILL, about 27 years of age, about five feet six inches high, somewhat of a yellow complexion, a spry lively fellow, very talkative; had on when he went away, a butter-nut coloured coat, felt hat, tow cloth trowsers; he has part of his right ear cut off, and a mark on the backside of his right hand.

Whosoever takes up said Negro and brings him to his master, or secures him in gaol, so that his master may have him again, shall have the above reward and all reasonable charges, paid by   JAMES BANKS

N. B. Masters of vessels are hereby warned not to carry off the above Negro.   74

Newspaper ad offers a $10 reward for the return of a runaway slave.

The **Ohio Anti-Slavery Society** employed lecturers to travel across the state. They tried to persuade Ohioans to join the abolitionist movement. An **abolitionist** was a person who wanted to abolish or end slavery. By the late 1830s, there were more than 200 antislavery associations in Ohio.

One of the most famous abolitionists was **Harriet Beecher Stowe**. She came from Cincinnati. In 1852, she wrote *Uncle Tom's Cabin*, a popular novel telling the story of a slave named Tom.

Beecher's story told how, after a lifetime of loyally serving his master, Tom was badly beaten and died. Tom's owner was responsible for his death. The main theme of her book was that slavery was evil and immoral, and it had to be stopped. Stowe's novel helped win the support of many people in the battle against slavery.

Harriet Beecher Stowe

OHIO'S ROLE IN THE UNDERGROUND RAILROAD

Ohio became a magnet for runaway slaves, even after the **Fugitive Slave Act of 1850** made it illegal to help slaves trying to escape.

Many Ohioans secretly helped slaves escape from the South. They provided a place for runaway slaves to hide on their way north to Canada. This escape route, known as the **Underground Railroad**, was a system of secret routes, safe houses, and hiding places used by runaway slaves to escape to freedom.

Ohio was the northern "trunk line" of the Underground Railroad. Throughout Ohio,

Escaping along the Underground Railroad

one could find safe houses where slaves were concealed during the day. Most escaped slaves would travel during nighttime hours to avoid being found. Even today, cities throughout Ohio have buildings that served at one time as safe houses. These safe houses hid fugitive slaves as they moved north along the Underground Railroad.

Although slavery was prohibited in the State of Ohio, some people still favored the idea of slavery. These people were afraid that some of the escaped slaves would settle in the state and take away jobs from long time residents of Ohio. For this reason, many of these people strongly opposed the Underground Railroad. Some Ohioans even tried to return runaway slaves to their Southern owners in the hope of collecting rewards.

OHIO AS A FINAL DESTINATION

Some runaways slaves decided to stay in Ohio rather than move on to Canada. Many settled in various Ohio communities among other African Americans. At least eight cities in Ohio — Ashtabula, Painesville, Cleveland, Sandusky, Toledo, Huron, Lorain, and Conneaut — acted as jumping-off points for runaway slaves moving to Canada. It has been estimated that there were as many as three thousand miles of Underground Railroad trails in Ohio.

LEADING OHIO "CONDUCTORS"

Several Ohioans played a key role in the Underground Railroad. In the late 1840s, Cincinnati resident **Levi Coffin**, helped more than three thousand slaves escape to Canada. Coffin helped so many slaves escape their masters that he was given the nickname, "President of the Underground Railroad."

Levi Coffin

In Ripley, Ohio, minister **John Rankin** was also a conductor on the Underground Railroad. Living atop a 300-foot hill overlooking the Ohio River, Rankin used a lantern on a tall flagpole to signal to runaway slaves when it was safe to cross the river into Ohio.

Rankin also built a staircase leading up the hill to his house for slaves to climb on their way north to Canada. It is estimated that Rankin helped as many as 2,000 slaves to escape to freedom. The staircase and house in Ripley, known as the Rankin House, are now National Historic Landmarks.

CHECKING YOUR UNDERSTANDING

What role did Ohio play in the Anti-Slavery Movement?

_____

_____

_____

Now that you have finished reading the passage, fill in the diagram on the next page. Then complete the diagram showing the main idea and supporting details of the passage.

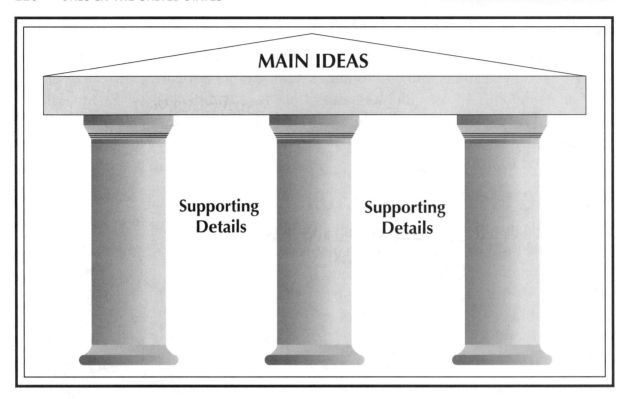

MAIN IDEAS

Supporting Details

Supporting Details

MAKING CONNECTIONS

READING POPULATION DISTRIBUTION MAPS OF OHIO AT DIFFERENT TIME PERIODS

Maps can be used for many purposes. For example, maps can show how a place looked in the past. By looking at maps of the same area in different time periods, we can see how that area has changed. Using our knowledge of historical events, we can then try to explain those changes.

A **population distribution** map shows how many people live in an area. For example, look at the population distribution map of Ohio on the next page. It shows the population of each county of Ohio in 1850.

The counties with light gray shading had less than 10,000 residents in 1850. The population of Ohio had dramatically changed just 50 years later. If you compare the two maps below, you will see how the population of counties in Ohio changed over this time. After you look over these historical maps, answer the questions that follow.

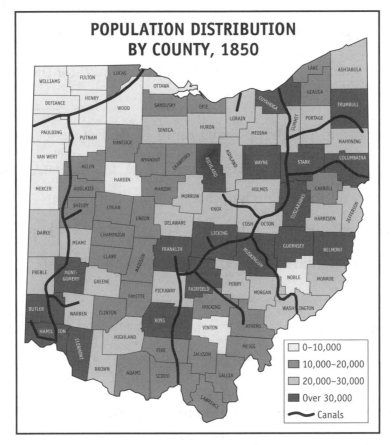

POPULATION DISTRIBUTION BY COUNTY, 1850

☐	0–10,000
■	10,000–20,000
▨	20,000–30,000
■	Over 30,000
∿	Canals

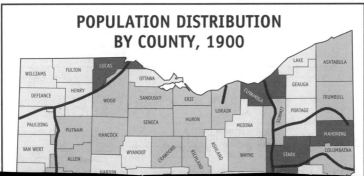

POPULATION DISTRIBUTION BY COUNTY, 1900

CHECKING YOUR UNDERSTANDING

1 In 1850, how many people lived in Darke County, on the western border of Ohio? _30,000-70,000_

2 Which county had a higher population in 1850: Lawrence on the southern tip of Ohio or Morrow in central Ohio? _Lawrence Morrow_

3 Which county on Lake Erie had the largest population in 1850? _Erie_
   What might explain why? _because Erie is the name of the county and the lake, it has transportation._

4 What do the thick black lines on these maps show? _Canals_

   _____

5 Name 3 counties that increased their population between 1850 and 1900:
   • _Clark_   • _Lawrence_   • _Mahoning_

6 Look at www.nationalgeographic.com/railroad/j4.html which includes inter-active information on the Underground Railroad. Then trace the route of the Underground Railroad on one of the maps on the previous page. Did the Underground Railroad go through areas that were thinly or densely populated?

STUDY CARDS

ACTIVITY 2J

HU_____ ____NOVATIONS OF OHIOANS BENEFITTED THE UNITED STATES?

■ Many technological innovations that originated in Ohio benefitted the United States.

In this activity, you will learn about Ohioans who have made important contributions to Ohio and the United States. After completing this activity, you will be able to describe the innovations of several Ohio inventors.

KEY TERMS

- Thomas Edison
- Garrett Morgan
- James Ritty
- Wilbur and Orville Wright
- Charles Kettering
- Thomas Midgley, Jr.
- Reference Books
- Biography/Autobiography
- Glossary

AKRON BEACON JOURNAL

Thomas Edison Invents the Lightbulb

Aurora Advocate

Garrett Morgan's Saftey Hood Saves 32 Men Trapped in Explosion

---

CINCINATTI SUN

James Ritty's Cash Register Reduces Employee Theft

❖ **CLEVELAND STAR** ❖

Wright Brothers Successfully Test First Airplane

COLUMBUS DAILY REPORTER

Charles Kettering's Invention Reduces Auto Deaths

MARIETTA TIMES

Thomas Midgley's Ethyl Gas Reduces Engine Knock

What do all of these newspaper headlines have in common? _____

_____

WHO WERE THESE PEOPLE?

You may have heard of some of the people mentioned in these headlines before. Each of them is famous for a special reason. Each was an Ohioan who made some technological innovation that has benefitted the United States. Let's take a closer look at each of these innovative men.

THOMAS EDISON (1847–1931)

Thomas Edison may well have been the greatest inventor of all time. Born in Milan, Ohio, in 1847, his family moved to Michigan when he was five. He left school at the age of 12 to work for the railroads. His first major invention was a printing telegraph. Edison was disappointed when Alexander Graham Bell beat him in the race to invent the telephone in 1876.

Edison invented the phonograph a year later. While working to make the telegraph more efficient, he discovered that the tape of the machine gave off a noise resembling spoken words when played at a high speed. His experiments led him to invent the phonograph, opening the field of home entertainment. It led to record players, and later to tapes, compact discs, and online music. Today, we enjoy music at home because of advances that came from Edison's phonograph.

Helped by investors, Edison next hired a team of assistants and invented the electric light bulb. Edison's light bulb made it possible for people to work and play after dark. He also invented motion pictures and alkaline batteries. To power his inventions, Edison invented the electric generator, which produced electricity. Edison patented more than a thousand inventions, earning the nickname of "The Wizard of Menlo Park."

When Edison died in 1931, President Hoover requested that electric lights throughout the nation be dimmed for one minute out of respect. Thomas Edison never stopped inventing during his lifetime. To this day, no other person has patented more inventions.

CHECKING YOUR UNDERSTANDING

1 What do you think was Edison's most important innovation? _____

_____

2 What evidence would you give in support of your opinion? _____

_____

GARRETT A. MORGAN (1877–1963)

Garrett Morgan was the son of former slaves. Born in Kentucky, he moved to Cincinnati when he was in his teens to find work. After witnessing a crash between an automobile and a horse-drawn carriage, Garrett Morgan set about to prevent such accidents in the future. He developed his own hand-operated traffic signal. In 1923, Morgan became one of the first people to obtain a U.S. patent for his traffic signal.

Morgan's "safety hood."

Morgan also invented his own "safety hood," a kind of gas mask for firefighters. It had a long hose so that it could pull up air from close to the ground. In 1916, he used his safety hood to rescue 32 men trapped during an explosion in a tunnel 250 feet beneath Lake Erie.

JAMES RITTY (1836–1928)

James Ritty owned a bar in Dayton, Ohio, in the years after the Civil War. He wanted to find a way to prevent his employees from taking money from customers and putting it in their pockets.

In 1878, he came up with a solution while on a trip to Europe. With the help of his brother, a mechanic, Ritty invented the cash register in 1879. His invention, known as the "thief catcher," stopped dishonest clerks by recording all sales. Cash registers made it difficult for employees to steal from their employers.

Ritty's cash register, 1879

In 1881, Ritty began to manufacture cash registers in Dayton while still running his bar. Ritty eventually sold his cash register business to John Patterson. Patterson renamed the business the National Cash Register Company. Patterson's company soon became very successful selling cash registers across the country.

CHECKING YOUR UNDERSTANDING

In your opinion, who made the greater contribution to American society: Garrett Morgan or James Ritty? Justify your answer.

_____

_____

_____

_____

WILBUR AND ORVILLE WRIGHT

Orville and Wilbur Wright

Every bird can do it, but the problem of flight had stumped well-known scientists and inventors for centuries. Did you know that two brothers from Ohio, working alone and with little scientific training, were the first men to finally fly?

Wilbur and Orville Wright grew up in Dayton, Ohio, after the Civil War. As children, the Wright brothers were fascinated with flying. They loved to make and fly kites. Even as adults, the Wright Brothers continued to dream of building a flying machine. The invention of a gasoline engine for automobiles seemed to make the dream of human flight possible.

The Wright brothers owned a bicycle shop in Dayton. In their spare time, the brothers began experimenting with kites. Next, they built a glider with wings that moved up and down. A glider is an aircraft that sails through the air without an engine or propeller.

In 1902, the Wright brothers designed propellers for their glider. The Wright Flyer, as they called it, was built on a wooden frame and covered with fabric. It was powered by a new, lighter engine that the Wright brothers designed themselves. The engine drove two propellers with chains. The propeller created a stream of air that lifted the plane as it blew across the wings.

Name _____

In December 1903, the Wright brothers took their invention to Kitty Hawk, North Carolina, to test it. The Wright Flyer took off and flew 120 feet, staying in the air for 12 seconds — making it the first manned flight! The Wright brothers tested their airplane three more times that day.

Orville lifts off in the Wright Flyer as his brother watches.

On one test, the plane was able to stay in the air for almost a minute. Later, the brothers improved the design of their airplane. By 1905, they developed a plane that could fly 34 miles and remain in the air for 40 minutes. Their improvements made it possible for people to travel longer distances in less time.

CHECKING YOUR UNDERSTANDING

1 How have Americans benefitted from the Wright Brothers' invention?

_____

_____

2 If the Wright brothers had not been able to fly their airplane in 1903, do you think someone else would have come along and invented one?

_____

_____

CHARLES KETTERING (1876–1958)

Charles Kettering was born in Loudonville, Ohio, in 1876. He first worked for the National Cash Register Company in Dayton, where he helped invent an electric cash register.

In the early days of the automobile, the only way to start a car was to use an iron hand-crank. Not only did this require some arm strength, but it also carried some risks: the car could backfire or roll forward onto the driver turning the crank.

Charles Kettering

In 1909, Kettering and a group of friends created a new ignition system still used today to start automobiles. To "ignite" something is to cause it to burn. With this ignition system, all the driver has to do is turn a key to start the engine of a car. Although electrical ignition was at first thought of as a convenience, in reality, this invention was one created for safety.

Kettering was something of a genius when it came to inventions. With Thomas Midgley, he later invented a quick-drying, weatherproof paint for cars, and high octane gasoline. Kettering also helped start the Dayton Engineering Laboratories Company (Delco). In the field of medicine, Kettering created an incubator for premature infants. Finally, he co-founded the world famous Sloan-Kettering Institute for Cancer Research in 1945.

THOMAS MIDGLEY, JR. (1889–1944)

Thomas Midgley, Jr.

Born in Pennsylvania, **Thomas Midgley, Jr.**, grew up in Columbus, Ohio. As a young man, Midgley witnessed the dramatic changes that were occurring in people's lives because of the invention of the first automobile. One of the flaws of early automobiles, was a loud and unpleasant knocking noise made by car engines.

In 1916, Charles Kettering hired Midgley to find a way to eliminate this annoying sound. Midgley soon realized that the noise was affected by the type of gasoline that was used. After several years of research, Midgley found that by adding a lead compound to the gasoline, the knocking noise would go away. In 1921, Midgley patented his new fuel. Many years later, it was realized that fuel containing lead was harmful to the environment. Today, cars no longer use leaded fuel.

CHECKING YOUR UNDERSTANDING

Who do you think made a more beneficial contribution to American society, Charles Kettering or Thomas Midgley, Jr.? Justify your answer.

_____

_____

_____

CHECKING YOUR UNDERSTANDING

Make a chart that classifies all the inventors identified in this activity. Across the top row, list the names of the inventors. On the left column, list the areas in which they made inventions: energy and power, transportation, manufacturing, construction, information and communication, medicine, agriculture, and biotechnology.

CREATING AN OHIO HALL OF FAME

Many sports honor their best players in a "Hall of Fame." For example, football honors its greatest players in the Football Hall of Fame, located in Canton. Rock musicians honor their greatest artists in the Rock and Roll Hall of Fame in Cleveland. Can you imagine what it would be like if Ohio had a Hall of Fame to honor its greatest inventors?

The Rock and Roll Hall of Fame.

Which inventor would you recommend to the Ohio Inventor's Hall of Fame? In this activity, your class will be divided into smaller groups by your teacher. Each group will nominate one person to the imaginary Ohio Inventor's Hall of Fame. Here are the qualifications for admission:

- Each nominee must either have either been born in Ohio or lived here for a good part of his or her life.
- A nominee must have invented something that has benefitted the United States.
- A nominee can be either a historical figure or someone still alive today.

Each group should research two possible candidates for the Hall of Fame. Then it should select one to propose to the class. The following list identifies some people who either were born in Ohio or who lived here. This list is only a starting point. Your group may also select an Ohioan not on this list for its nominee.

LIST OF POSSIBLE NOMINEES

Benjamin F. Goodrich. Goodrich was born in 1841 in New York. A former surgeon, he developed rubber fire hoses that would not burst under pressure. Later, he went on to found the B.F. Goodrich Corporation, a rubber company, in Akron, Ohio. In 1895, the company developed a tire for use on automobiles. From this, the company quickly rose to become a leader in the rubber industry.

Amos Tyler / William Semple. In 1869, Amos Tyler, a Toledo resident, patented chewing gum. Tyler never sold his gum commercially. A Mount Vernon Ohio dentist, William Semple, make his chewing gum out of rubber. Semple believed the licorice root and charcoal he added to the gum would help to keep a person's teeth clean.

Granville Woods. Born in Columbus, Ohio, in 1856, Granville is sometimes referred to as the "Black Edison." He had close to 60 patents, including a telephone transmitter, a trolley wheel, and the multiplex telegraph, which allowed people to communicate orally over telegraph wires. As an electrician, Woods invented 15 appliances for electrified railways.

Granville Woods

John William Lambert. Lambert was born in 1860, in Ohio City, Ohio. He is credited with building the first gasoline-powered, single-cylinder automobile in 1890. His car, a three-wheeled motor car, could reach speeds of up to 5 miles per hour. Later, Lambert produced four-wheel cars at his Buckeye Manufacturing plant.

Charles R. Richter. He was born in Overpeck, Ohio in 1900. In 1935, while working at the California Institute of Technology, Richter developed the "Richter Scale" to measure the size of earthquakes. The Richter Scale uses whole numbers and decimal fractions to show the strength of an earthquake. It is in wide use today. Richter also mapped out areas that he believed were prone to earthquakes, although he denied that earthquakes could be accurately predicted.

Roy J. Plunkett. Born in New Carlisle, Ohio, in 1910, Plunkett discovered Teflon as a result of an experiment gone wrong. In 1938, Plunkett found a mysterious white powder left over from his refrigeration gas experiment resisted heat but remained as slippery as ice. Rather than toss the powder away, he tested it to discover some of its unique properties. In the 1960s, Teflon began to appear as a miraculous non-stick surface for cookware. It is nearly impossible to set a value to his contribution to science, industry, and society.

Roy J. Plunkett

Murray Spangler. Born in Pennsylvania in 1848, Spangler settled in Stark County, Ohio. While working as a janitor in an Ohio department store, he developed a cough. Spangler soon came to realize that the cough was caused by the carpet sweeper he used on the job. In 1907, Spangler attached a soap box to a old fan motor, and fastened it to a broom handle. He used a pillow case as a dust collector. His portable vacuum cleaner became the first to use a cloth filter bag and cleaning attachments.

Albert Sabin. Albert Sabin was born in 1906 in Poland. In 1939, he took a position at Cincinnati Children's Hospital, where he remained for the next thirty years. While at the hospital, Dr. Sabin developed a vaccine that eliminated the possibility that someone could transmit the polio virus. His vaccine could also be taken orally, making it easy to administer. Sabin also developed vaccines against such diseases as encephalitis, an inflammation of the brain.

One of the first vacuum cleaners ever made.

Which of these individuals has your group nominated to Ohio's Hall of Fame? Explain your group's choice.

_____

_____

RESEARCHING YOUR NOMINEE

You and members of your group can find more about your nominee using a variety of sources.

REFERENCE BOOKS

Reference books are books with factual information on many topics. There are many kinds of reference books, such as encyclopedias, dictionaries, almanacs and atlases. Reference books are usually found in the "Reference" section of the library.

Encyclopedias, like *The World Book*, have articles about well-known people arranged in alphabetical order. An encyclopedia usually has guide words or letters on the spine of each volume. These guide words help you to locate the idea or name of the person you are looking for.

Some other reference books that might help you find information include:

- *Builders of Ohio: A Biographical History* by Warren R. Vantine, editor
- *Ohio Biographical Dictionary: People of All Times and All Places Who Have Been Important to the History and Life of the State*

BIOGRAPHIES AND AUTOBIOGRAPHIES

Biographies. A **biography** is a book about a person's life and achievements. Some Ohio biographies include:

- *Thomas Edison: Young Inventor* by Sue Guthridge
- *The Wright Brothers for Kids: How They Invented the Airplane* by Mary Kay Carson and Laura D'Argo
- *Charles Kettering: A Biography* by Thomas Alvin Boyd

Autobiographies. Sometimes a person writes a book about his or her own life. This kind of book is called an **autobiography**.

Most libraries have entire sections devoted to biographies and autobiographies. Biographies and autobiographies are listed in alphabetical order by the last name of the person the book is about. For example, a biography of Paul Lawrence Dunbar by Gossie Harold Hudson would be under the letter "D" for Dunbar, not the letter "H."

THE INTERNET

As you know, there are millions of websites on the Internet. That means there are billions of web pages. How is it possible to sort through all this information easily and quickly?

Soon after the development of the worldwide web on the Internet, searching for information became a major concern. Companies such as **Google**, **Bing**, **AOL**, and **Yahoo** offered their own search engines. These search engines played a critical role in helping people to search the Internet.

The Search Engine. A search engine is a program that searches the Internet by using one or more key words or search terms. After the search is performed, the program returns a list of results. All search engines have an indexing device that allows you to sort pages quickly. Search engines are able to produce results in a mere fraction of a second. One of the most frequently used search engines is Google.

To see how this works, carry out a search for your nominee using Google's home page. Here is what you might find:

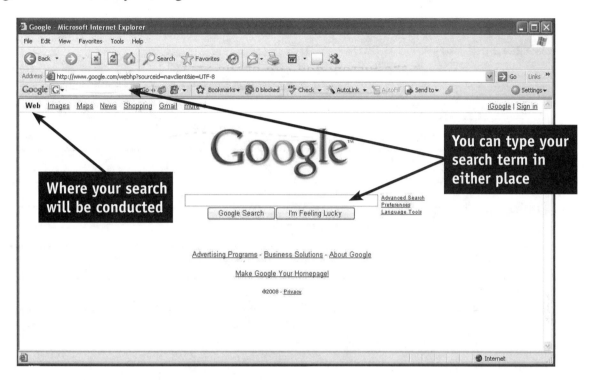

Enter Your Search Term. For the next part of your search, you must enter your search term into the blank window. A **search term** consists of a keyword or words that identify or describe the information you hope to find. Make your search terms as specific and focused as you can. For example, suppose you are searching for your nominee to the Ohio Inventor's Hall of Fame. Enter the person's name in the Google search window. Your search will provide thousands of results, in a fraction of a second.

Search engines are pretty advanced — some of them will even suggest corrections if you misspell a term or name in the search window. But search engines have no way of telling what you mean if a word has multiple meanings or can be interpreted in different ways. After you have completed your search, complete the following form to help focus your investigation. Complete a copy for each of the two candidates your group is considering as its nominee.

Some other websites you might want to consult are:

■ www.ohiohistorycentral.org

■ www.sos.state.oh.us/SOS/ProfileOhio/OhioTechnology.aspx

■ http://inventors.about.com/od/americaninventors/qt/Ohio.htm

NAME OF YOUR NOMINEE:

_____

- A brief summary of the person's life: _____

_____

_____

_____

_____

- The person's major inventions or accomplishments: _____

_____

_____

_____

_____

- What source did you use? Identify one source of information you consulted.

_____

_____

WHO WILL YOUR NOMINEE BE?

After your group has completed its research, it must come to a decision: Which of the people your group researched best meets the group's criteria for inclusion in the Ohio Inventor's Hall of Fame? Once you have selected a nominee, each group member should write a letter to the imaginary Hall of Fame. The letter should describe the nominee and explain why he or she should be admitted into the Hall of Fame.

After the members of your group have finished their letters, pass them around your group to read. The group should select one letter to be read to the entire class. When all the groups have finished choosing one letter, your teacher should bring the class together to listen to the letters. A member of each group should read the letter the group has chosen. When one letter has been read from each group, the class should vote on which nominee to admit to the Ohio Inventors Hall of Fame.

MAKING CONNECTIONS

USING A GLOSSARY OR BIOGRAPHICAL DICTIONARY

Some books end with a glossary. A **glossary** defines or identifies important words or terms mentioned in the book. A **biographical dictionary** usually identifies people. Both list their entries in alphabetical order. Examine part of the biographical dictionary below from a book about women in Ohio history. Then answer the questions that follow:

Mary Ann Ball Bickerdyke (1817–1901). Born in Knox County, Ohio. As a member of General Grant's staff, she established hospitals for wounded soldiers during the Civil War.

Hallie Quinn Brown (1849–1949). Born in Pennsylvania. She served as President of the Ohio State Federation and the National Association of Colored Women.

Eliza Bryant (1827–1907). Born in North Carolina. A reformer who worked in Cleveland to establish societies to support elderly African Americans. She established the Home for Aged Colored People.

Alice Carie (1820–1871). Born in Mt. Healthy, Ohio. In 1869, she founded the Sorority of Sisters, a club for women. Its purpose was to gain greater rights for women.

Victoria Claflin (1838–1927). Born in Homer, Ohio. In 1872, the Equal Rights Party nominated her to become the first woman to run for U.S. President. She lost to Ulysses S. Grant.

Frances Dana Gage (1808–1884). Born in Marietta, Ohio. She was a leader in the Temperance Movement, the Women's Rights Movement, and the anti-slavery crusade.

Annie Oakley (1860–1926). Born in Patterson, Ohio. A sharpshooter with Buffalo Bill's Wild West Show, she could hit a dime in the air with a rifle shot from 90 feet away.

Alice Schille (1869–1955). Born in Columbus, Ohio. Critics viewed her as one of the best American painters. Some of her most notable watercolors include "Mother and Child in a Garden," "Storytime," and "Poplars."

CHECKING YOUR UNDERSTANDING

1 How are the names in this glossary arranged? _____

2 Name two women who worked for greater rights for women in Ohio:

   A _____   **B** _____

3 Who was the first woman to run for President of the United States?

   _____

STUDY CARDS

Thomas Edison

- What were some of Edison's most important inventions? _Thomas Edison's most important inventions were the lightbulb, phonograph, and the printing telegraph._

- Why were Edison's inventions of such importance to the world? _Edison's inventions changed the world by giving I brghte future._

Orville and Wilbur Wright

- What did the Wright brothers do that helped changed the world? _They built a better airplane._

- Do the Wright Brothers deserve all the credit they have received? _Yes because thy did something that changes the world_

How Research Tools Help You Gather Information

- Reference Books: _are factual information on many topics._

- Biography/Autobiography: _is a book about a persons life and achievements._

- Glossary: _defines all the or identifies most important terms in a book._

Name _____

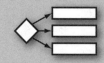

LEARNING WITH GRAPHIC ORGANIZERS

Directions: Complete the graphic organizer below by identifying an important invention of the person indicated, and how it benefitted the United States.

Thomas A. Edison: _Lightbulb_

Benefits: _It gave eletric like light_ _unlik cundles, It gave us_ _real light that we can use._

Garrett A. Morgan: _____

Benefits: _____

James Ritty: _____

Benefits: _____

Orville and Wilbur Wright: _Airplane_

Benefits: _Stoped us from crashing_ _so much. They made improvements_ _to the old airplne._

Leading Ohio Inventors

Charles Kettering: _eletric cas_ _register automobia_

Benefits: _____

Thomas Midgley, Jr.: _____

Benefits: _____

EXPRESS YOURSELF

The inventors born and raised in Ohio have made enormous contributions to the United States. They have changed people's lives and contributed to the growth of the nation.

Write a short essay explaining how innovations from Ohio have benefitted the United States. For more information you might want to consult the website: www.oplin.org/famousohioans/inventors/puzzler.html

Name _____

UNIT 3

GOVERNMENT

Ohio's State Capitol, Columbus.

Interior of Ohio's Statehouse. Columbus.

Edward Tiffin, Ohio's first governor.

A government protects its citizens by setting up and enforcing rules for them to live by. When your teacher establishes rules for your class, your teacher is actually acting as a kind of government. In this unit, you will learn about your national and state government.

ACTIVITY 3A

HOW WOULD YOU DEFINE A "GOOD" CITIZEN?

■ Individuals have a variety of opportunities to participate in and influence their state and national government. Citizens have both rights and responsibilities in Ohio and the United States.

In this activity, you will learn how to conduct a survey. You will also learn about some of the duties and responsibilities of a good citizen.

KEY TERMS

- ■ Citizen
- ■ Right
- ■ Privilege
- ■ First Amendment
- ■ Duties
- ■ Responsibilities

WHAT IS CITIZENSHIP?

A **citizen** is a member of a particular nation. The idea of citizenship can be traced back to ancient Greece and Rome. In modern times, every nation has developed its own rules to define citizenship.

You are an American citizen if you were born here or if your parents were American citizens at the time of your birth, even if you were born outside the United States. People who were not born here and whose parents are not citizens can become American citizens. To become a citizen, a person must live in the United States for a number of years and pass a citizenship test. People who become citizens in this way are called **naturalized citizens**.

Individuals being sworn in as naturalized U.S. citizens.

WHAT MAKES SOMEONE A GOOD CITIZEN?

Now that you know what a citizen is, what makes someone a "good" citizen?

THINK ABOUT IT

Let's start by exploring your own ideas. What do you think makes someone a "good" citizen?

_____

_____

Would adults in your community agree with your answer? Let's find out. In this activity, you will speak with two adults to see how they define a "good" citizen.

CONDUCTING A SURVEY

The purpose of an **opinion poll** is to find out what people think about a topic or issue. Opinion polls provide a sample of how people feel about a particular issue. In this poll, you will find out how two adults in your community define a "good" citizen. Remember, there are no right or wrong answers in a survey.

After you finish, thank your volunteer for his or her help.

GETTING STARTED

To conduct your opinion poll, ask your parent to recommend two adults willing to participate in your opinion poll. One of these might be your parent, relative or a neighbor. After you select your two volunteers, begin by reading the following statement to each adult:

For a school project, I am polling two adults to find their opinion to the question: "How would you define a good citizen?"

COLLECTING DATA AND COMPARING ANSWERS

Complete the sheet below to record the answers provided by your two volunteers. A **respondent** is someone who responds to your questions.

HOW WOULD YOU DEFINE A GOOD CITIZEN?
First Respondent's Answer: _____   _____   _____   _____   **Second Respondent's Answer:** _____   _____   _____   _____

After your sheet is completed, share your answers with your classmates. After each student has reported his or her results, the class should select those answers your class believes represent the best definition of what a "good" citizen has.

HOW EXPERTS DEFINE GOOD CITIZENSHIP

How does your classmates' definition of a good citizen compare with ones provided by experts? The following are qualities most experts believe a "good" citizen has.

■ **Respectful.** Good citizens treat others with respect, even when they disagree with other people's opinions. They are polite and courteous to others' viewpoints.

■ **Civic-Minded.** Good citizens give their time and money to help improve their community. They are concerned and are active in community affairs.

■ **Responsible.** Good citizens are responsible for their actions. They show self control and follow their community's rules. They keep their promises and are willing to pay the penalty when they do something wrong.

■ **Open-Minded.** Good citizens listen to others' opinions and can sometimes be persuaded to change their minds. Good citizens will compromise to solve problems. They accept others with different customs and ways of living.

THINK ABOUT IT

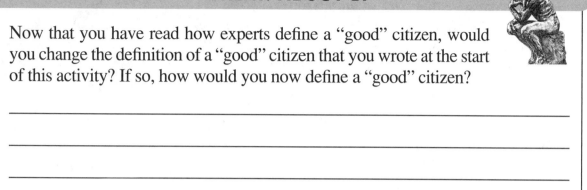

Now that you have read how experts define a "good" citizen, would you change the definition of a "good" citizen that you wrote at the start of this activity? If so, how would you now define a "good" citizen?

_____

_____

_____

THE RIGHTS AND RESPONSIBILITIES OF A GOOD CITIZEN

RIGHTS OF A CITIZEN

A **right** is something that everyone in a society is entitled to or permitted to do. All U.S. citizens enjoy certain rights. For example, every American has the right to freely practice his or her own religion. This right is protected by the U.S. Constitution. It cannot be denied to anyone by the government.

A right is different from a **privilege**. A right is something you are born with. You don't need permission to exercise a right. A privilege is granted to you by the government and may be taken away. It is an advantage that some have and others don't. For example, you have a right to live, but you do not have a right to drive a car.

As a student, you also have the right to be treated fairly and with respect. You have the right to attend school in a classroom that is orderly and safe. In addition, as a student you have the right to be encouraged and challenged to do your best. You have the right to eat lunch in school when everyone else eats lunch. However, it is a privilege to sit at a particular table with your friends and eat lunch.

Throughout history, there have been leaders in government who have wanted to stay in power. These leaders feared anyone who spoke out against their policies. They thought that if they allowed such criticism, others might start to agree with these critics. That is why some leaders punish and silence those who try to speak out against them.

The authors of the U.S. Constitution wanted to make sure that American citizens would be protected from possible abuses by those who held government power. The U.S. Constitution came up with several ways to prevent government from abusing its many powers.

One of the most important of these was a set of ten amendments, or additions to the U.S. Constitution, known as the **Bill of Rights**. The **First Amendment** guarantees our personal freedoms from government interference — freedom of religion, freedom of the press, freedom of speech, and freedom to gather together with others. Here is what the First Amendment says:

> **Congress shall make no law respecting an establishment of religion, or prohibiting the free exercise thereof; or abridging (*reducing*) the freedom of speech, or of the press; or the right of the people peaceably to assemble, and to petition the Government for a redress (*remedy*) of grievances.**

CHECKING YOUR UNDERSTANDING

- In your own words, describe what this amendment says. _____

    _____

    _____

    _____

    _____

- Which rights does it guarantee to citizens of the United States? _____

    _____

    _____

THE OBLIGATIONS OF A CITIZEN

Along with these rights of a citizen of the United States come certain duties.

Duties are the "musts" of citizenship — things that the law says you must do. If you refuse to perform your duty, you may have to pay a fine or even go to jail.

Obey the laws of local, state and federal government	Pay taxes to support the costs of government

DUTIES OF A CITIZEN

Serve on a jury if called upon	Attend school to get an education
Defend the nation by serving in the armed forces if called upon	Testify in a court of law if called upon to present evidence

RESPONSIBILITIES OF A CITIZEN

Citizens of the United States have several additional responsibilities. **Responsibilities** are the "shoulds" of citizenship. A citizen is not punished for failing to meet a responsibility, but each responsibility is something that a good citizen would normally do.

The success of our democracy depends on people acting in a responsible way. For example, responsible students attend school and try their hardest to learn. Being responsible means doing the right thing. A responsible person respects other students and listens to what they have to say. In so doing we learn that everyone has something to offer.

Stay informed about the activities of your local, state and national government	

RESPONSIBILITIES OF A CITIZEN

Vote in local, state and national elections	Participate in local events
Inform elected representatives about your issues of concern	Serve in government if elected or appointed
Join a political party or act as an independent voter	Help enforce laws by cooperating with the police

Although many of these responsibilities do not apply to students, there are ways you can act as a "good" citizens too. You can volunteer to participate in your community by working with others to clean up a vacant lot. You can visit hospitals or senior centers and talk with someone who simply needs a friend. You can offer to help a sick neighbor, or mow a lawn or shovel a driveway for an elderly person. By volunteering and helping others, a student can show a sense of responsibility as well as feel good about himself or herself.

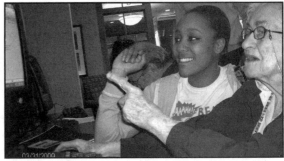
A student volunteer visits a nursing a home.

THINK ABOUT IT

Now that you have finished learning about the duties and responsibilities of good citizenship, would you call yourself a "good" citizen? Explain why or why not.

_____

_____

_____

_____

_____

MAKING CONNECTIONS

CREATING A "GOOD" CITIZEN SCRAPBOOK

Have you ever read a newspaper story about a person who rushed into a burning building to save someone else? Or a flight attendant who helped people evacuate from a plane crash before saving himself or herself? Most people would agree that that person was performing an act of bravery. In addition, he or she was also acting as a "good" citizen.

Name _____

Your daily newspaper or magazine often features stories about people who are outstanding citizens. Some of these citizens may commit acts of bravery. Others may donate large sums of money or volunteer their time to a good cause.

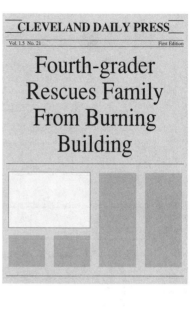

CLEVELAND DAILY PRESS

Vol. 1.5 No. 21   First Edition

Fourth-grader Rescues Family From Burning Building

Let's look at some examples of "good" citizenship. To do this, you will need to create a **scrapbook** of "good" citizenship. A scrapbook is similar to a photo album. It is a personalized, hand-made work that focuses on a specific topic. Your scrapbook will have stories from your local newspaper or ones you found on the Internet.

- Over the next few weeks, locate and cut out at least two articles that deal in some manner with an act of "good" citizenship.
- Paste each article into your "Good Citizen Scrapbook" that you created for this activity.
- Write a brief summary about each of the articles in your scrapbook. In your summary, be sure to explain why you think the person displays characteristics that exhibit "good" citizenship.
- Create a unique cover for your scrapbook. Your cover might use tinfoil or glue on a picture. Or you could cover it in paper and create your own illustration. Your cover may be as simple or elaborate as you desire. Remember, it's all up to you!

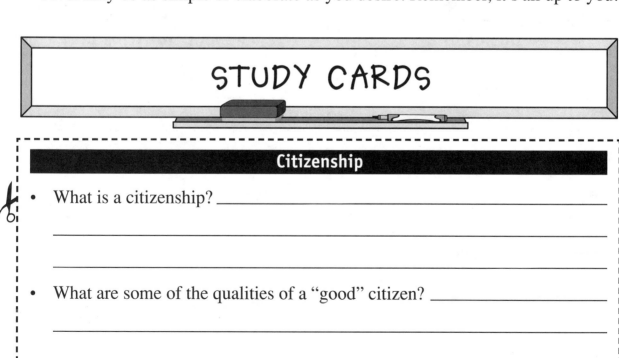

STUDY CARDS

Citizenship

- What is a citizenship? _____

_____

_____

- What are some of the qualities of a "good" citizen? _____

_____

_____

First Amendment

What rights are protected by the First Amendment to the U.S. Constitution?

1 _____

2 _____

3 _____

4 _____

5 _____

 # LEARNING WITH GRAPHIC ORGANIZERS

Directions: Complete the graphic organizer below about citizenship.

Citizenship

Duties of a "Good" Citizen:

_____

_____

_____

_____

_____

_____

_____

Responsibilities of a "Good" Citizen:

_____

_____

_____

_____

_____

_____

_____

EXPRESS YOURSELF

Dr. Carl Sagan, a famous scientist, once said, "I wish that the Pledge of Allegiance were directed at the U.S. Constitution and Bill of Rights rather than to the flag and the nation." What do you think Dr. Sagan meant by this? Do you agree or disagree with his statement. Explain your answer.

HOW DO PEOPLE INFLUENCE THEIR STATE AND NATIONAL GOVERNMENTS?

■ Individuals have a variety of opportunities to participate in and influence their state and national government. Citizens have both rights and responsibilities in Ohio and the United States.

In this activity, you will explore some of the ways citizens influence their state and national governments. After completing this activity, you will be able to explain how by participating in elections people influence their leaders and decide issues. You will also be able to describe some of the ways in which citizens promote the common good and participate in their government.

KEY TERMS

- ■ Democracy
- ■ Representative Democracy
- ■ Will of the People
- ■ Common Good

- ■ Majority Rule
- ■ Minority Rights
- ■ Candidates
- ■ Political Party

- ■ Election Day
- ■ Voting
- ■ Constituent
- ■ Line Graph

Imagine that your school is holding a contest. Fourth grade students are asked to see who can create the best poster on the theme:

How people influence their state and national governments.

POSTER GUIDELINES

Your teacher announces the guidelines for the poster contest:

> **Students must create a poster about
> how people influence their state and national governments.**
>
> ■ The poster should illustrate the actions that people take to influence their state and national governments. The focus of the poster must be on that theme.
>
> ■ The poster should include at least three illustrations. These illustrations can be pictures from newspapers, magazines, the Internet or your own drawings. Remember, creativity is more important than artistic talent.
>
> ■ Winning posters will be displayed in the school library, the local public library, and in store windows throughout the community.

After hearing the guidelines, you become excited by the contest and think it would be a lot of fun to enter the contest. However, you soon realize that you need more background information before you can create your poster.

After school, you decide to pay a visit to your school library to learn about the theme of the contest. You ask your school librarian for more details. The librarian gives you some books. Here is what you find in looking through these books:

INFLUENCING YOUR GOVERNMENT

The United States and all 50 state governments are democracies. A **democracy** is a form of government in which the real power of government is in the hands of its citizens. This means that the people are the highest form of authority.

In a **representative democracy**, voters elect their own "representatives" as government leaders. These representatives make decisions for the people based on the **will of the people** they represent. Power flows from the people to the leaders of government, who only hold power temporarily. The key advantage is that people are free to live their lives without having to vote on every issue that comes up.

CHARACTERISTICS OF DEMOCRACY

The most basic principle of democratic government is the belief that final power rests with the people. This idea is reflected in the first words of the U.S. Constitution: "We the people …"

■ **Free to Speak Your Mind.** In a democracy, people are free to express their opinions, to speak freely with one another, and to exchange ideas. They are free to criticize their elected leaders and representatives.

■ **Promote the Common Good.** People are able to promote the common good and to influence their government in a number of different ways. The **common good** is

The United States is admired around the world for the democratic rights its people enjoy.

working towards what will benefit the community as a whole. The root of the common good is that citizens will devote their time and energy to public causes and will contribute to bettering society. This is done by attending town meetings, volunteering, and participating in elections.

■ **Majority Rule.** In a democracy, decisions are made by **majority rule**. A majority is more than half of the voters who participate in an election.

■ **Minority Rights.** People have the right to disagree. A democracy protects the **rights of the minority**. The minority is made up of those people who disagree with the majority on an issue. Regardless of decisions by the majority, they cannot violate the rights of the minority.

THINK ABOUT IT

Which feature of democracy do you think is the most important?

_____

_____

_____

THE ROLE OF ELECTIONS

Citizens express their will by voting in elections. Elections either select government officials and representatives, or they decide on key issues.

In an election of government officials or representatives, different people — known as **candidates** — offer to serve. Candidates explain their ideas to voters during a campaign. Each candidate is helped by a **political party** — a group of people with similar beliefs. On **election day**, voters casts their ballot. The candidate with the most votes wins. In a democracy, elections are used as a fair and peaceful way for people to present their views. Elections allow the majority of people to decide what to do.

Sometimes, voters in state and national elections also decide issues. For example, voters may be asked to decide if local taxes should be increased. On election day, voters will vote either "yes" or "no" on the issue. The majority vote decides if the tax increase is adopted or not.

In societies without elections, a king or dictator usually tells other people what to do. Ordinary citizens are not consulted and have no rights. Citizens have only those freedoms that the king or dictator allows.

WAYS CITIZENS INFLUENCE GOVERNMENT

In a democracy, there are several ways citizens can get actively involved in influencing their government. This is what makes a democracy work. Here are some of the ways people in a democracy can help promote the common good and influence their state and national governments.

VOTING, CAMPAIGNING, AND RUNNING FOR OFFICE

Voting is a basic right of a democracy. When citizens vote it is their opportunity to be heard, to hold government officials accountable for their decisions. On Election Day, every vote matters. Voting gives a person a voice in who will be the next President or leader of the state or community. It is the single most effective way for a citizen to make his or her voice be heard. When citizens choose not to vote, they give away their right to influence their national or state government. You can also volunteer to help in an election campaign. Another way to participate is to run for an elected office. Citizens can run to become representatives in local, state, or the federal government. You can also run for office in a community organization or encourage a parent to run for the school board.

COMMUNICATING WITH OFFICIALS

In the United States, your voice is important. Elected officials are responsible for making sure that our laws represent the wishes of the majority of people. The most direct way of expressing your wishes is by voting. You also have the right to voice your opinion any time you wish. Letting your officials know your views on issues lets them know you are keeping track of their votes and encourages them to vote your way.

Citizens express their views to their elected representative.

Direct Meeting. The best way is to meet directly with your state or national representative. Meeting directly with your representative is the "purest form of democracy," since you are participating directly in making laws and raising issues. Meeting with members of Congress or their staff is an excellent way for citizens to communicate directly with policymakers. Through these visits, you can educate your representative about what concerns you and establish a relationship that can prove helpful in the future.

A group of voters meet directly with their elected representative in Washington, D.C.

Write a Letter. Often it's not possible to travel to Washington, D.C. or to a state representative's office. It might be difficult or too costly to travel to have such a meeting. In those cases, there are several useful alternatives to communicating with your representatives. A letter is often the most effective way to contact an elected official. A letter often provides an excellent way to tell your government representatives how you think they should vote on a particular issue, and explain how a particular issue affects people back home. Representatives enjoy hearing from their **constituents** — the people in their district.

Make a Telephone Call. Your representative wants to hear from people in his or her district. You can call your elected official's office and leave a telephone message. Every federal, state and local government office has a telephone number to allow the public to contact it. Your elected official's telephone number can be found by using websites like **usa.gov**. The White House, for example, has a public switchboard and a message line that allows citizens to leave a recorded message. When calling an elected official, it is rare that you will speak to them directly, but you can expect to leave a brief message with an assistant.

Use the Internet to Send an Email. You can use the Internet to find an official's email address and send an email. Most government officials today have an email address. The addresses of federal government representatives, including the President, can be found by looking up **USA.gov** or **whitehouse.gov**. Your state or local officials can be found by using such sites like **statelocalgov.net**.

THINK ABOUT IT

Have you or your parents ever communicated with a public official? _____ If so, ask your parents to explain the circumstances of that communication.

_____

_____

_____

_____

PARTICIPATING IN CIVIC AND SERVICE ORGANIZATIONS

Another way to influence your government is by participating in the community through volunteer service. In 2011, the number of volunteers in civic and service organizations reached its highest level in five years. More than 64 million Americans volunteered in some sort of an organization.

Students participate in cleaning up their neighborhood.

Many of these organizations attempt to influence government leaders. They may picket an elected official's office, hold a sit-in at a representative's office, or gather signatures for a petition on a specific issue. Some organizations also educate officials about issues that are important to the group. Such organizations may hold a "door-knocking" campaign to pressure representatives to follow a particular point of view.

THINK ABOUT IT

There are many other ways for citizens to influence their state or national governments. Can you think of any other ways a person can influence their elected state or national representatives?

_____

_____

_____

AND THE WINNING POSTER IS ...

Now that you know how you can influence your local, state or national government, you need to decide how you are going to design your poster.

On the day that posters are due in class, all of the posters should be exhibited around the room. Students should take turns examining each other's posters. Each poster should be judged by a small committee of students selected by your teacher. The committee should narrow down all the posters to the five best ones. A vote should be held by the class to determine which is best.

THINK ABOUT IT

What features did the winning poster have that made it best?

_____

_____

_____

MAKING CONNECTIONS

HOW MANY AMERICANS VOTE IN ELECTIONS?

Are Americans taking their voting responsibility seriously? **Line graphs** are used to show how something has changed over time. A line graph is made up of a series of points connected by a line.

The line graph below provides some answers as to whether Americans are taking their responsibility to vote seriously.

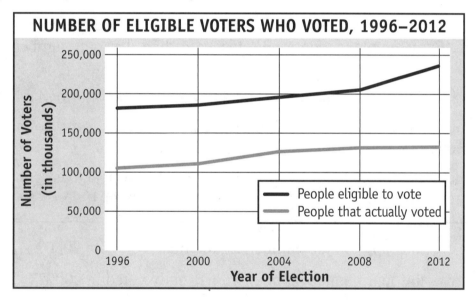

Before we analyze this line graph, let's examine how to "read" line graphs in general:

THE TITLE

The title of the line graph tells you the kind of information it presents. In this line graph, the title is *Number of Eligible Voters Who Voted, 1996–2012*. Based on the title, this line graph will provide information about the way eligible Americans voted in the years from 1996 to 2012.

THE VERTICAL AND HORIZONTAL AXIS

Line graphs have a **vertical axis** or line, which usually runs long the left side from the top of the line graph to the bottom. They also have a **horizontal axis**, which usually runs along the bottom from the left to the right. Each axis on the line graph is labeled.

- In this graph, what does the vertical axis show? _____

  _____

- What does the horizontal axis show? _____

  _____

INTERPRETING A LINE GRAPH

If a line graph has more than one line, a legend is often needed. Like the legend of a map, the legend of a line graph shows what each line represents. Here, you can see the legend on the right side of the graph. It tells us that the top line of the graph shows the "people eligible to vote."

You can use the legend and the location of the lines on the graph to find specific information. For example, suppose you wished to find the total number of Americans eligible to vote in 1996.

■ To find the answer, go to the horizontal axis and find the year marked "1996."

■ Next, run your finger up the "1996" line, until you reach the point where the "People eligible to vote" line crosses the "1996" line.

■ Then, slide your finger to the left until it reaches the vertical axis. You should see that about 180 million Americans were eligible to vote in 1996.

- What was the approximate number of American voters in 2000? _____

- What was the approximate number who actually voted in 2000? _____

- What year saw the greatest difference between the total number of eligible

  voters and the number of people who actually voted? _____

- What conclusion can you draw from this line graph about whether Americans take their responsibility to vote seriously?

  _____

  _____

  _____

  _____

  _____

STUDY CARDS

Democracy

- What is a democracy? _____

  _____

  _____

- What is the difference between democracy and a representative democracy?

  _____

  _____

  _____

Characteristics of Democracy

What are the main characteristics of democracy?

_____

_____

_____

_____

_____

_____

Voting

How is voting an effective tool for people to influence their elected representatives?

_____

_____

_____

_____

_____

_____

LEARNING WITH GRAPHIC ORGANIZERS

Directions: Complete the graphic organizer below by explaining the various ways that citizens can influence their elected representatives.

Ways Citizens Can Influence Their Government Officials

EXPRESS YOURSELF

Imagine that your street has a large pot-hole. Cars that drive down your street keep hitting the pothole. Some of these cars actually suffer damage. If left unchecked, the pothole can also become an issue for those who ride bikes, motorcycles or scooters. To put a stop to this situation, you decide to write the mayor of your city. You wish to make the mayor aware of this troubling pothole.

When writing a letter, you should keep the following hints in mind:

■ **Write Neatly and Legibly.** If you handwrite your letter, make sure your writing is clear, neat, and readable. If someone cannot read what you wrote, they will often not read your letter.

■ **Get the Name Right.** Be sure that you address the recipient of your letter in a respectful way. You should open the letter in an official manner using such terms as Dear, Mr., Ms., or Dr. and the official's full name.

■ **Explain the Purpose of your Letter.** Let the reader know immediately, in the first paragraph, what your letter concerns. Tell the mayor why your are concerned about the pothole on your street.

■ **Explain your Position.** Using as much detail as you can, describe why you feel the situation presents a safety hazard and must be repaired before someone is seriously injured.

■ **Describe What Action you Want.** State specifically what action you want the official to take. Indicate the time period you feel the repair should take. For example, in the next week or two.

■ **Close Your Letter.** Thank the official and sign your name in full. Make sure your address and telephone number are included in your letter. Check that your spelling and grammar are correct.

■ **Show It to Someone Before Mailing.** "Two heads are better than one." It will help if you show your letter to an adult or relative to review. Ask if he or she might make some suggestions to improve or strengthen your letter.

Name _____

ACTIVITY 3C

HOW CAN INFORMATION BE USED EFFECTIVELY TO MAKE AN INFORMED DECISION?

■ Civic participation requires individuals to make informed and reasoned decisions by accessing and using information effectively.

A successful democracy requires its citizens to make informed and reasoned decisions about public issues. Citizens need to use both print and electronic resources to evaluate information. In this activity, you will learn how to use these resources to obtain and evaluate information on a public issue. After completing this activity, you will know how to make an informed decision based on a variety of sources.

KEY TERMS

- Petition
- Newspaper Editorials
- Electronic Sources
- Internet
- Websites
- Web Pages
- Hyperlinks
- Internet Search
- Problem-solving

One evening at dinner, you are busy telling your parent what you have learned in school about good citizenship and problem solving. Just then, the doorbell rings. It is your next door neighbor, Mr. Smith, holding pamphlets and a petition.

Mr. Smith tells your parent that a **petition** is a demand for action sent to a government official. He then reads the petition. It states that the violence shown on television is a major reason for the rise in violence throughout your community. The petition concludes:

We the undersigned believe that Congress should pass a new law limiting the amount of violence shown on television.

Signatures	Signatures	Signatures
Robert Adams	Sally Tinsley	Kathleen Martin
Gary Freno	Michael Sampson	Vickie Abrams
Mary Jordan	Elizabeth Thorpe	Thomas Drew II

Your neighbor asks your parent to sign the petition. By signing the petition, citizens show that they support whatever action it demands.

Your parent tells Mr. Smith, "This is an important issue. Before I make a decision about whether or not I will sign the petition, I would like a little more time to learn more about it."

After Mr. Smith leaves, your parent says to you: "I really don't know enough about this issue to make an informed decision. You said at dinner that in school you recently learned how to use both print and electronic resources to find out about an issue. I have a great idea that would help both of us. Why don't you describe what you learned about how to gather information about an issue to help me make an informed decision?"

FOCUSING ON YOUR ISSUE

You agree to help your parent. You explain that the first step is one of the most important. The topic should not be so large that you cannot describe or explain it fully. Often it helps if you think of your topic as a specific question you wish to answer. To decide whether to sign the petition, you might focus on this question:

> *Should the government limit the amount of violence shown on television?*

PRINT RESOURCES

Next you need to gather information. This process requires you to do some research or investigation about your issue. Let's first focus on traditional, printed resources. You might look at reference books, such as encyclopedias and almanacs. **Reference books** are generally used to confirm facts and other information. You might also look at newspapers, magazines, and books.

BOOKS

You begin by looking at page 123 of your first source of information: a book. The title of the book is *The History of Television* (2006) by John Morris. Here is what you find in the book:

The History of Television   123

The first television broadcasts began in the 1930s. The introduction of television raised an important question: Should television stations be run by the government or by private companies? In some countries, the government runs the television channels. In the United States, private companies run the television channels.

Americans have a tradition of free speech and a free press. The government cannot tell TV companies what to show. However, the government does have the power to refuse to allow certain shows to be aired, especially if they are dangerous. It rarely uses this right. Many people think the government should use this right more often, especially to limit violence on television. They propose that the government should rate television shows for violence. This is already done by the film industry. Others say America would have better programs if the government ran the television stations.

CHECKING YOUR UNDERSTANDING

What information about your issue did you learn from reading this page from the book, *The History of Television*?

1 In some countries, the government runs television stations.

2 In the United States, private companies run television stations.

3 _____

_____

_____

_____

4 _____

_____

_____

_____

A NEWSPAPER ARTICLE

The next source of information you find on this issue is a newspaper article:

The Cleveland Daily

June 2, 2014   Page 3

TWO TEENS DIE IN HIGHWAY "DARE"
by Jim Marks

It all began as a joke. On Thursday night, Channel 3 was showing the latest action-adventure picture. In the movie, several teenagers lie down on the center-divider line of a highway to show their friends that they are not afraid.

After watching the movie, teenagers living near Toledo began daring each other to lie down on the center line just as the teenagers in the movie had done. Two teenagers took the dare. They are now dead, run over by a motorist who did not see them in the dark.

This is part of a growing number of violent, senseless deaths in America. Movies and television shows often influence us. Sometimes we imitate what we see, as these teenagers did. Other times, we are influenced without even knowing it.

Parents, teachers and doctors are alarmed at the increasing violence on television. Children watching television see thousands of acts of violence before they are old enough to go to school. Cartoons often show violence between the characters. Some experts believe television violence may be partly responsible for the increasing violence in America. They are demanding a new law banning all television violence before 10 o'clock at night.

CHECKING YOUR UNDERSTANDING

• What happened to the two teenagers discussed in the newspaper article?

_____

_____

• What does this newspaper story tell you about violence on television?

_____

_____

NEWSPAPER EDITORIAL

Newspaper editorials express opinions on issues. They appear in newspapers and magazines. They are not news articles that report facts. Instead, editorials state the views of the editors of the newspaper. Their purpose is to persuade their readers.

The Akron Times

January 29, 2014   Page 38

OUR VIEW OF TELEVISION VIOLENCE

A growing number of people are seeking a new law to limit the violence shown on television. Have these people carefully thought about the issue? They think that violence on television is the main cause of violence in America. But poverty and the large number of guns are the main causes of violence, not what is shown on a television screen.

Have these people thought about the dangers of government control? Who in government will decide which programs are violent and which are not? Will the government also prevent television stations from reporting violent news stories? Once government controls some subjects on television, it will try to control others. Soon, they will control everything we see. This could violate our rights of free speech and a free press.

We believe it is better to let private television stations show what they want. Parents should decide what their children watch. If parents don't want their children to watch a show because it is violent, there is a simple remedy—change the channel or turn off the set! If government controls what we can watch, where will government controls end? A growing number of people are seeking a new law

CHECKING YOUR UNDERSTANDING

- What stand does this editorial take on the control of television programs by the government?

  _____

  _____

- Why should someone reading this editorial be cautious about the information it provides?

  _____

  _____

ELECTRONIC RESOURCES

The Internet is a collection of millions of **websites**, or locations where information is stored. Each website consists of one or more **web pages** — pages of information provided by the creator of the website. Web pages usually display text, but they can also include graphics, sound, video, and animation. In fact, many websites are multimedia presentations.

The **Internet** therefore offers users a unique type of reading. It is more interactive than a book, magazine, or newspaper. A user chooses what and when to read, similar to a captain in control of a ship at sea. Searching the Internet is like having a huge library on your desktop. Unlike library researchers in the past, though, Internet users usually find the information they are looking for in seconds or minutes, rather than hours or days. People conducting research — from fourth-graders to scientists and engineers — are especially helped by the **World Wide Web**.

On the Internet, websites are often connected by links called hyperlinks. **Hyperlinks** are the backbone of the Internet. A hyperlink allows one website to link to another file or page on the Internet. For example, suppose you wanted to look up a science magazine on the Internet. The magazine's website includes several hyperlinks. Part of the information about *Science Magazine* might look like this:

---

http://www.sciencemag.org/content/295/5564/2377.short
The Effects of Media Violence on Society

1.   Craig A. Anderson and Brad J. Bushman (authors)

Evidence is steadily growing that continued exposure to violent television programming during childhood is associated with children becoming more aggressive. In their article, Anderson and Bushman discuss new research (Johnson *et al.*) that clearly demonstrates this association in adolescents and young adults. Their research broadens the range of individuals that are affected by media violence.

This short passage actually contains four hyperlinks. Each link is underlined and appears in a different type, so it is easily recognized. If you click on the link for *Craig A. Anderson*, you will be connected to a different page or website. This new page will focus on information about that author.

If you click on the link for _Anderson and Bushman_, you will discover more information about their article. This is the magic of the Internet. Exploring resources on the Internet is truly a voyage of discovery!

CHECKING YOUR UNDERSTANDING

By reading the magazine article, "The Effects of Media Violence on Society" by Anderson and Bushman, what information are you likely to find?

_____

_____

_____

SEARCHING THE INTERNET FOR INFORMATION

One of the most important features of every website is its website address. Just as every student in your class lives at a unique address, every website also has its own unique address or location. Suppose you wanted to visit the website of the Federal Communications Commission. This agency is in charge of regulating the television airwaves.

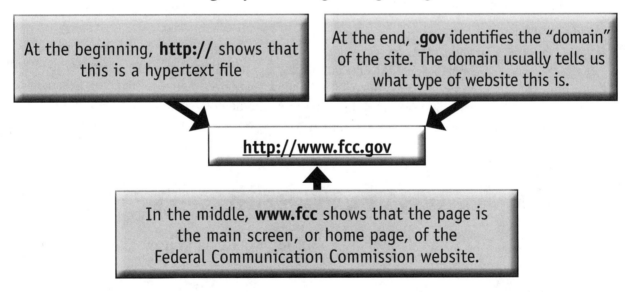

At the beginning, **http://** shows that this is a hypertext file

At the end, **.gov** identifies the "domain" of the site. The domain usually tells us what type of website this is.

http://www.fcc.gov

In the middle, **www.fcc** shows that the page is the main screen, or home page, of the Federal Communication Commission website.

Some other common domains include **.com** which identifies a commercial website; **.org** tells us this is an organization or association; **.net** is a network-related site; while **.gov** identifies a government agency.

To search for information on the Internet, you must specify what you are searching for in the blank search box. Use **keywords**, or "search terms," to describe the information you hope to find. Make sure that your search terms are as specific and focused as you can make them.

Suppose you are looking for information about violence on television. If you enter the term "Television" in the search window, you will receive over a billion results! Most have nothing at all to do with your topic. If you narrow your search to "Amount of violence on television," you will still get 91 million results — this is far less than 1 billion "hits" but still quite a large number of websites.

You would probably want to limit your search to the top five or six of these "hits." Imagine that the box below is one of the first "hits" you investigate. It is a section from a book by Dr. Benjamin Block, a noted authority on raising children, *How to Raise Children: Advice for Parents*.

---

230   **How to Raise Children: Advice for Parents**

Nightmares

Nightmares are dreams in which the dreamer feels helpless, afraid or sad. Children are the ones most likely to suffer from nightmares. Children may seem to enjoy television programs that show violence. However, once the children are asleep, they often suffer from terrible nightmares. These nightmares are caused by the same television programs. For this reason, many parents and educators support the use of a computer chip in televisions to prevent children from watching violent programs. The chip would get signals that would prevent the television set from showing programs considered violent.

Educational Television

Since the 1960s, there have been many attempts to create interesting television programs. Many have been created that are both educational and fun for children to watch. The most successful of these has been "Sesame Street." Tests show that three-year-olds watching Sesame Street regularly do better in learning skills than those who do not watch the program. For this reason, many parents are asking the government to sponsor more educational programs.

CHECKING YOUR UNDERSTANDING

• What does this Internet site say about nightmares and how television can shape our behavior?

_____

_____

• How does this information relate to the issue of television violence?

_____

_____

In evaluating sources, you should keep the following in mind:

- ■ Distinguish between facts and opinions in what you read.
- ■ Consider each author's purpose in writing.
- ■ Identify any important cause-and-effect relationships.
- ■ Compare points of agreement and disagreement.

MAKING A DECISION ABOUT THE ISSUE

Now that you have researched the topic, write a brief essay advising your parent on whether to sign the petition. Give your point of view on the question: Should the government limit the amount of violence shown on television? Be sure to explain how you arrived at your decision. In your answer, you should refer to some of the sources you read in this activity and any others you may have found in your school or public library or on the Internet.

THINK ABOUT IT

Should the government limit the amount of violence shown on television?

_____

_____

_____

_____

_____

_____

_____

_____

_____

_____

_____

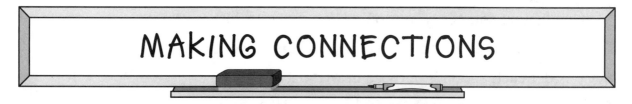

MAKING CONNECTIONS

STEPS TO APPLY IN SOLVING A PROBLEM

Does your family drive a car, throw things in the garbage, or use products made in factories? Although these acts seem innocent enough, each of them can produce harmful effects to the environment. It is no wonder that protecting the environment from pollution has become a major public concern. Today it is unusual to read a newspaper or listen to the news on television without the topic of pollution coming up.

In this *Making Connections*, you and your classmates will evaluate the problem of pollution and consider what can be done to reduce it. Let's take a look at some of the key steps involved in solving a problem, such as pollution.

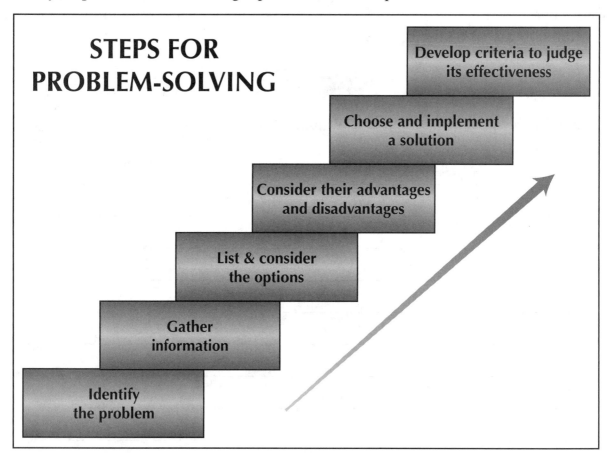

STEPS FOR PROBLEM-SOLVING

- Develop criteria to judge its effectiveness
- Choose and implement a solution
- Consider their advantages and disadvantages
- List & consider the options
- Gather information
- Identify the problem

Let's learn more about this problem-solving approach by applying each of these steps to the problem of pollution.

STEP 1: IDENTIFY THE PROBLEM

The first step is to identify the problem. You might want to focus on one type of pollution: solid waste and how it pollutes our environment. Here is the problem it raises:

> ***Where should we put the billions of tons of garbage that are thrown away each day?***

STEP 2: GATHER INFORMATION

Next, you must gather information about the problem. You can often find information on the Internet or in your school library. Look for information both on:
  (1) what causes the problem, and
  (2) the solutions people have proposed for it.

STEP 3: LIST AND CONSIDER THE OPTIONS

Now you need to explore all the ways or options you can think of for solving the problem. You should look through the sources you found for helpful ideas and information. Then you should "brainstorm" ideas with your classmates, listing as many possible solutions as you can think of.

STEP 4: CONSIDER THE ADVANTAGES AND DISADVANTAGES OF YOUR OPTIONS

Next, consider the advantages and disadvantages of each option. Here is what a sample chart might look like that considers the advantages and disadvantages of some options:

Option	Advantage	Disadvantage
Recycle the garbage	• Reduces the amount of garbage • People in the community support it	• Expensive to establish recycling centers • Requires a great deal of work • Requires cooperation of the entire community
Place the garbage in landfills	• Inexpensive to place garbage in landfills • Creates new land areas out of areas that were wastelands	• Encourages people to create even more garbage • May put poisons in the ground that can pollute underground water wells • Existing places for landfills are rapidly being used up
Dump garbage at sea	• Does not add to existing landfills	• Pollutes the oceans

STEP 5: CHOOSE AND IMPLEMENT A SOLUTION

Now you are ready to make a choice. Compare the proposed options to come up with a solution. Decide which advantages are most important, based on your own values. Your proposed solution will depend on what you most value. People value different things and often disagree about what should be done. Once you choose a solution, think about how you can put it into effect. For example, here are some actions you might take:

- **Sign a Petition.** Get people who support your plan to sign a petition.
- **Inform the Media.** Write a letter to your local newspaper, television or radio station explaining your proposal.
- **Contact Your Representatives.** Write a letter to local public officials or your elected representatives in the General Assembly.
- **Speak to Community Leaders.** Invite one or two community leaders to your school to discuss the problem and your proposed solution.

Petition signing is a popular method used to build support for a solution.

- **Volunteer for a Community Organization.** Volunteer to work for a community organization that will help put your ideas into action.

STEP 6: DEVELOP CRITERIA FOR JUDGING ITS EFFECTIVENESS

Once you carry out a possible solution, you need to determine its effectiveness. **Criteria** are standards for judging something to see how well your proposed solution actually works. For example, you might use these criteria to judge the effectiveness of recycling or landfills:

- What will it cost?
- What effect will it have on the environment?
- Will people in the community be successful in carrying it out?

The most effective solution will be the one that best reduces garbage, limits pollution, and is something that people are willing and able to afford.

Now it is your turn. Your teacher should divide your class into groups. Each group should use the problem-solving approach you just learned to come up with other solutions to an environmental problem facing your community.

Identify the Problem: _____

_____

Gather Information: _____

_____

_____

_____

List and Consider the Options: _____

_____

_____

_____

Consider the Advantages and Disadvantages of Each Option: _____

_____

_____

_____

_____

_____

_____

_____

_____

_____

Choose a Solution to the Problem: _____

_____

_____

_____

_____

_____

CONTINUED

Develop Criteria to Judge the Effectiveness of the Solution: _____

_____

_____

_____

_____

STUDY CARDS

Printed Sources of Information

What are some printed sources of information? _____

_____

_____

_____

_____

_____

_____

Electronic Sources of Information

- What advantages do electronic sources, such as the Internet, have over traditional sources of information?

_____

_____

- What disadvantages do they have? _____

_____

_____

Conducting an Internet Search

- Describe how to go about searching the Internet for information. _____
  _____
  _____

- Why is it important to be specific when searching the Internet for information?
  _____
  _____

LEARNING WITH GRAPHIC ORGANIZERS

Directions: Complete the graphic organizer below by identifying the various sources of information that can be used when conducting research.

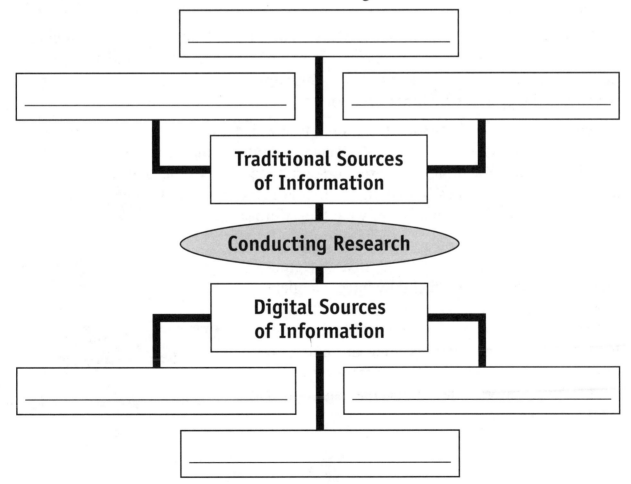

Traditional Sources of Information

Conducting Research

Digital Sources of Information

ACTIVITY 3D

HOW GOOD ARE YOU AT COMPROMISE?

■ Effective participants in a democratic society engage in compromise.

In this activity, you will learn how people in a democratic society act when they compromise. You will also explore one of the most important compromises that took place at the Constitutional Convention of 1787.

KEY TERMS

- ■ Compromise
- ■ Issue
- ■ Negotiation
- ■ Constitution
- ■ Constitutional Convention
- ■ Articles of Confederation

Dr. Martin Luther King, Jr. once said that Americans "must learn to live together as brothers or perish together as fools." He recognized that disagreements are a part of life and are sometimes unavoidable. Situations often occur where one person wants one thing, while another wants something else.

What needs to be done? Dr. King's point was that we are foolish if we refuse to learn how to resolve disagreements. A successful **compromise** is one in which both parties give up something in return for something else. Compromise involves the settlement of differences by having each side make concessions. This means that each side gets some, but not all, of what they were seeking.

There are some good reasons why compromise is sometimes called an "art." In a disagreement, both sides usually feel they have excellent reasons why they should not give in on an issue. Figuring out what to give, where to hold firm, and how to achieve one's goal is often difficult. But this is what a person needs to do to bring about an effective compromise and reach an agreement with the other side.

Compromising is especially important as one goes through life. Let's take a look at an example to see how this is done. Imagine you are out with your family for the day. Your sister wants the family to spend the day at the beach. You have waited all week long for everyone to go on a family bicycle ride. You may not get to do what you want, but if you are good at making compromises, you'll probably enjoy yourself just the same.

THINK ABOUT IT

What would be a good compromise to end this disagreement between you and your sister?

_____

_____

_____

_____

Remember: in all compromises each side gives in a little in order to get some of what they want. This can go a long way towards avoiding major problems in your life. In the imaginary disagreement above, you might make the following compromise — you agree to go to the beach with the family in the morning, and to go for a family bike ride in the afternoon.

THE ART OF COMPROMISING

In a democracy, ordinary citizens hold the final power in government. These citizens, acting through their representatives, decide the issues of the day. An **issue** arises when there are two or more opposing views on what should be done. For a democracy to work effectively, people with opposing viewpoints must engage in compromise.

As we have just seen, reaching a compromise is not always easy. But resolving issues in a democracy without compromise is nearly impossible. Let's examine more closely what is involved in resolving disagreements in government through compromise.

UNDERSTAND WHAT'S AT STAKE

Sometimes you may be involved with someone who has a difference of opinion or a different way of handling an issue. The first step is to make sure that both of you are really interested in reaching some kind of a solution. Even if you think that you know the other person's views, you should still ask yourself: "What is my real concern? What are the real concerns of the other side?" The first step to reaching a compromise is to always make sure that each side fully understands what the other side wants.

BE RESPECTFUL

Each person needs to be given an opportunity to speak his or her mind without being interrupted. Both parties need to avoid pointing blame, name calling, or using offensive or abusive language. If someone thinks you are really listening to them thoughtfully, he or she is far more likely to respond positively. A phrase such as "I understand how you feel" or "I see what you are saying," can go a long way in reaching a compromise. You need to recognize when emotions are high. It is often best not to have a conversation about what is at issue until each of you has a "cool head."

BE OPEN TO NEGOTIATE

Both parties in a disagreement need to come up with solutions that work for both of them. It is very important that the proposed solution works for both, and not just one of the parties. Each party needs to understand the other's viewpoint.

A compromise doesn't have to be exactly equal to be acceptable. However, it is important to understand that both parties are giving up something to reach a solution. You may not feel happy about the compromise, but you have to feel that you can accept it and live with it. Each side must give up something in the bargain. In a true compromise, neither side will walk away feeling they have achieved all that they wanted.

THINK ABOUT IT

What do you think is the most important step in trying to reach a compromise with someone?

_____

_____

_____

_____

_____

THE GREAT COMPROMISE

You might not realize it but the art of compromise played a very important role in the beginning of this nation. The people who met in Philadelphia in 1787 to write the U.S. Constitution had many disagreements. They argued about the slave trade, export taxes, whether slave populations should count towards representation, and many other issues.

One of their disagreements threatened to break the new nation apart before it had a chance to get started. Let's see whether you and your classmates would be able to reach a compromise if you were presented with the same situation on this key issue.

THE CONSTITUTIONAL CONVENTION OF 1787

In 1787, representatives from the 13 states met in Philadelphia to revise the **Articles of Confederation** — our first national constitution. The delegates quickly decided that a new plan for government, or **constitution**, was needed to replace the existing Articles of Confederation. Most of the delegates were in agreement that a stronger central government was needed.

Delegates at the Constitutional Convention.

They also agreed that the new government should be led by a strong executive who would carry out the laws, known as the *President*, and that there should be a national legislature to make the laws, known as a *Congress*.

However, the delegates at the Constitutional Convention did not agree on all issues. For example, they could not agree on how the states should be represented in the new Congress. Under the Articles of Confederation, each state had been given only one vote. Under this system, all states had equal political power.

Some delegates at the Constitutional Convention now argued that this system was unfair to states with larger populations. The representatives from the larger states felt that states with larger populations should not have the same number of votes in Congress as states with smaller populations. For a short time, it seemed that the Constitutional Convention might even break up over this important issue.

A TRIP BACK IN TIME

If you and your classmates had been at the Constitutional Convention would you have been able to work out a compromise to resolve this dispute? Let's see if we can find out.

Below is a list of the thirteen states and their populations at the time of the Constitutional Convention in 1787. Your teacher should divide the class so that each state has a number of student representatives generally in proportion to the size of its population. For example, Delaware or Rhode Island might have only one person. Larger states, such as Pennsylvania or Virginia, might have four students as representatives. The goal of the "Convention" (*your class*) is to reach a compromise about how states should be represented in the new Congress.

STATE POPULATIONS IN 1787

Large States	Population	Student Representatives	Small States	Population	Student Representatives
South Carolina	249,100	3	Delaware	59,100	1
Maryland	319,700	3	Rhode Island	68,800	1
New York	340,100	3	Georgia	82,500	1
Massachusetts	378,800	3	New Hampshire	141,900	1
North Carolina	393,700	3	New Jersey	184,100	2
Pennsylvania	434,400	4	Connecticut	237,900	2
Virginia	691,700	4			

Source: Thirty-Thousand.org Information Brief

Now discuss this issue: how should states be represented in the future Congress? Should larger states have more votes or should all the states have the same number of votes in Congress, regardless of their size?

THINK ABOUT IT

- What do you think the larger states wanted regarding the issue of representation in the new Congress?

  _____

  _____

  _____

- Can you think of a compromise in which all the different states would agree?

  _____

  _____

  _____

  _____

You and other class members should now propose your ideas for a good compromise to the class. Then the class should discuss these ideas further. Finally, the class should vote on a compromise solution.

THINK ABOUT IT

- Was the class able to reach a compromise? If so, what was it?

  _____

  _____

- If the class was able to achieve a compromise, how does their compromise compare to the actual comprise reached by the delegates at the Constitutional Convention*?

  _____

  _____

* See the results of the actual compromise on page 295.

MAKING CONNECTIONS

COMPROMISING ON A STATE OR NATIONAL ISSUE

Now that you have learned about the art of compromise, let's put your skill at compromise to use to solve a state or national issue. For the next week or two, each student should read a newspaper or check the Internet. You should look for two controversial issues that affect your local community, your state, or the United States.

The issue must, of course, have two opposing sides. You should then explain what each side seeks, and how you might suggest a compromise that would resolve the issue. The chart below will help you to organize your answers:

TOLEDO DAILY PRESS

Vol. 15 No. 21   First Edition

Mayor and Union Workers Reach a Compromise

FIRST ISSUE: _____

What does each side want?	What compromise would you suggest to solve the issue?

Name _____

SECOND ISSUE: _____

What does each side want?	What compromise would you suggest to solve the issue?

STUDY CARDS

Compromise

What steps are necessary for a compromise to take place?

_____

_____

_____

_____

Constitutional Convention of 1787

Describe the compromise that was finally reached at the Constitutional Convention in 1787? _____

_____

_____

_____

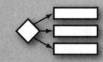

LEARNING WITH GRAPHIC ORGANIZERS

Directions: Complete the graphic organizer below by explaining the key points to keep in mind when making a compromise.

The "Art" of Compromise

The Great Compromise: At the Constitutional Convention in 1787, larger states felt they should have a greater say in the national government since they had larger populations. Smaller states felt each state should have an equal voice. In this compromise, a two "house" legislature, called Congress, was created. In the House of Representatives, states were to be represented based on the size of their population. This allowed states with larger populations to have a greater number of representatives. In the Senate, each state, no matter what its size, was to be represented by two Senators. This satisfied the smaller states. All laws would need the approval of both houses of Congress.

Name _____

EXPRESS YOURSELF

In a democratic nation, a majority in the legislature is required to pass laws. Compromise is often needed before a majority can be reached. Compromise brings opposing groups together and helps to bring about agreements to pass laws acceptable to a majority of people. To reach a compromise, supporters of one side often make concessions to attract enough support to build a majority. The laws that are passed often do not include all of the wishes of its supporters.

Write an essay explaining why compromise is essential for a democracy to work.

ACTIVITY 3E

WHAT RULES WOULD YOU CREATE FOR YOUR CLASS?

■ Laws can protect rights, provide benefits, and assign responsibilities.

In this activity, you will learn how governments work by creating a set of rules for you and your classmates. After completing this activity, you will be able to explain the benefits of the rule of law.

KEY TERMS

- ■ Rules
- ■ Laws
- ■ Rule of Law
- ■ Protection of Property
- ■ Jury Duty
- ■ Obtaining a License

We are all social beings. We need to live with other people in groups or communities. We need the help of others to get our food, to build shelters, and to defend ourselves. A community protects its members and reduces disagreements by developing rules of behavior that everyone agrees to obey.

A **rule** tells people what they can and cannot do. Under a system of rules, we know how we should behave and how we can expect others to behave. Can you imagine what life would be like without any rules?

RULES

1. you can....
2. you can't....
3. you can....
4. you can't

MAKING RULES FOR YOUR CLASS

Imagine it is the first day of school. Your teacher begins discussing the rules for class behavior. Your teacher explains that rather than dictate the rules, the class will make up these rules. Your teacher says that the rules should establish order and protect the rights of class members. The rules should allow class members to do their work without being distracted. Finally, each rule should include a penalty for breaking it.

Name _____

As an example, your teacher suggests the following rule: In class discussions, only one student may speak at a time. Your teacher recommends that any student who breaks this rule should have to write a note of apology to the student who was interrupted. This is the penalty for breaking this rule.

THINK ABOUT IT

- Why does your teacher recommend the classroom rule that only one student should speak at a time?

  _____

  _____

  _____

- What would happen in your class if this rule were not adopted?

  _____

  _____

  _____

Now it's your turn to make rules for the class and to set penalties for breaking them. What rules and penalties would you suggest? Some topics for rules are listed below.

YOUR SUGGESTIONS FOR CLASS RULES

TESTS

Rule: _____

Reason: _____

Penalty: _____

CLASSROOM BEHAVIOR

Rule: _____

Reason: _____

Penalty: _____

CONTINUED

HOMEWORK

Rule: _____

Reason: _____

Penalty: _____

GRADES

Rule: _____

Reason: _____

Penalty: _____

LATENESS

Rule: _____

Reason: _____

Penalty: _____

OTHER: _____

Rule: _____

Reason: _____

Penalty: _____

AGREEING ON YOUR CLASS RULES

Are your rules and penalties similar to those proposed by your classmates? Compare your list of rules and penalties with those of other members of your class. See what your teacher is willing to accept. Try to reach an agreement on a single set of class rules. Be sure to include a penalty as part of each rule. Have one of the students write these rules on the chalkboard. Each student in the class should then copy these rules and penalties in their notebook.

THE BENEFITS OF HAVING LAWS

A **law** is a rule enacted by a government that tells people to do or not to do something. Usually there is a penalty for breaking a law. Laws provide many benefits to citizens:

THE RULE OF LAW

Americans live under the "**rule of law**." This system protects each American from reckless acts by government or unfair treatment by neighbors. When people live under the rule of law, they live in a society in which the rules are clear, just, and applied equally to all members of society. In a society governed by the rule of law, even the government and its officials are required to obey the law. The government must exercise its power according to well-established and clearly written rules, regulations, and legal principles. No one, not even the President, is above the law.

PROVIDE ORDER IN OUR DAILY LIVES

Laws help to keep society orderly and predictable. For example, traffic laws tell us how to behave when driving so that we do not have accidents.

PROTECT PEOPLE'S PROPERTY

Laws restrain people who would might otherwise try to take from others what is not theirs. Our laws protect us from theft. If someone takes something from us unlawfully, there are procedures (*a way of dong things*) for us to get it back. In fact, property can only really be owned in a society where property is legally protected. If a person's property is not protected, economic freedom cannot exist.

PROTECT PEOPLE'S RIGHTS

Another function of law is to protect our rights. In the United States, people's rights are identified in the U.S. Constitution and the Bill of Rights. These rights include the right to life, liberty, and freedom. People have the right to pursue happiness, to speak out freely, and to worship in their church, synagogue or mosque without fear of being arrested for their religious beliefs. Laws protect our rights to assemble, to publish our ideas in the press, and to petition the government.

Laws also make sure that no one is abused by others. Laws even protect the rights of people who are physically weak. They help protect us and keep us safe. Governments establish laws to protect these rights.

PROTECT PUBLIC EDUCATION

One of the most important functions of law is to provide public education for young citizens. By law, each community must provide free public education to the children that live in its area. The law requires children to attend school until they reach a certain age, usually between sixteen to eighteen.

Listed below are a series of situations. For each situation, identify whether a law is involved and explain why it is important for society.

The Situation	Does it Involve a Law?	Why is this important for a society?
Drivers are required to stop their cars when the traffic light turns red.	❏ Yes ❏ No	
You are forbidden to take a person's property without their permission.	❏ Yes ❏ No	
You are free to express yourself to others.	❏ Yes ❏ No	

LAWS ASSIGN RESPONSIBILITIES

Laws also define our responsibilities as citizens.

SERVE ON A JURY

For example, laws tell adult citizens when they have to serve on a jury. As an adult citizen, you may be called to appear in a court to serve on a jury. This responsibility is assigned by law. If you fail to appear or respond, you will face fines and other penalties. Only persons who have a court accepted reason for not serving on a jury are excused.

Citizens are expected to serve on a jury when called.

PAY TAXES

Our government raises money by taxing its citizens. Laws define the amount of taxes we should pay. With the ability to collect taxes, federal, state, and local governments are able to meet their financial needs and to pay for projects that benefit their citizens. Every citizen is required by law to pay his or her taxes. People that fail to pay their taxes are subject to civil and criminal penalties.

OBTAIN A LICENSE

Laws also state when we need to obtain a license in order to do certain things. A license may be required for acts that might be dangerous. For example, state governments require individuals to obtain a driver's license before they can drive a car or motorcycle. Usually, you have to take a driving test and pay a fee. The driver's license serves as official identification if you are in an accident. This insures that people who drive can handle that responsibility safely.

States provide drivers licenses to make sure you are a safe driver.

Other laws require licenses for such activities as fishing, getting married, running a restaurant, or being a teacher, lawyer, doctor or other health professional.

Below are a series of situations. For each situation, explain why it is important for a society to have such a law.

The Situation	Why is this important for a society?
You receive a summons to report to a court in your city to serve on a jury.	
You receive a notice from the government that you owe a sum of money for taxes.	
You apply to your county government for a business license to open a new restaurant in your community.	

RESEARCH A RECENT LAW

The General Assembly is Ohio's law-making body. Each year, they pass laws that affect the lives of its citizens. In this section, you will focus on one recent law passed by the General Assembly. Using the Internet, enter *Laws of Ohio* in a search box on Google, Firefox, Bing or AOL. Most likely, one of the first sites to appear in your search will be *Ohio State Laws-Findlaw.com*. This link contains a summary of various laws passed in Ohio. Select one of the topics shown and answer the following:

What issue did the passage of this law seek to resolve?
_____
_____
_____
How has this law changed the lives of Ohioans?
_____
_____
_____

MAKING CONNECTIONS

HOW IS YOUR SCHOOL GOVERNED?

In many ways your school is a community of groups — students, teachers, administrators, parents and a school board. Like most communities, your school is a sort of government. What role do these groups play in governing your school?

HOW YOUR SCHOOL IS GOVERNED

How is your school "government" organized? You probably know that your principal is the main authority figure in your school. A principal is similar to a mayor of a town, or the governor who is the central authority in your state.

THINK ABOUT IT

Can you think of another central authority figure that is similar to a school principal?

_____

_____

Typically there is a whole network of people in a school that helps the principal run the school. For example, who decides when students should eat lunch or go home? Who decides if your class can go on a school trip or what books to use in class? Who decides what time the class will go to the cafeteria for lunch?

To find the answer to these questions, work with your teacher to find the answers to the following questions:

THINK ABOUT IT

- Is there a student government in your school? _____

- If so, how are its members chosen? _____

  _____

  _____

  _____

- What procedure does your school follow in making its rules?

  _____

  _____

- Who is in charge of carrying out your school's rules? _____

- What parts do the principal, teachers, and parents play in school decisions?

  _____

  _____

  _____

  _____

USING THE INTERNET TO LEARN ABOUT OTHER SCHOOLS

How does the way your school is governed compare to other schools in Ohio or the rest of the nation? There are many ways to find out. Your class can write to students in other schools. Or you can conduct a search of the Internet to find out about other elementary schools. Many other schools make information about themselves available on Internet websites. Enter the key words "**Ohio Public Elementary Schools**" in a search engine like Google, Firefox, Bing or AOL to find schools with Internet websites.

Name _____

STUDY CARDS

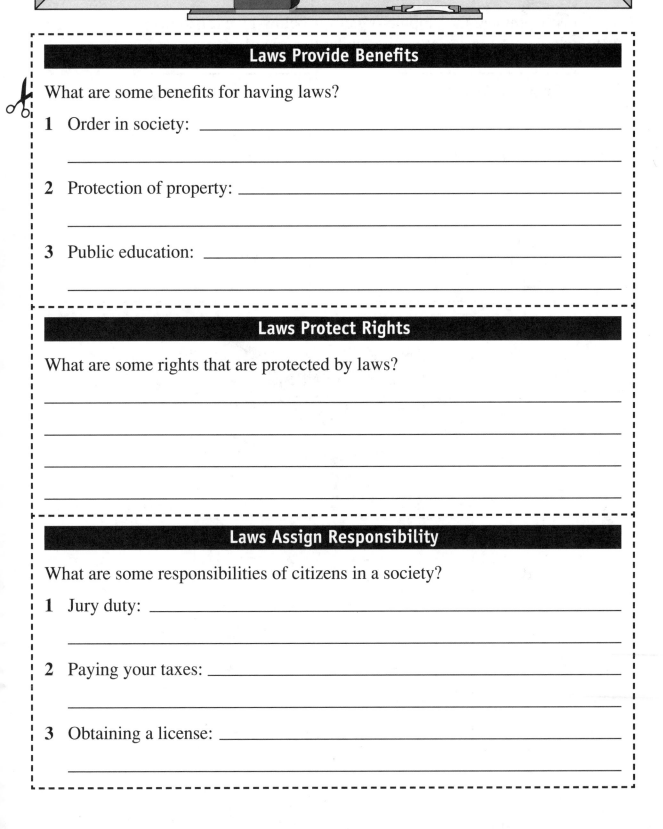

Laws Provide Benefits

What are some benefits for having laws?

1 Order in society: _____

_____

2 Protection of property: _____

_____

3 Public education: _____

_____

Laws Protect Rights

What are some rights that are protected by laws?

_____

_____

_____

_____

Laws Assign Responsibility

What are some responsibilities of citizens in a society?

1 Jury duty: _____

_____

2 Paying your taxes: _____

_____

3 Obtaining a license: _____

_____

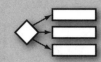 # LEARNING WITH GRAPHIC ORGANIZERS

Directions: Complete the graphic organizer below by explaining the various benefits to individuals and society living under the rule of law.

Protect Rights:

_____
_____
_____
_____
_____
_____

Provide Benefits:

_____
_____
_____
_____
_____

Laws Protect Rights, Provide Benefits and Assign Responsibilities

Assign Responsibilities:

_____
_____
_____
_____
_____
_____

EXPRESS YOURSELF

In 1955, *The Lord of the Flies* was published. It told the story of a plane that crash landed on a remote island in the Pacific Ocean. The only survivors were a group of boys in their teens. The theme of the book is the conflict between two competing desires that exist in all humans — on the one hand, the drive to live by rules, to live peacefully, and to value the good of the group. On the other hand, the desire to gratify our immediate desires, to act violently, and to enforce our will over others.

Write an essay below that deals with your views on this conflict. If there were no laws, would civilization triumph over savagery? Would order be victorious over chaos? Would law succeed over lawlessness?

ACTIVITY
3F

HOW DOES THE U.S. CONSTITUTION LIMIT GOVERNMENT POWER AND PROTECT INDIVIDUAL RIGHTS?

■ The U.S. Constitution establishes a system of limited government and protects citizens' rights. Five of these rights are addressed in the First Amendment.

In this activity, you will learn about a key problem faced by the framers of the U.S. Constitution. After completing this activity, you will understand how the U.S. Constitution established a system of limited government in which the rights of its citizens are protected.

KEY TERMS

- Problem
- Constitution
- Limited Powers
- People's Sovereignty
- First Amendment
- Bill of Rights

IDENTIFYING THE PROBLEM

A **problem** is something that is harmful and has to be overcome, or a situation that has to be resolved. Often a problem involves a conflict or a choice between different alternatives. For example, you may have to explain a poor grade on a test to your parents. Or have to tell a friend you cannot go to her party. Or you may have trouble understanding what a relative is saying. What do you do when faced with a problem? The first step is to identify the problem.

After declaring their independence from Great Britain in 1776, American leaders identified a problem they faced. They recognized the nation's need for some type of central, or national, government. Because of their recent experience under British rule, the former colonists were fearful of creating a central government that would be too strong.

The leaders of the new nation drafted the Articles of Confederation in 1776 to resolve this problem. This was our nation's first constitution.

A **constitution** provides a framework for government and establishes the rules for the government. It defines what a government can and cannot do. Leaders of the new United States feared that individual freedom might be threatened by the national government if it was given too much power over the lives of its citizens. Fearful of a strong national government, the Articles of Confederation deliberately placed more power in the hands of the thirteen individual states. This had the effect of creating a national government that was generally weak.

The Articles of Confederation

The government under the **Articles of Confederation** was a loose association of states — a "league of friendship" — with only one branch of government, a Congress. Since the states held the real power, the Articles of Confederation soon proved inadequate as a national government. Some citizens feared that if a foreign country attacked the United States, the government was so weak the new nation would be unable to survive.

American leaders decided a stronger government was needed. They invited delegates from each of the thirteen states to meet in Philadelphia to revise the Articles of Confederation. The **Constitutional Convention** was held in Philadelphia in 1787.

When the delegates met, they decided it would actually be easier to abandon the Articles of Confederation and just write a new constitution.

The signing of the U.S. Constitution at Independence Hall

CHECKING YOUR UNDERSTANDING

What problem did the nation face under the Articles of Confederation?

_____

_____

_____

CONSIDER THE OPTIONS

The next step in solving a problem is to consider the options, or possible courses of action you might take.

Americans had several types of government from which to choose after the **Declaration of Independence** was issued in 1776. They could have created a **monarchy** — a government ruled by a king. Or they could have created a government where a king and legislature shared power. Or they could have selected a government run by representatives chosen by the people. The colonists chose to establish a **democracy**. A decade later, when the delegates met at the Constitutional Convention they remained committed to a democratic government. They sought to make sure that power would be in the hands of the people, who vote to elect their representatives.

Members at the Constitutional Convention had to design a government that would create a balance between the powers of the government and the rights of the individual. The problem they faced in writing a new constitution was: How much power should be given to new national government? It had to have enough power to carry out its duties, but not have enough power to threaten the liberties of its citizens. A government would need to be strong enough to meet national goals, but not so powerful that it would threaten the freedom of its citizens.

They had several options to achieve this. They could create a central government that would make all important decisions. They could also leave all power to the states. Finally, they could attempt to design a system somewhere in between these two.

CHECKING YOUR UNDERSTANDING

Which of these options would you have preferred? Write a brief speech to members of the Constitutional Convention explaining your favorite option.

_____

_____

_____

_____

_____

_____

ARRIVING AT A SOLUTION

The final step in resolving a problem is to select and apply a solution. In 1787, the members of the Constitutional Convention decided that the best way to control government was to **limit the powers** of government.

The path the writers of the U.S. Constitution chose was completely new. Instead of a government limiting the power of its citizens in the new constitution, the government's power itself would be limited for the benefit of the people. The government would only be given specific powers. These powers would be listed in the Constitution.

The principle of limited government is actually the other side of the coin that political power comes from the consent of the governed. If the people are the source of government authority, then the government only has the limited authority that the people want it to have. The Constitution is the place where Americans spelled out which powers were given to the government and which powers it did not have.

CHECKING YOUR UNDERSTANDING

What was unique about the role given to the people of the nation by the writers of the U.S. Constitution?

_____

_____

_____

_____

_____

_____

A system was created to prevent the government from gaining to much power. To accomplish this, the U.S. Constitution adopted some important measures:

THE PEOPLE HOLD SUPREME POWER

As we have seen, one way that the writers of the Constitution sought to limit the power of government was to give the people of the nation the real power. The U.S. Constitution says that the people are **sovereign** — they hold the supreme power.

The national government receives its powers from the consent of the people. This means that the people of the United States are the real source of the government's power. The government has only those limited powers the people want it to have. It is for this reason that large sections of the Constitution lists things the government cannot do.

PROTECTION OF INDIVIDUAL RIGHTS

The original U.S. Constitution included only a few protections of individual rights. As a result, many Americans felt the Constitution did not provide enough protection to individuals. They wanted additional limits on the power of the national government. They demanded that a **Bill of Rights** be added to the U.S. Constitution. These amendments protected citizens' individual liberties.

Five of these liberties are included in the **First Amendment**.

Freedom of Speech

Freedom of the Press

Freedom of Assembly

Right to Petition Government

Freedom of Religion

Our government cannot tell us what to read, what to think, where to pray or even whether to pray. Some of the most important words in the First Amendment are *"Congress shall make no law…"* The leaders who founded our country believed greatly in individual freedom — in the rights of citizens to be protected from a government that was too powerful and too controlling.

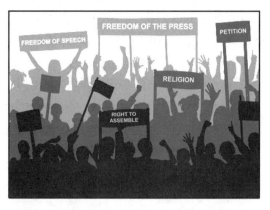

Let's look more closely at each freedom protected by the **First Amendment**.

FREEDOM OF SPEECH

Freedom of speech is the right to communicate one's ideas to others. The government cannot prohibit someone's own expression. It cannot force someone to express certain views. However, there are some limits to freedom of speech, such as lying about a person or causing a danger.

FREEDOM OF THE PRESS

Freedom of the press is the right to publish ideas, written in newspapers, magazines, and electronic media.

FREEDOM OF RELIGION

This part of the First Amendment supports a person or group's right to practice its religion. It also allows us the freedom to change our religion or not to follow any religion if we should so choose.

FREEDOM OF ASSEMBLY

Don't like something and want to demonstrate against it? Well, the First Amendment protects your right to do so. Freedom of assembly is the right to get together to express, promote or defend a common interest.

THE RIGHT TO PETITION GOVERNMENT

You already know that a **petition** is a written request by citizens to government to change or do something. The right to petition means we have the right to ask our government to correct a wrong or problem. It allows us to demonstrate against our government when we do not agree with its actions of policies.

Other amendments in the **Bill of Rights** guarantee the right to a fair trial and other protections to persons accused of a crime.

How well do you think the authors of the Constitution and the Bill of Rights solved the problem of creating a strong government that still respected citizens' rights? Did limited powers and protection of citizens' rights solve the problem? Write an essay on how well you think these features solved the problem.

MAKING CONNECTIONS

WRITING AND PERFORMING A SKIT ABOUT OUR FIRST AMENDMENT RIGHTS

When our nation was founded, its leaders believed that the open and free exchange of ideas was essential for the survival of democracy. The most basic liberties guaranteed to Americans are found in the First Amendment.

Its 45 words assure citizens that their government is responsible to its citizens. These words are as meaningful and important today as they were 230 years ago. The First Amendment symbolizes the right of "a minority of one" to express views that are different from those of the majority.

In this *Making Connections* you will create and perform a skit demonstrating the five freedoms of the First Amendment. A skit differs from a play. A play is a story that is created to be acted on a stage or in a theater. A **skit** is a short play performed in a more informal setting such as a classroom. The text for a skit is called the **script**. To carry out your skit:

■ Your teacher will divide your class into five groups. Each group of students will be assigned one of the five freedoms found in the First Amendment.

■ Each group will write its own script. Decide in advance who will play each part. After the script is written, everybody should receive a copy of the skit.

■ The students will perform their skit illustrating the idea of freedom in front of the class. Each group member must have a role in the skit. The focus of the group's skit should be about how Americans exercise these rights.

■ To get ready for the skit, you might want to practice saying your lines in front of you parents or a friend. This will help you get used to saying your lines and allow you to get a feel for performing in front of people.

■ Speak clearly and in a voice that can be easily heard. Be polite to your audience.

STUDY CARDS

Articles of Confederation

What major problem faced the nation living under the Articles of Confederation?

_____

_____

_____

_____

_____

Problems Facing the U.S. Constitution

What problem did the authors of the Constitution face in writing a Constitution?

1 Too much power: _____

_____

_____

2 Too little power: _____

_____

_____

Limiting the National Government's Power

How does the U.S. Constitution protect its citizens against the abuse of power by the national government?

_____

_____

_____

_____

LEARNING WITH GRAPHIC ORGANIZERS

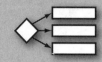

Directions: Complete the graphic organizer below by explaining how the First Amendment protects the individual liberties of its citizens.

First Amendment Protections of Individual Liberties

EXPRESS YOURSELF

When the U.S. Constitution was written it provided a government with limited powers. It then added the First Amendment to further protect the rights of its citizens against government abuse. In the space below, explain how the Constitution limits the power of the national government and protects the rights of its citizens.

Name _____

ACTIVITY 3G

WHAT DO OHIOANS KNOW ABOUT THEIR GOVERNMENT?

- A constitution is a written plan for government. Democratic constitutions provide the framework for government in Ohio and the United States.
- The Ohio Constitution and the U.S. Constitution separate the major responsibilities of government among three branches.

In this activity, you will conduct a survey to find out what adults know about their national and state governments. In conducting your survey, you will learn about the U.S. Constitution and the Ohio Constitution. You will also learn how the structure these documents provide for the national and state government. After completing this activity, you will be able to explain the main responsibilities of each of the three branches of government in both Ohio and in the national government.

KEY TERMS

- Hypothesis
- Government
- Constitution
- Legislative Branch
- Executive Branch
- Judicial Branch
- Ohio Constitution
- General Assembly
- Senate
- House of Representatives
- U.S. Congress
- Supreme Court of Ohio

WHAT DO YOU KNOW?

Some government experts claim that most people do not know much about their state and national government. What do you think?

Do most adults know enough about their government to answer nine basic questions? ❏ Yes ❏ No

At this point, your answer is only a **hypothesis** — an educated guess. In this activity, you will try to find out if your hypothesis is correct. To do this, you will conduct an informal survey of adult knowledge about our national government in Washington, D.C. and Ohio's state government. In a survey, you ask questions to a sample group. In carrying out your survey, use the following procedures:

- The questions below will form the basis of your survey. First, take the survey yourself. Record your answers. Then check your answers with the **Fact Sheets** found later in this activity. Give yourself 11 points for each correct answer.
- Next find two adults you know — your parents, relatives or neighbors. Ask them to help you with a school project by answering nine questions about their government. Carefully record each person's answers.
- After the survey, show your adult volunteers the **Fact Sheets** in this activity. Remember to thank your volunteers for their help.

SURVEY OF KNOWLEDGE ABOUT
THE NATIONAL AND OHIO GOVERNMENTS

1　**All communities set up an authority to make rules, settle disagreements and protect their members. What is this authority called?**

◆ Your answer: _____

◆ Volunteer 1: _____

◆ Volunteer 2: _____

2　**What is the main purpose of a constitution?**

◆ Your answer: _____

◆ Volunteer 1: _____

◆ Volunteer 2: _____

3　**Both our state and national governments have similar branches to carry out their duties. What is the responsibility of the legislative branch of both governments?**

◆ Your answer: _____

◆ Volunteer 1: _____

◆ Volunteer 2: _____

CONTINUED

4   What is the responsibility of the executive branch of both governments?

◆ Your answer: _____

◆ Volunteer 1: _____

◆ Volunteer 2: _____

5   What is the responsibility of the judicial branches of both governments?

◆ Your answer: _____

◆ Volunteer 1: _____

◆ Volunteer 2: _____

6   Our national law-making body is made up of two parts, a Senate and a House of Representatives. What is this law-making body called?

◆ Your answer: _____

◆ Volunteer 1: _____

◆ Volunteer 2: _____

7   Ohio has a Chief Executive, who is responsible for carrying out Ohio's state laws. What is Ohio's Chief Executive called?

◆ Your answer: _____

◆ Volunteer 1: _____

◆ Volunteer 2: _____

8   The highest court in the United States is the Supreme Court. What is the highest court in the State of Ohio called?

◆ Your answer: _____

◆ Volunteer 1: _____

◆ Volunteer 2: _____

9   Ohio's state government is a democracy. What is a democracy?

◆ Your answer: _____

◆ Volunteer 1: _____

◆ Volunteer 2: _____

After you record each volunteer's answers, hand him or her the following **Fact Sheets** to look over.

FACT SHEET #1

WHAT IS A GOVERNMENT?

The organization that protects a community is called a **government**. All governments are given certain powers to carry out their authority over the members of society. These powers include:

A *legislative* power to make laws	An *executive* power to carry out the laws	A *judicial* power to interpret laws

WHAT IS A CONSTITUTION?

A **constitution** is a written plan of government. It establishes how a government is organized. It also tells government officials what they can and cannot do. Government officials can only use those powers given to them by their constitution. This is done so that government officials cannot abuse people's individual liberties. A constitution has three main functions:

To provide a plan or framework for government	To limit the power of government	To define the authority of elected officials

Both Ohio and the U.S. governments are democracies. A **democracy** is a form of government in which its citizens have the final say in how their government acts.

THE GOVERNMENT OF OHIO AND OF THE UNITED STATES

In the United States, there are 51 constitutions: one for the national government and one for each 50 state government. Our national government handles matters that affect the entire nation, such as raising an army and creating a money system.

Ohio's state government, like other state governments, handles matters that affect people throughout the state. For example, Ohio provides a system of justice and protects the safety and health of Ohio citizens.

FACT SHEET #2

OUR STATE AND FEDERAL CONSTITUTIONS

The U.S. Constitution was written in 1787 and adopted soon afterwards. It created three branches of government. Ohio's written plan of government is the **Ohio Constitution**. The Ohio Constitution also organized the state government into three branches — a *legislative*, *executive*, and *judicial*. These constitutions spell out what each branch's powers are and tells how these powers may be used.

THE LEGISLATIVE BRANCH

Where Ohio's General Assembly meets.

Ohio's law-making, or *legislative*, branch is the **General Assembly**. Like the national government, Ohio's legislature is made up of two chambers — a **Senate** and a **House of Representatives**. There are 33 Senators in the Ohio Senate. Each Senator is elected to a four-year term.

Ohio's House of Representatives has 99 members. Each member serves for a two-year term. The General Assembly passes laws concerning the state budget, education, crime, the environment, workers safety and public projects.

The chamber where the Ohio House of Representatives meets.

Our national law-making branch is called **Congress**. It is made up of a **Senate** and a **House of Representatives**. There are 100 Senators in the U.S. Senate. Each U.S. Senator is elected for a six-year term. The U.S. House of Representatives has 435 members. Each member serves a two-year term.

FACT SHEET #3

THE EXECUTIVE BRANCH

The President of the United States and Ohio's Governor are elected to serve for a four-year term. Ohio's Governor has many powers. The Governor's main responsibility is to enforce the laws passed by the General Assembly and to maintain order in the state. The Governor also recommends new laws to the General Assembly and is the Commander-in-Chief of Ohio's National Guard. Similarly, the President recommends new laws to Congress and is Commander-in-Chief of the nation's Armed Forces.

This house is the official residence of Ohio's Governor.

THE JUDICIAL BRANCH

The role of Ohio's judicial branch is to interpret and apply state laws. It does this by deciding specific court cases. The state's highest court is the **Supreme Court of Ohio**. There is no appeal from their decisions except to the U.S. Supreme Court. The Supreme Court of Ohio has a Chief Justice and six Associate Justices. All Ohio judges are elected for a term of six years.

Our nation's highest court is the **U.S. Supreme Court**. Its most important power is to decide whether laws or government actions violate the U.S. Constitution. The U.S. Supreme Court has a Chief Justice and eight Associate Justices. All judges are nominated by the President, but must also be approved by the U.S. Senate. They serve for life.

The room where Ohio's Supreme Court meets.

THE BILL OF RIGHTS

Like the U.S. Constitution, the Ohio Constitution has a Bill of Rights, which protects each individual's rights. The Bill of Rights guarantees free speech, a free press, and the right to a trial by jury. It also protects the rights of victims of a crime.

Now that you have read the **Fact Sheet**, how well did you and your volunteers do in answering the survey? To find out:

ANSWERS TO THE SURVEY QUESTIONS:

❶ This authority is called a **government**.

❷ There are three **main purposes for a constitution**:

   (1) to provide a plan of government;

   (2) to limit the powers of government; and

   (3) to define the authority of elected officials.

❸ The legislative branch is responsible for **making the laws**.

❹ The executive branch is responsible for **carrying out the laws**.

❺ The judicial branch is responsible for **interpreting and applying the laws**.

❻ Our national law-making body is **Congress**.

❼ The Chief Executive of Ohio is the **Governor**.

❽ The highest state court in Ohio is the **Supreme Court of Ohio**.

❾ A **democracy** is a government in which the people have the final say in how their government acts. The people in a democratic government usually elect their government officials.

Now that you have read the three **Fact Sheets**, how well did you and your two volunteers do in answering the questions of the survey? To figure the grade for each of your volunteers, use the following guide:

Number of Correct Answers: _____ x 11 points = _____

Points: You: _____ Volunteer 1: _____ Volunteer 2: _____

THINK ABOUT IT

- In general, did your volunteers have a good, fair or poor understanding of our state and national governments? _____
  Explain your answer. _____

  _____

  _____

- What would you suggest to improve people's knowledge about our state and national governments?

  _____

  _____

CHECKING YOUR UNDERSTANDING

In what ways is our national government under the U.S. Constitution similar to our state government under the Ohio Constitution?

Characteristics	Under the U.S. Constitution	Under the Ohio Constitution
Form of Government		
Branches of Government		
Legislative Branch		
Executive Branch		
Judicial Branch		
Protections of Individual Liberties		

MAKING CONNECTIONS

CREATING A TIMELINE ABOUT OHIO'S STATE CONSTITUTION

The passage below describes some of the key events in the history of Ohio's State Constitution. Use this information to complete the timeline on the next page:

In **1802**, Ohio's first constitution was approved. This was the first step in Ohio's admission as a state. The Constitution of 1802 established a relatively weak government. It gave most government powers to the legislative branch. It provided all white males with the right to vote, and prohibited slavery. However, it failed to give voting rights to women or to African-American men. Ohioans later came to realize this constitution needed to be changed.

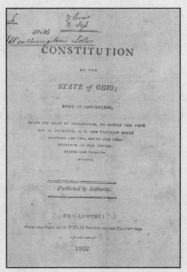

Ohio's first Constitution (1802)

In **1851**, a new state constitution was adopted to create a more democratic system in Ohio. It reduced the power of the General Assembly. It provided that all judges would to be elected directly by voters. The Constitution of 1851 further provided that Ohio voters would decide whether to hold a Constitutional Convention every 20 years.

In **1871**, Ohio voters decided to call a Constitutional Convention. However, the constitution drafted by that Constitutional Convention was later rejected by the voters of Ohio.

In **1911**, voters again called for a Constitutional Convention believing that Ohio should do more to protect the rights of its citizens. The 1912 Constitutional Convention added a several **amendments** that further protected individual liberties. Now citizens accused of a crime in Ohio had the same rights that they enjoyed under the Bill of Rights.

Since **1912**, Ohio's constitution has been amended many times. These changes have involved selling bonds (*loans*) for economic development, environmental cleanups and other purposes. Today, the **Constitution of 1851** and its amendments still provide the basic framework for governing Ohio.

Below is a blank timeline of *Key Events in the History of Ohio's State Constitution.* Use the information in the passage above to complete the timeline:

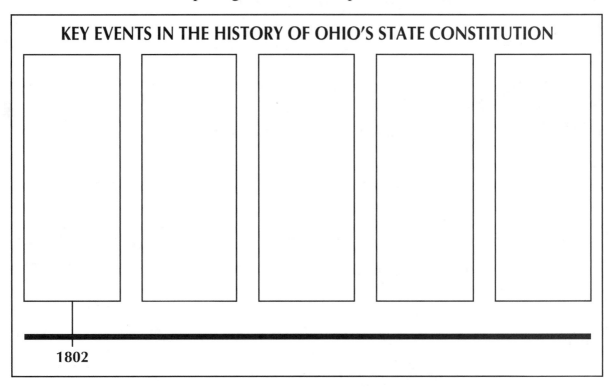

KEY EVENTS IN THE HISTORY OF OHIO'S STATE CONSTITUTION

1802

STUDY CARDS

Functions of a Government

Name and explain three functions that are carried out by all governments.

1 _____

_____

2 _____

_____

3 _____

_____

Functions of a Constitution

- What is a constitution? _____
  _____
  _____

- What functions does a constitution perform?

  1 _____

  2 _____

  3 _____

Ohio and U.S. Constitution

Describe how the U.S. Constitution and Ohio's Constitution are similar:

_____

_____

_____

_____

_____

_____

The Ohio and U.S. Bill of Rights

Describe how the Bill of Rights in the U.S. Constitution and the Bill of Rights in the Ohio Constitution are similar:

_____

_____

_____

_____

_____

_____

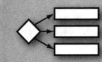

LEARNING WITH
GRAPHIC ORGANIZERS

Directions: Complete the graphic organizer below by explaining the three main functions carried out by all governments.

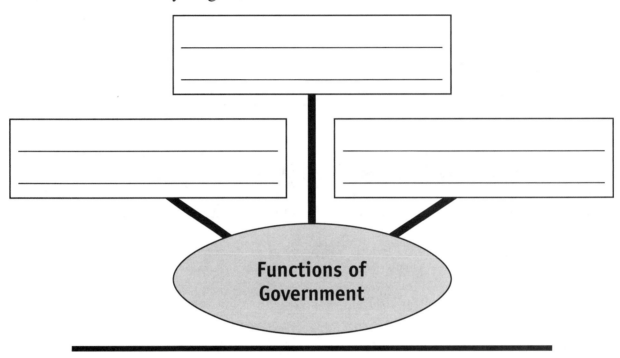

Functions of Government

Directions: Complete the graphic organizer below by explaining how the Ohio Constitution is in some ways similar to the U.S. Constitution.

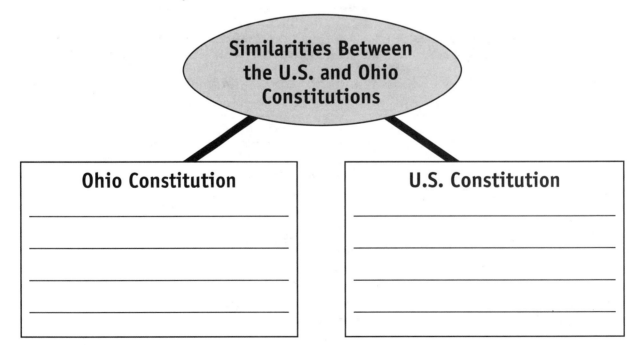

Similarities Between the U.S. and Ohio Constitutions

Ohio Constitution

U.S. Constitution

Name _____

UNIT 4

ECONOMICS

Workers pose at one of Ohio's early coal mines.

Open furnace at the Republic Steel Mill in Ohio (1940)

Worker at the B.F. Goodrich tire factory in Akron, Ohio.

Economics **explains how people make and spend money to meet their needs. In this unit, you will learn about the things that consumers buy and how producers provide goods and to provide services. You will also learn about how to create a budget and to use it to help you save some money.**

ACTIVITY 4A

HOW VISUALLY LITERATE ARE YOU?

■ Tables and charts help people to understand information and issues. Tables organize information in columns and rows. Charts organize information in a variety of visual formats (pictures, diagrams, graphs).

In this activity, you will learn how to read various types of data. After completing this activity, you will be more "visually literate" and be able to analyze information when it is presented in different formats.

KEY TERMS

- ■ Visual Literacy
- ■ Diagrams
- ■ Pictographs
- ■ Line Graphs
- ■ Relevant Information
- ■ Irrelevant Information

WHAT IS VISUAL LITERACY?

Someone who is **literate** is able to read and write. But literacy also refers to the ability to "read" things other than words. "**Visual literacy**" is becoming increasingly important in the twenty-first century. We are constantly presented with images in newspapers, magazines, television, movies, and on the Internet. As a result, visual literacy — the ability to "read" images — has become a vital skill in our modern society.

Seeing things in a visual format adds power to the information. Charts, graphs, maps and diagrams help to clarify something where words alone may be inadequate. They make a stronger impression on our minds and help us to remember the information longer.

BAR GRAPH   PICTOGRAPH   LINE GRAPH

"Visual literacy" also includes reading and understanding maps, timelines, tables, pictures, diagrams and graphs. All of these can provide important information and ideas. Some of these — *maps*, *timelines*, and *tables* — have already been explored in this book in previous activities.

THINK ABOUT IT

In general, why is "visually literacy" so important in today's world?

_____

_____

_____

_____

In this activity, you will learn about tables and charts, including *diagrams*, *pictographs*, and *line graphs*. Let's begin with diagrams.

WORD DESCRIPTIONS vs. VISUAL PRESENTATIONS

Have you heard the expression, "a picture is worth a thousand words"? It means that it is often easier to understand something that is visual rather than written. To see how this works, read the following description:

THE ORGANIZATION OF A SCHOOL

My school is headed by our principal. The principal of my school is assisted in running the school by two assistant principals. Each of these assistant principals is in charge of supervising several teachers. Each teacher is responsible for his or her class of students. The job of the teacher is to work with the students in his or her class and to teach these students.

Here is how this same word description might look in a visual format:

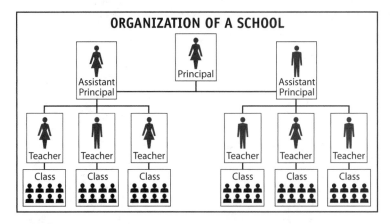

CHECKING YOUR UNDERSTANDING

Which of these descriptions was easier to understand? _____

Explain your answer. _____

_____

_____

UNDERSTANDING A DIAGRAM

A **diagram** is a simplified picture that shows how something is organized, how several things are related, or how the different parts of something work. Each part of a diagram is usually identified. Arrows or lines in the diagram often indicate important relationships.

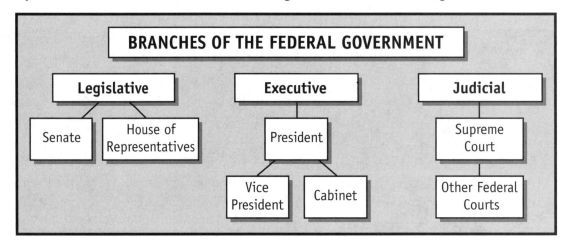

Name _____

STEPS TO UNDERSTANDING A DIAGRAM

EXAMINE THE TITLE

The title tells you what kind of information is presented in the diagram. For example, the title of the diagram above is: "Branches of the Federal Government." It shows three the three main parts of government: a legislative, executive, and judicial branch.

LOOK AT THE LEGEND

Sometimes a diagram will have a legend to show what each symbol stands for. In this diagram, each part is clearly labeled so there is no need for a legend.

STUDY THE DIAGRAM

The diagram shows the three branches of the federal government. The lines indicate their relationships. For example, in this diagram, the lines that come from the three branches of the Federal Government show how each branch is divided. In the Executive Branch, we see it is led by the President. Below the office of President are the Vice President and the President's Cabinet or advisors.

CHECKING YOUR UNDERSTANDING

If you wanted to add to this diagram, how would you show the Federal Court of Appeals and the Federal District Courts? Explain how you would present this information.

_____

_____

UNDERSTANDING TABLES AND PICTOGRAPHS

You already learned in previous activities how to read a table. You may recall that in a **table**, information is displayed so that it is easily found. Information is placed in cells. The cells are organized into rows and columns. Headings are usually listed along the top row. In the table below, the first and third columns give the year and the second and fourth columns give the amount of income.

AVERAGE PERSONAL INCOME IN OHIO: 2005–2012

Year	Amount of Income	Year	Amount of Income
2005	$32,445	2009	$35,001
2006	$34,008	2010	$35,931
2007	$35,183	2011	$37,836
2008	$36,401	2012	$39,289

The information in this table can also be turned into a pictograph. In a **pictograph**, a symbol or illustration is used to represent a number of something, such as money or people.

AVERAGE PERSONAL INCOME IN OHIO: 2005–2012	
YEAR	AMOUNT OF INCOME
2005	$ $ $ $ $ $ $ $ $ $ $
2006	$ $ $ $ $ $ $ $ $ $ $ $
2007	$ $ $ $ $ $ $ $ $ $ $ $
2008	$ $ $ $ $ $ $ $ $ $ $ $ $
2009	$ $ $ $ $ $ $ $ $ $ $
2010	$ $ $ $ $ $ $ $ $ $ $ $
2011	$ $ $ $ $ $ $ $ $ $ $ $ $
2012	$ $ $ $ $ $ $ $ $ $ $ $ $ $

LEGEND
Each $ = $3,000

To understand a pictograph, you need to look at its various parts:

EXAMINE THE TITLE

Start by examining the title. It provides the overall meaning of the information in the pictograph. In this pictograph, the title is: *The Average Personal Income in Ohio: 2005–2012*. This title states that in this pictograph, we see how much the yearly income of an average Ohioan was in the years from 2005 to 2012.

WHAT THE SYMBOLS SHOW

Each symbol or picture in the pictograph represents an amount. In our example, the legend shows that each dollar sign ($) is equal to $3,000 in annual (*yearly*) income. Thus, two and a half dollar symbols ($$$) represent $7,500 in yearly income:

$ + $ + $

$3,000 + $3,000 + $1,500 = $7,500

INTERPRETING THE INFORMATION IN A PICTOGRAPH

If you want to find the average yearly personal income in Ohio in 2008, here is what you need to do:

- Start by looking at the years listed on the left side of the pictograph. Find the year "2008."
- Now slide your finger along the "2008" row. As you do, count the number of $ symbols on that line.
- The year "2008" has 12 complete $ and a partial $ symbol. Remember that each full $ symbol represents $3,000 in annual (*yearly*) income.
- Thus, in 2008, the average person in Ohio earned about $36,400 in income.

CHECKING YOUR UNDERSTANDING

- What advantages does a pictograph have over a table? _____

  _____

  _____

  _____

- What was the average yearly income in Ohio in 2012? _____

- In which two years was the average yearly income of Ohioans similar?

  _____ and _____

- In which year was the average annual income of Ohioans the highest?

  _____

- In which year did personal income decline from the previous year? _____

UNDERSTANDING LINE GRAPHS

A **line graph** is a graph composed of a series of points connected in a line. Line graphs are used to show how something has changed over time. Taking information from a chart and making it into a line graph is an important skill.

HOW TO MAKE A LINE GRAPH

Below is a table that shows the population of four Ohio cities over a 40-year period. Each number represents a thousand people. For example, in 1970 the population of Akron was 275 — that number represents 275,000 people.

City	1970	1980	1990	2000	2010
Akron	275	237	223	217	207
Cincinnati	454	385	364	331	333
Cleveland	751	574	506	478	431
Columbus	540	565	633	711	769

Let's use the information in the table to create a line graph.

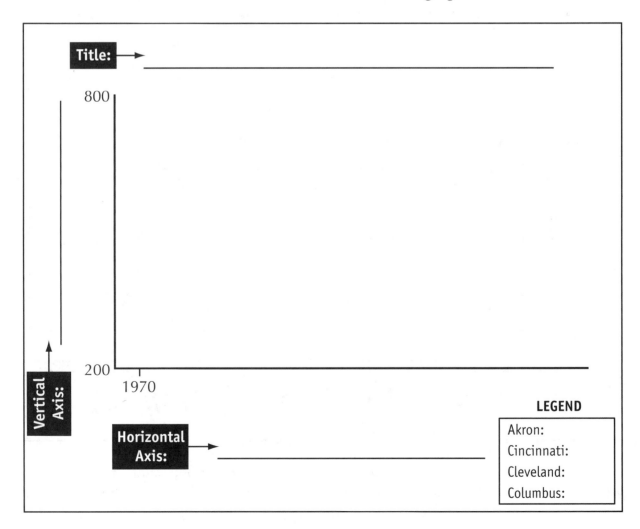

THE TITLE

The first step in creating a line graph is to select an appropriate title. The table provides information about four cities in Ohio between 1970 and 2010. What do you think would be an appropriate title for a line graph with this information?

THE VERTICAL AXIS

Now you need to draw and label a **vertical axis** (*up and down*). The vertical axis runs along the graph's left-side and usually measures amounts. Here the vertical axis should show your scale. The numbers in the chart range from **207** to **769**. You might start your scale at 200 and end it at 800. Since you do not want your graph to be too large, each number might increase by **50**. Thus, your vertical axis would start at 200, next would be 250, then 300, then 350 and so on.

THE HORIZONTAL AXIS

Next draw and label the **horizontal axis** (*across*). The horizontal axis usually runs along the bottom of a line graph. In the chart, the years appear at ten-year intervals. Here you might list the years, starting with **1970** and ending with **2010**.

MARK THE POINTS

Now you are ready to locate each point on the graph. Let's begin with Akron. Along the horizontal axis, find the year **1970**. Slide your finger up until you are midway between **250** and **300** on the vertical axis. Mark a point half way between both numbers, since you are showing **275**. Do the same for all the remaining years for Akron. Then connect each of the points with line segments. Do the same for Cincinnati, Cleveland, and Columbus.

THE LEGEND

Sometimes it can get confusing telling one line from another. To distinguish each line, you need a **legend** to identify what each line represents. For example, you might make one line black, another red, a third one green and one blue. Or you might make one line solid, another with dots, another with dots and dashes and so on. Your legend identifies what each color or type of line shows.

TRENDS

Sometimes a line graph will reveal a trend. A **trend** is the general direction in which things are moving. We can often see a trend by examining the movement or general direction of a line. To describe the trend in a line graph, terms such as *upward*, *rising*, *climbing*, *dropping*, *downward*, *falling*, *declining*, *leveling off*, and *unchanging* are often used.

CHECKING YOUR UNDERSTANDING

Use your line graph to answer the following questions:

1   In what year was the population of Columbus the highest? _____

2   In what year was the population of Cincinnati the lowest? _____

3   In what year did Cleveland's population fall below that of Columbus? _____

4   Do you see any trends in the populations of these cities? _____

_____

_____

MAKING CONNECTIONS

DISTINGUISHING BETWEEN RELEVANT AND IRRELEVANT INFORMATION

In this activity, you examined different types of information. One important skill in examining data is the ability to tell what information is important (**relevant**) and what is unimportant (**irrelevant**) information. It is important to recognize that the same information can be relevant or irrelevant depending upon what it is that you need to find out.

RELEVANT INFORMATION

Relevant information is information that is connected to what you are looking for. In general, such information will be useful and appropriate. It is "related" to what you are looking for.

IRRELEVANT INFORMATION

Irrelevant information is not related or connected to what you are looking for. It is either not useful for what you are working on, or it has no connection with what you are trying to find. For example, if you wanted to buy a notebook in a store and did not know which aisle to find it. If the salesperson tells you where to find pens in the store, that would be irrelevant to what you are looking for.

Name _____

How well do you understand the difference between relevant and irrelevant information? Let's see how well you do. Imagine you wanted to find the name of a state from certain information provided to you. You will need to decide which clues are relevant and which are irrelevant.

---

1 The state borders Michigan. Is this clue relevant?   ❏ Yes ❏ No

2 The state is governed by a governor. Is this clue relevant?   ❏ Yes ❏ No

3 The state has more than seven letters but less than ten letters in its name.
   Is this clue relevant?   ❏ Yes ❏ No

4 The state has a state flag. Is this clue relevant?   ❏ Yes ❏ No

5 The state has two major league baseball teams.   ❏ Yes ❏ No
   Is this clue relevant?

What is the name of the mystery state? _____

WHAT IS THE NAME OF THE MYSTERY STATE?

A THIS STATE BORDERS MICHIGAN

This information is relevant. It narrows your search from 50 states to the four states that border Michigan:

(1) Wisconsin   (3) Indiana
(2) Illinois   (4) Ohio

B THE STATE HAS A GOVERNOR

This information is correct, but irrelevant and not useful. Since every state has a governor, this information does not help you to identify the unknown state.

C THIS STATE HAS MORE THAN SEVEN BUT LESS THAN TEN LETTERS IN ITS NAME

This information is relevant. We already know that this state borders Michigan. There are only two states that border Michigan that also have more than seven letters but less than ten letters in their names: **W-i-s-c-o-n-s-i-n**, and **I-l-l-i-n-o-i-s**. This information is very relevant. It helps us to narrow the search to only two states.

CONTINUED

D THIS STATE HAS A STATE FLAG

This information is correct, but again is not relevant. Every state, including the two states we have narrowed our search to, have a state flag.

E THIS STATE HAS TWO MAJOR LEAGUE BASEBALL TEAMS

This final clue is relevant. It rules out Wisconsin, since it has only one major league baseball team. However, Illinois has two major league baseball teams: the Chicago White Sox and the Chicago Cubs.

Now that you understand the difference between relevant and irrelevant information, let's use this to help identify the mystery state.

STUDY CARDS

Diagrams

- What is a diagram? _____
  _____

- Why do people sometimes prefer to use a diagram? _____
  _____
  _____

Pictographs

- What is a pictograph? _____
  _____

- What advantages does a pictograph have over other visual formats?

  1 _____

  2 _____

  3 _____

  4 _____

Name _____

Line Graphs

- What are line graphs? _____

  _____

- Why do people use line graphs? _____

  _____

  _____

  _____

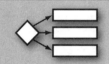 # LEARNING WITH GRAPHIC ORGANIZERS

Directions: Complete the graphic organizer below by explaining the function of the various parts of a diagram.

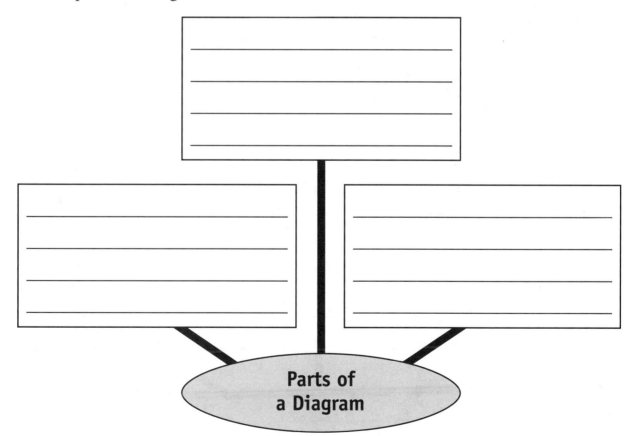

Parts of a Diagram

Directions: Complete the graphic organizer below by explaining the function of the various parts of a pictograph.

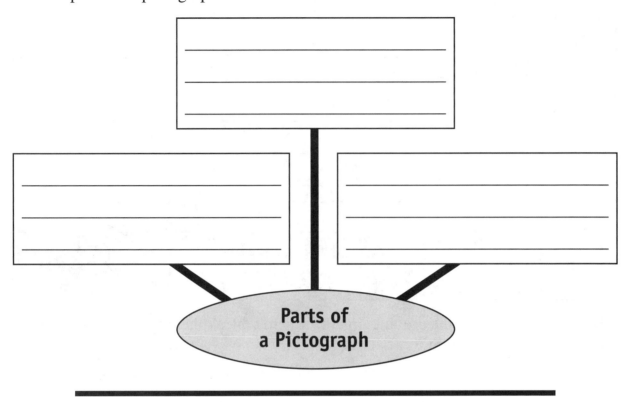

Directions: Complete the graphic organizer below by explaining the function of the various parts of a line graph.

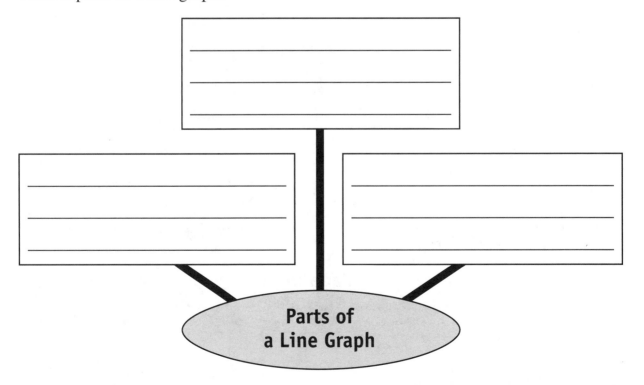

Name _____

ACTIVITY 4B

WHAT RISKS WOULD YOU TAKE AS AN ENTREPRENEUR TO START A BUSINESS?

■ Entrepreneurs in Ohio and the United States organize productive resources and take risks to make a profit and compete with other producers.

In this activity, you will learn what it might be like to start your own business. After completing this activity, you will be able to identify the productive resources needed to produce a particular good or service. You will also be able to explain how entrepreneurs organize productive resources and take risks to make profits.

KEY TERMS

■ Business
■ Free Market Economy
■ Consumer
■ Consumption

■ "Opportunity Costs"
■ Producers
■ Entrepreneur
■ Risk and Benefits

■ Productive Resources
■ Capital Goods
■ Technology
■ Specialization

PRODUCTION AND CONSUMPTION

A **business** is an activity that makes goods or provides services to others. The economy of the United States is a free market economy. A **free market economy** is one in which anyone has the right to start a business. It is based on the interaction of two groups — consumers and producers.

CONSUMERS

A **consumer** is someone who buys and consumes goods and services made by businesses. To consume is to use up. Food, for example, is **consumed** or eaten up, by consumers. The consumer "consumes" clothes by wearing them, and "consumes" a barber's services by getting a haircut.

Consumers examine different products, buy goods and services, and sometimes return goods they have purchased. The buying and using of goods and services is called **consumption**.

Every economic decision you make as a consumer has an "**opportunity cost**." Its "cost" is the opportunity you give up to do other things. For example, suppose you have saved money from your allowance to buy a toy or a book. You

When you make a purchase, you are acting as a consumer.

decide to buy the toy. That purchasing decision allowed you to buy the toy instead of the book. The "opportunity cost" of purchasing a new toy is giving up the opportunity to have bought the book instead.

CHECKING YOUR UNDERSTANDING

Think of an economic decision you made to recently purchase something.

1   What were some of the things you were thinking of buying? _____

_____

2   What did you finally decide to buy? _____

3   What was the opportunity cost of your decision? _____

_____

PRODUCERS

Businesses are active in the production of goods and services. Producers can be individuals, firms, or companies. Producers of certain goods are often influenced by the availability of resources and the climate where they are located. If enough consumers buy a product, a business will make a **profit**. No wonder that almost nine million new businesses are started each year in the United States.

CHECKING YOUR UNDERSTANDING

In your community, what are some goods and services that are produced?

1   Name an item that is produced in your community: _____

_____

2   Name an item that is not produced in your community: _____

CHECKING YOUR UNDERSTANDING

For each of the following, indicate if the action is consumption or production:

Action	Consumption or Production?
Sam drinks milk.	❏ Consumption / ❏ Production
Acme Construction builds a house.	❏ Consumption / ❏ Production
Samantha buys a book.	❏ Consumption / ❏ Production
Peter opens a new restaurant.	❏ Consumption / ❏ Production
Derrick grows corn on his farm.	❏ Consumption / ❏ Production
General Motors makes new cars.	❏ Consumption / ❏ Production
James rides on a roller coaster.	❏ Consumption / ❏ Production
Robert makes a wristwatch.	❏ Consumption / ❏ Production
William buys a new bicycle.	❏ Consumption / ❏ Production

STARTING A BUSINESS

What would it be like to be a young business owner? In this activity, you will have an opportunity to look at all that goes into starting a business. Then you will decide if you would like to start your own business.

A person who starts his or her own business is known as an **entrepreneur**. Starting a business can carry some risks. It requires money to start a new business without knowing if it will succeed. An entrepreneur is willing to take this risk and overcome the challenges of starting a business in order to be rewarded by making a profit.

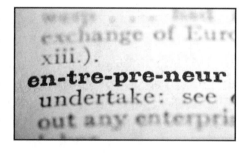

Now you are ready to think about starting your own business. Every business begins with an idea. Your class should break up into small groups. Members of your group should think of some kind of work that you would enjoy and be good at. Below is a list of suggestions. You are not limited to the ideas on this list. Your group may have an even better idea for a business.

- **Pet Care:** Caring for household pets by feeding, walking and caring for them.

- **T-Shirt Sales:** Selling T-shirts decorated with different designs.

- **Car Wash Service:** Washing people's cars.

- **Bottled Water Sales:** Selling bottled water at school events.

- **Notebook Covers:** Making personalized book covers with unique designs on them.

- **Other:** (Your group's original idea): _____

This student earns money by mowing lawns. What business are you thinking about?

THINK ABOUT IT

Now it's time for your group to make a decision. Which business would your group like to try?

The business we chose was _____.

We decided on this type of business because _____

_____

GETTING INFORMATION AND SOME ADVICE

Before starting a new business, it helps to get advice from people with experience. Members of each group should consult with their parents. You might also invite a business person from your community to speak to the class. Explain that you need advice and want to understand some of the advantages and disadvantages of starting different types of businesses.

Looking at the Risks and Benefits. Members of each group should make a list of the risks and benefits of the type of business they are planning. Risks are costs or disadvantages. For example, you risk losing the time and money you put into your business if it fails. Benefits are the possible gains or profits you stand to gain from your business if it is successful.

You should also consider what changes might happen to the costs for your materials. For example, you may want to sell homemade cookies to family members, neighbors and friends. What happens if the price of the cookie dough rises dramatically? How will the business be affected if the cost of packaging the cookies were to double?

Benefits	Risks
1.	1.
2.	2.
3.	3.
4.	4.

If the risks seem too great, your group may want to rethink its proposed choice for a new business.

PRODUCTIVE SERVICES

Each society has limited resources that it can use to make the goods and services that it needs. People starting a new business must first think about the resources they will need to run their business. These resources are called **productive resources**. Such resources include all the things needed to produce goods and services.

There are four main types of productive resources. Sometimes these are also called the **factors of production**.

Natural Resources	Human Resources	Capital Goods	Entrepreneur-ship

NATURAL RESOURCES
Natural Resources are the resources found in nature. These natural resources include metals, minerals, water, plants and soil. These are the raw materials that are made into the products we use. Natural resources like coal and oil also provide energy to make goods and services.

CAPITAL GOODS
Capital goods are those things used to make other goods or to perform services. For example, machines and tools are capital goods. **Technology** (*ways of making and doing things*) is constantly improving as new ways are invented to do things. As a result, capital goods are constantly changing and improving.

PRODUCTIVE RESOURCES

A house under construction.
What productive resources can you identify?

HUMAN RESOURCES
Human resources refer to the work people do to produce goods or provide services. Under *specialization*, or the division of labor, workers specialize in performing particular jobs. Specialization allows each worker to perform better and more efficiently, producing more with less effort.

ENTREPRENEURSHIP
Natural resources, human resources, and capital goods must be combined in an organized way to make something. People who bring these three factors of production together are called **entrepreneurs**. They are the owners and managers of businesses. Entrepreneurs risk investing their money in a business in the hope of making a profit.

WILL THERE BE A PROFIT?

Starting a business takes money. You need money to rent space and to buy raw materials (*land*), tools and technology (*capital goods*). Sometimes you may also need money to hire others or to pay someone to produce something for you. Think about the different productive resources you will need and how much each will cost.

Now your group is ready to figure out how much money it will need to start its business. Use the chart below to estimate the costs of your first month of business (*see the left side of the chart*). An **estimate** is an educated guess. Figure out how much money your group might earn from selling its good or service (*see the right side of the chart*). The money left over after you have paid all of your costs is your **profit**.

Our First Month of Business

Estimate of Monthly Costs			Estimate of Monthly Income		
A. Cost of materials:			Selling price of the good or service:		
B. Costs of tools and technology:					
C. Cost of advertising:			Number of goods or services you think you can sell each month:		
D. Other:					
(add A, B, C, D, for monthly costs)			?		
			Multiply selling price by number of items sold.		
These are your monthly costs:		?	This is your monthly income:		?

Being able to figure your profit is a valuable tool for anyone in business. Figuring out your possible profits will help you to know how much to charge for your goods and services. To figure out if your business will be profitable, you need to subtract your monthly **costs** (*left column*) from your monthly **income** (*right column*):

Total Monthly Income: $___?___
− (minus) Monthly Costs: $___?___
Monthly Profit or Loss: $___?___

However, your costs also have to be low enough to compete with other producers. If you sell lemonade for $1.00 a glass, and another group of students sells glasses of lemonade for 50 cents, most consumers will buy the lemonade for 50 cents. So you cannot make your price higher than that of competing producers unless you are offering something better, such as better-tasting lemonade.

SHOULD YOU START YOUR OWN BUSINESS?

You now have some idea of what you will need, as well as the risks of starting your own business. If your costs are more than your income, then your group will have a **loss**. If your group loses money for too long, you will be forced to go out of business. However, if your income is more than your costs, you will make a profit.

THINK ABOUT IT

Based on what you have learned in this activity, do you think you would like to start your own business?

❏ **Yes**   ❏ **No**. Explain your answer. _____

_____

_____

_____

MAKING CONNECTIONS

INTERVIEWING A LOCAL ENTREPRENEUR

Imagine you and a classmate have been hired as reporters by your local newspaper. Your first assignment is to write an article based on an interview with an entrepreneur in your community. As a reporter, here are some things you will need to consider before your interview.

- Ask family members if they know a local entrepreneur they might suggest for you to interview. It could be an owner of a local business or a professional, such as a barber, plumber, lawyer, or doctor.

- Before the interview, get your parent's permission to meet with the entrepreneur you wish to interview.

- Call or contact that entrepreneur in advance to request a time for your interview. Be sure to contact the person the previous day to confirm your appointment.

- Use the information you have learned in this activity about consumers and producers, productive resources, profits, and starting a business as the basis for the kinds of information and questions you will use in your interview. Do as much research as possible in advance on the person you are going to interview.

- Questions need to be short. Remember to listen carefully to the answers. Try not to dominate the conversation.

- Be sure to come with a pad and a pen or pencil to the interview. It is advisable that you take notes or bring a small tape recorder to record your interview.

- As soon as practical, find a place to review your notes. Underline or put stars around answers that seem most interesting for your article.

Some of the topics you might discuss during the interview should include how long that entrepreneur has been in business, why he or she started the business, how he or she obtains his or her productive resources, and how that entrepreneur sets prices. After your interview, be sure to thank the person for his or her help.

In the space below, write a short newspaper article about your interview. Include information about the *who*, *what*, *where*, *when*, and *why* of the interview.

STUDY CARDS

Opportunity Costs

- What is an opportunity cost? _____

  _____

  _____

- Provide an example of an opportunity cost.

  _____

  _____

  _____

Consumers and Producers

- What is a consumer? _____
  _____

- What is a producer? _____
  _____

- Provide an example for a consumer and a producer.

  Consumer: _____

  Producer: _____

Productive Resources

- What are productive resources? _____
  _____
  _____

- List the four types of productive resources:

  1 _____   3 _____

  2 _____   4 _____

Entrepreneurship

- What is an entrepreneur? _____
  _____
  _____

- Why are profits so important to an entrepreneur? _____
  _____
  _____
  _____
  _____

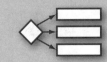

LEARNING WITH GRAPHIC ORGANIZERS

Directions: Complete the graphic organizer below by explaining the difference between a consumer and a producer.

Consumers and Producers

Directions: Complete the graphic organizer below by explaining the role of productive resources in making goods and providing services.

Productive Resources

EXPRESS YOURSELF

In our economy, making profits is often considered the main reason a business exists. Some critics suggest that a business has a greater responsibility to society than just making profits.

Does a business have a responsibility that goes beyond making a profit? For example, a business has decided to cut its expenses by laying-off three workers. However, if the company president would reduce his million dollar salary by $100,000, it would eliminate the need to layoff workers. In the space below, write an essay that deals with your views on this subject.

ACTIVITY 4C

HOW CAN A BUDGET HELP YOUR FINANCIAL WELL-BEING?

■ Saving a portion of income contributes to an individual's financial well-being. Individuals can reduce spending to save more of their income.

In this activity, you will learn how saving a portion of your income will contribute to your financial well-being. After completing this activity, you will know all about how to create a budget. You will know what a budget is, and how to save your money to get more of the things you want to buy for yourself.

KEY TERMS

- ■ Budget
- ■ Earnings
- ■ Saving
- ■ Expenses
- ■ Income
- ■ Trade-off

MY FIRST JOB!

WOW, you just landed your very first job. Mrs. Jones, our neighbor, hired you to help her by walking her dog each day. Mrs. Jones was in an automobile accident and broke her ankle. She will be unable to get around for the next several weeks, and has asked you to exercise her dog, Peppy, each day. She has agreed to pay you $4.00 each day. You are so excited.

In addition to helping Mrs. Jones and her dog, you will be earning some spending money for yourself. **Earnings** include the money you make from wages. You may even earn enough money to buy a bicycle that you have wanted for some time.

Mrs. Jones' dog, Peppy

Your parents have suggested that, now that you are going to earn some money, you should create a budget. You tell your parents, "I have no idea what a budget is. Why do I even need a budget." As usual, instead of just giving you the answers to your questions, they point you in the direction of where you can find the answers.

After a search on the Internet, you find what you are looking for and print it out to read so you can create your own budget.

WHAT IS A BUDGET?

A **budget** can help give you greater control over your money. It estimates how much money you will make and how you will spend your money over a period of time. A budget helps you to decide what to spend your money on and if you should spend less money on some things in order to spend more money on other things.

A budget helps you to be sure that you will have enough money every week or month to spend on what you need. Without a budget, you might run out of money before you get your next week's money from Mrs. Jones.

HOW TO MAKE A BUDGET

Let's assume you want to create a monthly budget. You must first list all of your expected income for the month. Then you need to list all of your expected expenses that you will have for the month.

One of your "expenses" should be an amount that you set aside for **savings**. The goal is to have your income be equal to or greater than your expenses. To find out, subtract your **expenses** from your **income**.

- If you have less than zero, you are spending more money than you are receiving in income. You will need to review your monthly expenses to see what spending you can reduce or eliminate.

- If the amount is greater than zero, you have the opportunity to spend it on things you want or to increase the amount of your savings.

CREATING A BUDGET

Below is a worksheet to prepare your budget. Assume you are dog-sitting for your neighbor. She pays you for 25 days of dog-sitting at $4.00 per day. Based on this rate, estimate the costs of your expenses and see if you have any money left at the end of the month.

MY BUDGET FOR THE MONTH

INCOME: My income this month will be $4 per day
times the number of days in the month $ _____

EXPENSES: My expected expenses this month will be:

Go to Movies	$ _____
Video Game	$ _____
Food and Drink	$ _____
New horn for bike	$ _____
Other: _____	$ _____
Other: _____	$ _____
Money for Savings	$ _____
TOTAL EXPENSE	$ _____

THINK ABOUT IT

- How much money did you have left at the end of the month?

  _____

- If you did not have any money left at the end of the month, what could you do to balance your expenses with your income?

  _____

  _____

THE BENEFITS OF SAVING

Making a budget can make it easier to save money. Why should we try to save money and not spend it all the moment we earn it? Why are people encouraged to save their money? There are a number of good reasons for not spending everything the moment you have money.

For most people, it's a good idea to put some money aside for a "rainy day." You might need money at a future time for an emergency. You also might need to buy something more expensive, like that new bicycle you had your eye on for some time. **Saving** money might let you buy the bicycle or pay for something else that is expensive. Putting money away regularly is the simplest way to save for an expensive item. People who save their money make a short-term sacrifice by not spending some money in order to get a greater benefit in the future.

It can be difficult to save money. Saving money is a **trade-off**. In a trade-off, you give up something to get something later. Saving money becomes more difficult when the amount of things you want to buy keeps increasing, but the amount of money you have to spend does not.

Did you have enough money left over for savings? Saving money should be very important to you. It does not just mean getting a discount on something that you buy. It means putting away money for a rainy day and pretending you never saw it

Setting aside some money each week or month is very important to your "financial well-being." Ideally, you are never too young to start saving. Being young gives you more time to grow your "nest egg." The more money you save now, the more you will have available when you need it. There is never a shortage of the things we want. Being able to put aside money can be very hard, but it is never too soon to start. That is why you need to be very disciplined.

You need to want to save for a goal. The simplest way to save money is by reducing the amount of money you spend. By finding ways to lower your everyday spending, you will build positive financial habits that can change your life and help with your future.

By setting aside a certain amount for savings, you are contributing to your own financial well-being. Here are some tips on how to save money:

- **Create a Budget.** Probably the simplest first step is to have a plan. This why establishing a budget is so important. You need to know what you are spending to keep track of where your money is going.

- **Do You Really Need It?** Stop spending money on things that are unnecessary. Place your emphasis on what you need, not just on what you want.

- **Piggy Bank.** Piggy banks are not just for children to save money. The oldest discovery of a box used for saving money dates back to the time of the Greeks in the 2nd century B.C. So don't think saving money in a "piggy" bank is childish. Anyone can have a piggy bank — be they adults or grandparents.

Tang Dynasty (618-906) "piggy bank"

- **Limit Temptation.** If you are someone who knows you cannot hold onto money without spending it, find a place to put it. If you do not want to put it in a bank or a savings account, then give it to someone you trust who won't spend it, such as your parent or guardian.

MAKING CONNECTIONS

HOW CAN JACK IMPROVE HIS FINANCES?

Jack is 25 years old. He lives alone and has two jobs. His first job pays $1,205 each month, while his weekend job pays another $855 per month. Jack has a lot of trouble living on what he makes. Below is his monthly budget. Review his income and expenses for each month and see if you can make some recommendations for his monthly spending.

JACK' MONTHLY BUDGET

MONTHLY NET INCOME

Income from First Job...$1,205

Income from Second Job $855

Monthly Net Income Total...**$2,060**

MONTHLY EXPENSES

Savings..$20

Rent...$750

Food $470

Car Payment...$270

Car and Home Insurance..$100

Health Insurance $90

Heating..$60

Clothes/Personal Care...$110

Cable/Telephone...$90

Other Items..$100

Monthly Net Income Total...**$2,060**

THINK ABOUT IT

Jack wants to buy a better car. So far, he has been able to save only $20 each month for a car. He has $300 in savings. He needs to save $1,000 more in the next year for his car. What recommendations would you make to Jack for adjustments to his monthly budget? Justify the reasons for your budget suggestions.

_____

_____

_____

_____

_____

STUDY CARDS

Budget

- What is a budget? _____

  _____

  _____

- How can a budget help you to achieve "financial well-being"? _____

  _____

  _____

Income and Expenses

- What kind of things are counted as income?

  _____

  _____

- What things are counted as expenses?

  _____

  _____

  _____

Savings

How can a budget help you to save more?

  _____

  _____

  _____

  _____

  _____

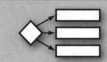

LEARNING WITH GRAPHIC ORGANIZERS

Directions: Complete the graphic organizer below by explaining the role played by each of the following items in a budget

Why is a budget necessary?

_____

_____

_____

_____

What counts as income in a budget?

_____

_____

_____

_____

What counts as an expense in a budget?

_____

_____

_____

_____

Budgets

Why are savings an important part of a budget?

_____

_____

_____

_____

EXPRESS YOURSELF

One day a fourth grader asked her parent why her parent encouraged her save money. She wanted to know if her parent wanted her to buy something specific in the future. Her parent responded, "You are not saving to spend, you are saving to save. Your goal is not to save money so that you can spend it on something later. It's fine to save for a specific goal, but you also should be saving to build wealth." Do you think this parent was giving her child good advice? Explain your answer.

INDEX